The New Perennials Preferred

The *New* PERENNIALS PREFERRED

Helen Van Pelt Wilson

Foreword by Elvin McDonald

COLLIER BOOKS
Macmillan Publishing Company • New York

Maxwell Macmillan Canada • Toronto

Maxwell Macmillan International
New York • Oxford • Singapore • Sydney

Collier Books
Macmillan Publishing Company
866 Third Avenue
New York, NY 10022

Maxwell Macmillan Canada, Inc.
1200 Eglinton Avenue East
Suite 200
Don Mills, Ontario M3C 3N1

Macmillan Publishing Company is part of the Maxwell
Communication Group of Companies.

Library of Congress Cataloging-in-Publication Data

Wilson, Helen Van Pelt, 1901–
    The new perennials preferred/Helen Van Pelt
Wilson; foreword by Elvin McDonald.
        p.   cm.
    Includes index.
    ISBN 0-02-082661-3
    1. Perennials.   I. Title.
SB434.W5   1992
635.9'32—dc20   91-15996   CIP

Macmillan books are available at special discounts for
bulk purchases for sales promotions, premiums, fund-
raising, or educational use. For details, contact:

Special Sales Director
Macmillan Publishing Company
866 Third Avenue
New York, NY 10022

First Collier Books Edition 1992

10 9 8 7 6 5 4 3 2 1

Printed in the United States of America

Acknowledgments

For assistance in the preparation of this extended revision of 1961, my gratitude goes particularly to Léonie Bell, who has generously shared with me her vast horticultural knowledge and also accompanied me on a number of wonderful gardening expeditions; to Roderick W. Cumming of Bristol Nurseries, Inc., for up-to-date information on chrysanthemums; to Louis Smirnow, for the same on tree peonies; to Harold Calverley of White Flower Farm for discussions on perennials in general.

Appreciation is likewise expressed to the *New York Times, House Beautiful, House and Garden, Better Homes & Gardens,* and especially to *Flower Grower, the Home Garden Magazine* since the subject matter of certain chapters has been used in articles previously written for these publications.

I am particularly grateful to my friend, Margaret Henderson Bailie, L.A., who devised the small planting schemes which were added to the 1953 edition and are used again here; and to Kathleen Bourke, the artist for the many new planting plans in this 1961 edition. Working at a great distance, she was apparently endowed with second sight which enabled her to transcribe my own *rough* sketches to the clear and attractive drawings of this presentation.

I am also most grateful to my secretary, Isobel F. Sherwood, for her cheerful and patient assistance, far, far beyond the call of duty; and to Herbert C. Bardes for his meticulous editorial attention to the multitudinous "finalities" of the manuscript.

Contents

Foreword

A Garden of One's Own

When the first edition of this book was published in 1945 as *Perennials Preferred*, its author, a young mother who lived in Philadelphia, was beginning to carve a niche for herself as a real gardener who wrote about the experience so that it outwardly taught practical gardening how-to but also looked inwardly at affairs of the human head and heart. I became an ardent fan after reading *The African Violet, Saintpaulia*, published in 1948. It was the first book ever on what became almost overnight America's favorite flowering houseplant. After we became friends some fifteen years later she told me that *"Saintpaulia"* had been added by the publisher so that would-be readers would not mistake it as the story of an African girl named Violet.

By the time the book you are now beginning to read was published in 1961, the original slender volume had grown into *The New Perennials Preferred*, and the small but mighty Helen Van Pelt Wilson had become an important editor in the New York book-publishing establishment, one who specialized in books about gardening and flower arranging. She had followed her vision and become a self-reliant, independent woman who found success doing what almost nobody else had thought of. I visited her garden in Connecticut only

once, and then in the dead of winter, but evidence of the
gardener consciousness was apparent throughout the house,
in the form of beautifully grown and trained potted plants as
well as sensitively arranged cut flowers. I never actually pulled
weeds or planted seeds with HVPW but there isn't a shred
of doubt that she had the gift of helping things grow, people
as well as plants. Today she lives in a retirement community
and, except for some potted plants, has given up cultivating
her own patch of earth.

Having written and edited books for HVPW, several attributes of her personality and ways in which she did things
come to mind and suggest why *The New Perennials Preferred*
has achieved classic status:

HVPW was a superb organizer, always busy with a variety
of goals and projects, each of which she ordered and prior-
itized with gusto. She could be wickedly irreverent and was
almost invariably fun. HVPW constantly built files on every
subject that was of particular interest, most destined to be
sorted out eventually to become books that included thoughts
and ideas and experiences from as many sources as possible.
Helen was meticulous about giving proper credit.

The way HVPW tackled editing a book can be well applied
to a variety of tasks in the garden or elsewhere: She first
divided a manuscript into lots of ten pages each, which were
then crisscrossed in one pile. It was her belief that unless
broken into manageable steps, getting through a manuscript
consisting of several hundred pages was simply too daunting
a prospect to even consider.

With regard to writing, HVPW's policy was never to finish
one article or chapter or book without beginning the next.
While she composed by handwriting or by dictating to her
secretary, those of us who used our own typewriters were

admonished to follow the last page of one project with the first page of the next before we ever got up from our machines.

Keeping garden upkeep down was a favorite theme in the works of HVPW, while much was made of the garden's sensual pleasures, especially the mindful placement of plants having fragrant blossoms that could be enjoyed in the everyday course of coming and going through or from one's home. *The Fragrant Year,* a book she wrote in the late 1960s with watercolorist Leonie Bell, is another classic, surely as worthy of study as any other published on the subject.

If HVPW were revising *The New Perennials Preferred* today, I think these are some of the changes she would make:

1) Page 47, in discussing winter covering, HVPW says, "The tall tops are, of course, cut down before mulching." This practice is being rethought as gardeners learn to appreciate the appearance of any given plant in all seasons and in all stages of growth. Excessively long or wayward branches may be cut back at the end of the growing season, so winter winds do not whip them about to the point of causing root breakage, but normal stands of stems and deadheads may be left in place until spring cleanup.

2) Other than new cultivars of such popular flowers as daylily, lily, and iris, the greatest outright changes since 1961 have to do with the management of garden pests and plant diseases, discussed in Chapter 7, Guides to Garden Health, beginning page 55. As published originally in 1961 HVPW listed and recommended a veritable arsenal of what were then considered the most modern garden pest and disease controls that had ever been placed at the disposal of the home gardener. Only a year later Rachel Carson's *Silent Spring* (1962)

began to change all that. In the spirit of HVPW we have updated this chapter in such a way as to preserve her sound basic philosophy about garden pest management but to suggest controls that are effectual and safe by today's more enlightened standards.

3) Present trends HVPW would no doubt include would be to encourage the use of more native plants and ornamental grasses. The ground rules of Xeriscape gardening would probably also be included, which is to say that it is sound policy not to set in motion any garden that will require large amounts of irrigation in order to survive normal periods of dry weather. The idea of Xeriscape also embraces esthetics, good design, mulching, and drip irrigation, all consistent with the common-sense practices set out in this book as it was originally published.

4) HVPW was one of the first authors and editors of gardening books to include a list of resources for the plants and products mentioned in the text. In keeping with her high standards, "Sources of Plants," beginning page 295, has been completely updated for this edition. The new list contains, along with numerous additions, all the resources from the original that are still in business.

I also call to your attention the line drawings, "garden floor plans," as HVPW called them, especially those signed "Kathleen Bourke" or bearing the initials "K.B." Katie Bourke was herself an accomplished gardener who was at the time art director of *Flower and Garden* and was thus able to consult with Rachel Snyder, a peerless plantswoman who was then editor-in-chief of the Kansas City–based gardening magazine. The results of this collaboration are exceptionally fine plans, as timely today as when they were drawn more than thirty years ago. True, some cultivar names may be outdated, but the basic plant relationships and site-specific plans are as valid as ever.

Today's new reader of Helen Van Pelt Wilson will find solace in the way she worked out life's hitches and heartaches through her gardening, all the while stopping to celebrate the pleasures and triumphs that may be experienced daily in a garden of one's own.

—Elvin McDonald
New York City, August 1991

My Garden Is a Citadel

Perennial—through the years. How pleasant to me is the intrinsic meaning of this word characterizing the many lovely flowers which through the years have afforded me both solace and joy. Recalling childhood, I have no memories earlier than those of our garden where spicy old-fashioned pinks, early peonies, scented August lilies and dark pungent chrysanthemums marked the passing seasons. More sturdy and fragrant than many flowers we grow today, they were often less handsome, but still dearly loved by the child who also "played store" with canna seeds, sucked nectar from honeysuckle tubes and with daisies made a crown for her little sister's head.

We who have early known gardens intimately have a most precious heritage. Not only do they afford us an ever delightful and rewarding occupation but as time unfolds, our love for gardening proves a bulwark against life. In happy years we women consider our gardens simply as part of our homemaking. We design them as outside living or dining rooms with sky for ceiling, grass for floor and encompassing walls of evergreens or flowering shrubs. They are background for summer parties or the setting for great family events like weddings or anniversary celebrations. We plant in them a wealth of flowers for bouquets to blend with the wallpaper in the hall or draperies in the library.

But to all of us come times when our gardens are much more than this pleasant attribute of good living. My garden is a citadel where I turn to unravel intricate matters or seek valor to face crisis or sorrow. For a garden never fails the one who plans and tends it. The night after my young sister's death it was the tall grandeur of the lilies and the splendid blue verticals of the delphinium which alleviated the anguish of my spirit. The first moon she will never see, I thought. But even the impact of that terrible finality was eased by a vivid, mystical assurance that now her beauty was merged with the loveliness of these scented moonlit flowers.

A garden always welcomes us whether we return from a journey or an illness. I recall a June I never saw my garden. But I did enjoy its background when the first day I sat up I found my window framing a new picture of the peach orchard richly carpeted in purple vetch. The next year I missed June again. This time it seemed not to matter until one day my nurse broke off a stalk of a lily. What a regal rattle of enamel and gold Benvenuto Cellini might have made with such a model, I thought, only my new daughter will prefer the original. So I hastened to recover and show her her first lilies before they faded for the year.

Often in my garden I have experienced the incomparable joy of an hour or a season's climax of grace. When in autumn, masses of chrysanthemums have gleamed like a fallen sunset against a blue, cloud-driven sky I have felt the pressure of beauty beyond bearing and cried out with Millay,

"Lord, I do fear
Thou'st made the world too beautiful this year;
My soul is all but out of me,—let fall
No burning leaf; prithee, let no bird call."

But essentially it is the doing in a garden rather than the seeing which is dearest to us all. It is our close preoccupation with the timeless verities of seed and soil which yields both peace and delight. For seed sowing is an act of faith. The cultivation of the soil is creative and the gathering and giving of flowers grown by ourselves deeply gratifying.

When my dear Louise protests, "It ain't fittin', you like that in the afternoon and the Mister, he comin' in any minute. You should be a settin' on that bench with some sewin'. Look at them knees. It just ain't fittin'."

"You're right, Louise," I admit, "but don't scold me. On the outside I'm a sight. I know it. But you should see what a clean and shining spirit I have within."

Philadelphia, 1945

SIXTEEN YEARS LATER

It seems impossible that sixteen years have passed since I first wrote this account of my garden. Yet so it is, and now I have a great many more gardening experience to share. Today I incline to plant more casually than in 1945, and my garden no longer has the formality of the simple balanced layout of the plot in suburban Philadelphia. In this Connecticut garden, the feature is a meandering shaded brook, and the perennial border has given way to a sprawling Apple-Tree Garden, to Door-Step and Look-Into plantings and to a Fern Walk. A Bog Garden is in the doing, and wild flowers have been added to my repertoire.

The emphasis, however, is still on perennials (I have never used many annuals). My respect for certain plants that take care of themselves has increased with time. My pleasure in fragrant flowers seems greater than ever, and I am always discovering new scented possibilities I must have. It is the disposition of my plants that has changed most, I think. This is partly due to both the opportunities and the limitations of this country site where acreage must be dealt with and shade taken into account. Different uses of plants have also been dictated by the cost and scarcity of outside help. The "yard man" is no more, at least where I live. So if there is to be any time left for enjoying the garden, all complicated plans must be avoided and limits set on how many hours we ourselves will work. I must admit I have never been very good at setting these limits. I always have more enthusiasms than sense and strength—as witness my new plantings of old roses and my plans for more iris and peonies—but anyway I am going to go right on urging *you* to plant with easy upkeep in mind and a comfortable chair as well as a kneeling pad in view.

This new edition, then, of *Perennials Preferred,* and *Perennials for Every Garden,* now called *The New Perennials Preferred,* is simply a sixteen-year extension of my gardening record with a number of my new "floor plans" to bring you up to date and, of course, all new variety lists. There is a change of emphasis, you'll see, but certainly no less enthusiasm. Once an ardent gardener, always so, with satisfaction and joy in the continuous pursuit. My wish is that your gardening hours may go on being as rewarding as mine, and that your garden, like mine, may also be a lovely citadel!

Helen Van Pelt Wilson
Westport, Connecticut, 1961

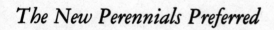

The New Perennials Preferred

1. First Principles
for Perennial Borders

Perennials are plants with many values. Yet more often than not we entirely overlook their simple landscape possibilities and place them in herbaceous borders. This is the most complex arrangement of all but the loveliest, it is true, when attractive color harmonies are achieved for each season. Frequently, however, disappointments occur because we expect of our perennials continuous bloom and eternal life.

Like people, perennials have their limitations. Until we allow for these, while emphasizing all their glorious assets, we can never create pictures which quite suit us. We must eventually admit, therefore, that a satisfactory border starts not with seeds, soil or plants but with the gardener's state of mind. It is, in fact, an exercise in evaluation.

I found this out years ago when I made my first border. I was greener then than the greenest plant I grew for I had no real information about perennials. I just loved them all and wanted for myself every variety I discovered. I was a one-of-each gardener trying to create a paradise from my neighbors' cast-offs.

THE EIGHT PRINCIPLES

Today I attempt less than in that first garden, yet I achieve far more. For now I apply to the making of a garden certain definite rules. I pass these principles on to you after repeated tests of their soundness.

1. Provide Background

First, provide a strong background. Few perennials can stand alone. They require a setting.

If you have ever planted free-standing borders you know what a thin appearance they make. Sometimes, to be sure, the site of the garden requires a free-standing border and you must get the best effect you can. In such cases plant the tall, late-flowering varieties of hardy aster along the back of your border. Hollyhocks, meadowrue and other tall subjects which must be cut down after early blooming are not so satisfactory.

Much more happily situated is the perennial border with a green hedge of yew behind it or a stalwart line of shrubs. Where possible I have planted double white lilacs as background for my borders and find their enduring green excellent while their scented flowering makes twice blessed the lavender, pink and yellow pageant of May perennials.

The mixed shrubbery boundary of small properties also provides a pleasing backdrop. Let the outline of your perennial borders follow its curves and bays and you will have charming pictures. A house wall, too, may be considered but dividing walls of brick or stone such as the English use are the ideal setting. Such walls are, of course, the goal of us all in our affluent years.

After the site is chosen, next consider the plants.

2. Important Roles for Big Five

In selecting perennials for a border, emphasize the relia-bles. Eliminate those which bloom briefly, sulk after flowering or are unduly rampant. Peonies, iris, daylilies, phlox, hardy asters and perhaps early chrysanthemums are worthy of lead-ing roles. Let columbines, flax, candytuft, meadowrue and such play the secondary parts. Omit entirely in limited spaces bleedinghearts, oriental poppies and other perennials which disappear completely after flowering. And think twice about admitting hardy ageratum, beebalm or heleniums which are of far too exuberant a nature for restricted areas.

3. Proceed by Plan

Proceed by plan only. Plant your perennials on paper be-fore you put them in soil.

Through the winter think out your border design. Work and rework it by drawings. Even then you will be tempted to make yearly changes in the actualities. A good plan, how-ever, saves a lot of useless effort and makes planting easier too. You can work your schemes out on graph paper, filling in the sections with crayons to test your color harmonies. Or you can just rule a large piece of plain paper into guiding squares. Well-illustrated catalogues will acquaint you with unfamiliar perennials. The ready-reference Cultural Index on page 252 will inform you as to heights, colors and seasons.

4. Emphasize and Repeat

As you plan, strive for emphasis throughout the garden by repeating drifts or colonies of the same plants. Place also the same single specimens at regular intervals for accent.

Such repetition gives a garden picture unity and strength. If the layout of the beds can also be balanced, that too helps

considerably. In a Philadelphia garden, I had two long borders
on each side of a wide grass panel. Three beds were planted
exactly alike while the fourth varied somewhat in the center
because it was shaded by an ancient apple tree. Yet I found
no monotony in that small garden, only the pleasant restful
result which orderly planting produces. The smaller the garden the more essential to effect is such repetition and emphasis. You will find that two peonies, three hardy asters or
four flax plants carelessly scattered in an undesigned border
say very little; but evenly spaced through four beds or
through a long border, composed of repeated units, they
produce a real harmony.

5. Design Wide Borders

From the start make your flower beds as wide as their
setting permits. Let them be one-third wider than the height
of the tallest plant they are to contain. Otherwise your important background giants will balance precariously.

Wide beds are essential to rich effects and greater variety
in plants. The beds must be wide enough, in fact, to hold
several masses of plants, so that one group will burst into
bloom as another quiets down. Perhaps, too, some groups
must be included to hide the complete retirement of others:
Chinese delphinium before oriental poppies, for example. In
an eight-foot-wide section you can manage a five-deep plant
line-up. That is little enough when the aim is continuous
color. A ten-foot-wide border would simplify the task.

Even with eight-by-thirty-foot sections which I have had,
it takes careful planning to get a fairly continuous parade of
flowers. With the often attempted three-foot-wide beds a
varied effect is impossible. It is better to give over such

narrow spaces to one-season plantings. Select peonies, for example, for the main show and edge the bed with tulips followed by petunias. You will not then attempt more in narrow limits than you can successfully achieve. And spring will be handsome while summer is pleasant.

Let me emphasize, however, that a garden can always be attractive and seem to be in full bloom when it really is not. If you plant long-blooming, easily managed perennials (with some bulbs), there can practically always be color. Usually there are five crescendo occasions, five peaks of flower color in the course of the season—in early May, early June, early July, early August and early September. (The plan for a Perennial Border Unit, on pages 302–303, shows how this can be worked out.) Five such glowing spectacles in one garden are about all we can expect. Between times the effect is necessarily quiet. But excellent color is always enhanced by a balanced design of beds and by good foliage on plants out of bloom.

6. Consider Foliage

Consider, therefore, the leaves as well as the flower of every perennial you select for your border.

At first I never thought of the looks of a plant out of bloom. Now dependable foliage seems to me as important as long flowering. Therefore I stress the evergreen hardy candytuft and iris. In the border I usually forgo bleedinghearts and Virginia bluebells, much as I admire them. With such perennials, there is an unattractive period when foliage is maturing and on the yellow side, and again when it actually disappears and the gardener beholds not flowers, nor leaves, but just bare ground. It is better, therefore, to rely on plants which look well both in and out of bloom. Of these there is a multitude—peonies, iris, daylilies, baptisia, gas plant, milfoil, stokesia, platycodon and veronica, for a start. Enduring foliage is particularly important for all edging plants. Coralbells, pinks and hardy candytuft are good examples.

7. *Plan Color from Front to Rear*

In general, plan for the color in your perennial border to start in spring at the rim and move to the rear as the season proceeds. Think of your design as composed of five not too well-defined waves. Call these arbitrarily the Edging, Foreground, Peony and Iris, Summer and Autumn strata.

This is a suggested principle, not an ironclad rule. You may, if you wish, use late dwarf asters for the edging or set a peony or so along the rear. Experience will indicate many pleasing variations. Consider, however, seasonal differences in heights. The tall, late asters really belong at the back, the medium-sized summer flax, daisies, milfoil and veronica in the foreground.

8. *Borders Should Be Neat*

Finally, to make the most of your border plantings, keep them neat.

Good grooming, you will discover, does as much for an out-of-bloom garden as it does for a plain woman. Therefore through the less vivid weeks cultivate your garden faithfully and keep it sharply edged and firmly staked. Divide your plants every three years or so to hold them within the confines you first selected. Sometimes discard them entirely and begin afresh. Perennials often live many years but not forever. You can achieve a fine and finished effect only with first quality material.

Here then, briefly, are your guiding principles to handsome perennial borders.

1. Provide a background.
2. Give important roles to the big five—iris, peony, daylily, phlox and hardy aster.
3. Proceed by plan only.
4. Emphasize and repeat.
5. Design wide borders.
6. Consider foliage as well as flower.
7. Arrange color in a front-to-rear wave.
8. Keep your borders neat.

DESIGN FOR FIVE CRESCENDOS

At this point I wish I could offer an absolutely satisfactory plan for a perennial border unit with a few annuals and bulbs introduced for supplementary color. But I have discovered that no one else's plan is ever quite right. Only *you* can evaluate your own factors, estimate the time you wish to give to culture and decide what plants are indispensable to you. However, here is a plan for a border unit to guide you. You can substitute as you wish. This unit, which appears on pages 302–303, illustrates the essential principles for borders which I have learned through many years of garden experience. Colors are basically pastel—white, pink, lavender and yellow.

In this particular scheme, on which I have had the always wise advice of my dear gardening friend. Léonie Bell, the five waves of bloom would work out this way, with italics to indicate time of peak bloom, capitals to show what plants are the stars in each:

1. April through   IBERIS and TULIPS
   May
2. May through   PEONIES, IRIS, pinks, gas plant,
   June   coralbells, flax, columbine
3. June through   LARKSPUR, LILIES, daylilies, mil-
   July   foil, shasta daisies, flax
4. July through   PHLOX, lilies, daylilies, milfoil,
   August   shasta daisies, flax, veronica, *Aster*
                        frikarti
5. August through   ASTERS, daylilies, phlox,
   September   veronica, *Aster frikarti*

Candytuft and Tulips

Notice that in this scheme the peaks of the five crescendos are reached during the first two weeks of each second month. The first crescendo occurs in late April and through May at the border's edge, when snowy candytuft blooms with colonies of yellow, lavender and pink tulips. These together sing a lovely spring song. (The tulips are planted eight to ten inches deep so that well-started annual petunias from the florist or low chrysanthemums can later be set among them, and cultivated through the summer without harm to the bulbs below.)

Peonies and Iris

Toward the end of May a second voice arises, paralleling the first like themes in a Bach fugue. Through June come the white and pink peonies and the blue iris, supported by white pinks, rose-colored gas plant, blue flax and yellow columbine, with coralbells at the edge. The columbine is particularly important. It brings an airy grace, a lilting beauty to the sometimes too solid look of a planting, and the pale yellow *Aquilegia chrysantha* blooms longer than the others—from May well into July.

But nothing exceeds the beauty of the peony and iris crescendo. See how the iris are clustered around the midseason peonies, the selection of iris made also from midseason varieties. Tall kinds are placed behind the clumps of peonies and seem particularly attractive there with the lower kinds massed in front. If the mats of pinks (dianthus) are allowed to creep up to the iris rhizomes, no harm is done; iris and pinks make a lovely pair all through the year, and their requirements are similar.

Larkspur with Lilies

In some gardens, delphinium (which actually is a perennial form of larkspur) might be the feature of the third peak for late June through July, but I hesitate to depend on this often unstable plant. Instead, for the delphinium spire effect, there is indicated a planting of a new kind of annual larkspur, Giant Imperial. This larkspur is double flowered and base branching, and comes in excellent colors. "Light azure," "clear lavender" and "rich violet" varieties would be perfect for our plan. Sow the Giant Imperial larkspurs in late October for bloom from mid-June to late July next year. After they bloom, pull them out.

With the larkspur, lilies make the lovely music of early summer. The July peak is marked by the glory of the white regal and Mid-Century Hybrid lilies—the lemon-yellow Prosperity beside the golden yellow daylily Cradle Song; the brilliant orange-gold Valencia next to the pale yellow daylily Fond Caress. Although both types of plants have flowers of lily form, the true lilies are upright and clustered, the daylilies are low and arching, a pleasant contrast of plant growth. Furthermore, after the wealth of rosiness in June and before the rosy pinks of August, early June seems a good time to bring in a bit of warm gold or apricot, as Valencia is sometimes described. You will notice that daylilies are not used as reigning stars and that in each of the last three periods there is something else that will probably attract more attention.

Importance of Daylilies

However, the daylilies have importance. The first pair—Cradle Song and Fond Caress—are early-midseason, quite low, extremely floriferous, open in the evening and fragrant. (Evening bloomers or those with extended blooming are essential when mixing daylilies with other perennials. There should be flowers through all daylight hours and also in the evening.) Only yellows are indicated, but with enough difference in tint between those in bloom at the same time to offer contrast. These daylilies are planted toward the back so that their fountaining leaves can fill in around the bases of phlox, peonies, and asters. The second pair of daylilies in the border unit—Shooting Star and Lark Song—is late midseason, blooming from the end of July through August, and without overlapping the season of the earlier two. The last daylily to open is Autumn King, September-blooming, tall and floriferous, the flowers still fresh by evening.

Three Foreground Plants

But to return to the early summer picture, there are three lower foreground plants to complete it. These are regularly spaced for accent and rhythm and all are long blooming. The milfoil *Achillea taygetea* has handsome gray-green foliage, a perfect setting for the pale yellow flower clusters. Actually this begins to bloom in May and continues all summer if faded flowers are removed.

The shasta daisy variety Mt. Shasta is another classic for all summer, and, though I always prefer single varieties, the single shastas do not seem to give the steady performance of this double one.

The bold clumps of flax, *Linum perenne*, bring "true" blue to this border. Flax often provides four months of color, for it begins in early May. The plants puff out charmingly over the low growers in front, and when flax passes, the petunias or chrysanthemums, filling in for tulips, spread enough to somewhat cover the flax departure as well.

Emphasis on Phlox

The fourth peak begins to shape up in late July and by August is in full beauty; the emphasis is on phlox, another of the strong plants of the border.

I prefer the pale beauty of the light-colored varieties with contrasting eyes; these phlox appear blush rather than white in the garden. You may want stronger shades but look out for salmons, which are yellow-pinks, if you plan to have in your fifth peak any of the pink hardy asters, which are blue-pinks. However, if you want brilliant color, you might choose phlox Sir John Falstaff, a fine salmon, and select some "matching" petunias like Fire Chief for the ends of the planting where the tulips were. Then you could have lavender or lavender and white asters. But I wanted to keep the plan to light phlox with the pink *speciosum* lilies to tower above it, and that left me then a free hand with the fall asters.

In addition to the continuing daylilies, the August peak is strengthened by more color in the foreground where the milfoil and shastas surely bloom on, and the flax may. There

Veronica holophylla, a good blue and lighter than the old *V.
longifolia*, sends up nice spires from glistening dark green
leaves, actually from July all through September if the faded
central spikes are cut out. It offers the excellent advantages
of contrasting flower form and fine enduring foliage. The
lovely, low-growing lavender *Aster frikarti* Wonder of Stafa
also has this asset and, as it increases in girth, it flops com-
fortably over whatever has been planted nearby and so helps
to fill in any possible vacancies.

Hardy Asters

For the fifth peak—late August through September—the
delicate, filmy perennial asters in soft shades of pink and
lavender put on the final show. The last daylily, Autumn King,
is softly beautiful in yellow, and that fine late phlox, World
Peace, comes handsomely into bloom. Meanwhile the *Aster
frikarti* and the veronica bloom on. If you planted low cushion chrysanthemums, preferably in a gold or yellow shade,
among the tulips, these bring fresh foreground color. Any
annuals, of course—petunias or something else you may have
preferred in the tulip areas—will also continue until frost.

So ends the symphony of the well-planned border, but you
will go on thinking about it, and next year and the next, you
will change it. I always do, though the reliance on the same
main plants continues.

You have noticed, I am sure, that there is a certain sym-
metry about this planting which helps to emphasize the effect
of bloom, but there is plenty of variation, too, through the
great variety of plants. As for color, as I have said, I do not
attempt unusual or subtle harmonies. Perhaps you will prefer
flower tones stronger than those of these pastel borders with
their pale emphasis. But where summers are very hot, a

white-and-green symphony appears pleasant and cool even on torrid days, and, of course, pale flowers tend to be more scented than others.

Furthermore, in twilight and moonlight it is the frost lily, the ivory phlox, the pale yellow daylily and the satiny white petunia which remain visible in the darkness. To me and my visiting friends their evening beauty affords gentle solace of spirit through trying summer weeks. And this is, indeed, the rewarding joy of a garden.

2. My Apple-Tree Garden

Although I know that one swallow does not make a summer, nor one crow a winter, for me one apple tree certainly makes a fine garden. It is the combination of handsome structure and lovely underplanting that does it. Actually there are other than apple trees which make beautiful umbrellas for gardens. You can grow flowers successfully under any deep-rooted, open-foliaged specimen that light can filter through. I have another garden under the high shade of an elm. Birches, dogwoods, oaks and sweet gums also offer possibilities, as do the sugar maples but not the other shallow-rooted maples and poplars, or the ground-poisoning black walnut. Where you find shade is a problem, try to make friends with it, and plan for a shade-tolerant or shade-loving garden under a favorite tree. There's surely no use in fighting shade with daisies and dahlias. Besides, under-tree gardens have special enchantment.

Indeed, almost by itself, my apple tree is a garden as I see its beauty changing through the seasons from stark and handsome silhouette to new leaves, a veil of blossoms, and then with globes of green fruit like ornaments on a Christmas tree. When underplanting with perennials, ferns and bulbs, an apple tree is an utterly satisfying canopy for a garden, and the picture is delightful. (There's a plan of my Apple-Tree Garden on pages 16–17.)

One or more old specimens have always been a part of my planning. I think of the first garden which was really mine. The place was called "Orchard Edge," for along the side was an ancient orchard planted to sod. A cool and pleasant outdoor living room it was, and as garden background, a lovely sight.

Then in my next garden, in Philadelphia, miraculously I possessed a great single ancient tree, gnarled and dignified, long past its youthful prime. The tree-man patched it up with cement and chained the weakest limb. But it wasn't that limb that finally went. One summer night in a thunderstorm, I stood alone on the wide veranda, watching the fury of the elements play about my treasured tree. Suddenly, there was a great flash of fire, a mighty rending, and before my eyes a great limb—the very arch of my garden—split apart and fell with a terrifying crash. It was as if God spoke there in the empty garden and with His hand parted the bough. I stood transfixed with awe and wonder.

But life goes on. The next day we cut the limb cleanly off, sawed it into logs, and burned it on winter nights. To my mind, there is nothing like apple wood for fires. Only I sighed for my lost garden beauty.

Garden in Connecticut

Now at Stony Brook I have another Apple-Tree Garden, the most pleasing of all, I think, as it should be for I have long been experimenting. This one constitutes an important part of my garden since, in keeping the upkeep down, I have had to limit myself to less extensive borders. But an area about ten feet deep by thirty-eight to forty feet long can hold

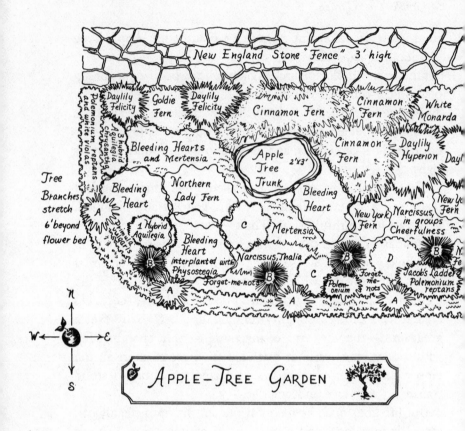

1' border of Arabis and Heuchera, alternated

A - Bold accents of Anchusa myosotidiflora, evenly placed
B - 4 Trollius, Lemon Queen
C - 4 Doronicum
D - 3 Dictamnus rosea

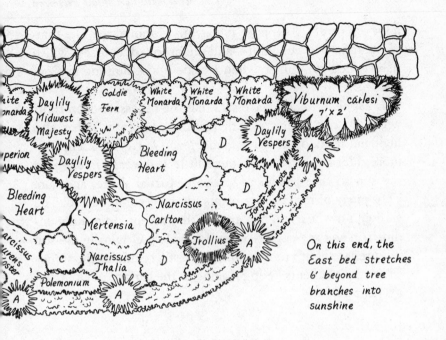

On this end, the
East bed stretches
6' beyond tree
branches into
sunshine

In summer pink Physostegia fills in – shows late
Bleeding Hearts and Mertensia interplanted and followed by
self-sown white Nicotiana.

Narcissus also followed by Nicotiana, but near front of bed
Single Petunias in purple and white also introduced.

Daylilies all yellow and summer flowering

Forget-me-nots self sow through front.

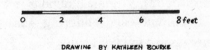

DRAWING BY KATHLEEN BOURKE

17

a lot of flowers. I suppose it was this glorious tree, the tumbling stone wall behind it—and the brook, of course—which determined my choice when I came house-hunting in Connecticut.

An apple tree, as I have said, has the necessary deep roots which do not interfere with plantings beneath. It has also high and fairly open shade, and I *prune to keep it so*. Furthermore, I let the bed stretch out a little at the eastern end into the sun so that I have deep shade, partial shade, and sun. Thus many of my favorite plants can be accommodated. The garden, now nearly ten years old, has accepted both my enthusiasm and my neglect when I traveled. Originally the soil was prepared but a foot deep. We are still removing the stones which the elements keep bringing to the surface of any Connecticut garden.

SPRING EMPHASIS

In this climate of sometimes hot, humid, buggy summers, my enthusiasm remains for the plants of spring. During the hot weeks, I am not one to wield the hoe and dust gun, so on most of the place a quiet green display contents me, but under the apple tree, I find it easy always to have some color. Indeed, from April to frost my Apple-Tree Garden enchants me—and everyone else, for that matter, since it lies along the drive where all who visit inevitably pause for a moment to admire—and to smell. Ferns, high and low, bleedinghearts (dicentra), Virginia bluebells (mertensia) and daylilies are the important—and enduring—basis of the garden, along with attractive edging plants.

Early spring starts at the edge where sections of white rockcress (*Arabis alpina*) flower intrepidly. Then come narcissus. There are five drifts of these: the early, soft yellow, single-trumpet Carlton; two of the fragrant Poetaz narcissus, the single, yellow-cupped, white Laurens Koster and the double, late, white Cheerfulness; and to the fore, the small, appealing white Thalia, a triandrus variety, easy to grow, sweet-scented and, like most narcissus, a dependable multiplier.

Early in June, clumps of coralbells (*Heuchera sanguinea*) between the arabis again define the edge. Heuchera blooms when roses are out, and I like to cut it for bouquets with the roses. Heuchera is practically the ideal perennial for edging since it is absolutely healthy and has year-round good looks. With the rockcress, there is a pleasant color sequence and at all times enduring green.

I have plenty of forget-me-nots, too, near the edge and also through the foreground. They self-sow readily so clumps can be lifted in spring, even at the bloom stage, and tucked into any bare spot as needed. The clear true blue, a color not common in flowers, is a joy.

Five spring-blooming perennials are fairly regularly spaced toward the front for accent and to "tie" things together, since this irregular planting necessarily lacks design. In the foreground, I have the lavender Jacob's ladder (*Polemonium reptans*), about twelve inches high, a spreader with excellent ferny foliage; clear yellow primroses (*Primula vulgaris*) rising from *almost* constant green crowns; fine-foliaged yellow globeflower or trollius; the yellow daisylike doronicum (yellow is important to "lift" pinks and blues), and the big-leaved forget-me-not-flowered anchusa (*Anchusa myosotidiflora* or, more accurately, *Brunnera macrophylla*), another fine true blue for stress between the lower arabis and heuchera. In summer, I relieve the anchusa of some of its huge leaves so its exuberance does not crowd out less vigorous growers.

Throughout the planting, bleedinghearts and mertensia make the prettiest possible spring symphony. They give power to the April-May picture which lasts some six weeks, with the dicentra still showing a few "hearts" early in July and the foliage not bad even to the end of the month. There are six or seven big plants of this through the center of the garden, and somewhat more mertensia, but this, of course, disappears more rapidly.

Ferns are the perfect accompaniment to bulbs. They make it possible decently to delay removing the bulb foliage. This really must turn yellow before it is cut if next year's daffodils are to be worth looking at, and it takes bulbs a good many weeks to mature. Cinnamon, New York and a goldie fern slowly take over as the spring plants grow shabby and are cut down, and it is these ferns which give beauty, grace and character to the summer picture.

June On

Toward the front appear the good foliage and low spires of the gas plant (*Dictamnus rubra*), a perennial of notable quality and one not to be moved about. The monarda Snow Queen fills in among the ferns; it is a thirty-inch or so, informal grower with long bloom—late June through August. In the center, that excellent, delicately scented, yellow daylily Hyperion, adds in July a bright note to the now almost all-white picture of summer. Two other pale yellow daylilies, the long-blooming Felicity and the very fragrant evening beauty, Vespers, light up the ends of the planting.

There are many marvelous daylilies available today in various colors, and most of them thrive in *light* shade. I like the pale yellow ones best, and these are mostly slow growing, not expansive. When necessary I keep them in bounds by pruning in summer and by some removal of side shoots. At the other end of the Apple-Tree Garden—separated from it and nicely silhouetted by the gray stone fence—is a great clump of the native (or do I mean escaped?) orange daylily, so common here we almost cease to see it. However, if this orange *Hemerocallis fulva* hadn't been right at hand, I would have chosen some other than this definitely 9 a.m. to 5 p.m. daylily to plant as a specimen here—Rajah, perhaps, which stays open in the evening and is of much longer bloom.

Three Annuals

Three annuals carry color right up to frost. The tall, white, very fragrant flowering tobacco (*Nicotiana affinis*) has been a favorite for many years, and it comes easily from seed. Its special asset is that it self-sows, so each spring all I have to do is to reset a few of the volunteers in appropriate vacancies. The rest stay where they come. This variety needs staking. Dwarf White Bedder grows only twelve inches high and could be used equally well. Daylight stays open all day, unlike my favorite night-blooming *N. affinis*. Both are scented, though not so heavily as *N. affinis*.

I also set out a few single white and purple petunias to the front where there is more light, and add impatiens plants if I can get them in separate colors of salmon or white, not mixtures. Impatiens will bloom in deeper shade than the flowering tobacco or petunias, both of which require fairly strong light.

About Tuberous Begonias

Then there are the tuberous begonias. Why *aren't* these more generally used for summer bedding? They are so entrancing yet much too little known. Around here folks think *I* invented them!

To leave the apple tree for a moment—one year I had a planting of tuberous begonias in shades of red in a narrow "difficult" area between house wall and walk. The location is northwest and quite shaded, yet they bloomed prodigiously. So, too, do they bloom under the apple tree in light and rather deep shade. Although I have never seen a variety I didn't like, the yellows, peachy pinks, and picotee whites are surely special. There's a glowing orange too that certainly sings out loud. In general, all the colors harmonize so that you can safely buy tuberous begonias "in mixture."

I suppose as easy gardening goes, tuberous begonias are slightly bothersome, yet not really in view of the dividends they pay. Also I usually have a florist start my tubers, which makes it all very simple. If you have a greenhouse, you can fill a couple of flats with the tubers in February or March with very little trouble. (Plant the tubers *concave* side up, and space them three to four inches apart each way. An inch covering of soil is enough.) My man delivers them well started, and four to five inches high, when frost danger is over in these parts, which is sometimes not till June! Usually, however, the third week in May is safe for setting out, and flowers appear very soon thereafter. I must tell you though that one year when I got behind on everything, I planted unstarted tubers outdoors in mid-June and I had a fine display from the end of July until frost. Of course, I did lose a good many weeks of enjoyment. It was just a something-is-better-than-nothing situation.

Each plant needs about three two-foot stakes, sturdy ones, and I fasten the main stems with twistems (much easier than string). Plants need plenty of *deep* watering during the usual summer droughts, and will bloom right through if you tend to it. A slow-running hose or a soil-soaker hose laid among them *for a couple of hours* at a time, and about once weekly, does the trick for them and the rest of the Apple-Tree Garden as well.

The first light frost usually finishes tuberous begonias so plants are lifted then (certainly before *hard* frost), and spread out to dry. When stems part *readily*, the tubers are cleaned and packed away until February in a basket of soil, sawdust, buckwheat hulls or peat moss. A 40 to 50° F. temperature is about right for storing. You may want to try the new method, useful for safe winter carry-over of other kinds of tender bulbous plants, in which the bulbs are coated with one of the antitranspirant sprays before being put into storage.

Way to Easy Upkeep

Speaking of peat moss reminds me again of the comfort—both to me and the Apple-Tree Garden—of a mulch. (There is more on this subject in Chapter 5.) After the nicotiana seedlings have been spotted and suitably placed, the petunias and the impatiens set out about mid-June, and the begonias staked, the garden is given a thorough cultivation and clean-up. Daffodil foliage can usually be spared by this time, mertensia foliage has already gone, and it's time to glide into summer. Then a two- to three-inch mulch of buckwheat hulls or damp peat moss is applied (the open bale has been absorbing rain for a month). The bed is then watered deeply, and that is pretty much that, as far as culture in summer goes. Aside from plant pruning to keep the hefties in line, and the removal of spent flowers, the Apple-Tree Garden is now all joy.

In autumn, a snowfall of bone meal is applied; in spring

the garden is given an application of whatever complete plant food is that year in favor, along with some wood ashes saved from winter fires.

The Apples!

One tiny fly remains in the ointment of this perfection— the apples! Some fall and fall from August on, and must on occasion be gathered. The tree gets two sprayings in spring, with the elms, and this keeps most of the apples *on the tree* until August when they ripen and descend. They are only just good enough for applesauce. (I think it takes twelve sprayings to produce *perfect* fruit.)

I questioned my tree man about a hormone spray which I read prevented fruit formation, but he advised me against it: too much danger of checking flowers too. So the unwanted fruit is picked up, which is after all not too arduous a job, and as good as Elizabeth Arden for the waistline!

Actually my Apple-Tree Garden is *all* satisfaction. For great enjoyment, I urge you all to have one—even if you must first plant the apple tree!

3. Doorstep and Dooryard Gardens for the Nearer View

Long ago I discovered that the plants I most enjoyed were those close to my comings and goings rather than those close to my sittings, since I don't seem to sit very much. I have therefore become more and more attached to small intimate plantings that can be enjoyed in the incidental way of life—while I cook, answer the telephone or talk to the mailman. Today, after long consideration and planning of doorstep and dooryard gardens, I have arranged it so that I cannot enter or leave Stony Brook Cottage without a rewarding glimpse of some favorite flower and usually a breath of fragrance too.

DOORSTEP GARDEN

At the kitchen door—which everybody uses here—I have planted a delicious sequence, as the planting plan shows (see "Kitchen Doorstep and Window Garden," page 26). Actually that little strip to the left of the step contains hardly fifteen square feet. Yet it holds spring weeks of blue hyacinth color and scent, summer months of nicotiana sweetness, and August loveliness from an espaliered mauve clematis, Mme. Baron-Veillard. In winter, I value the crisp green of the dwarf Japanese ilex, the sprays of ivy and the edging of pachysandra.

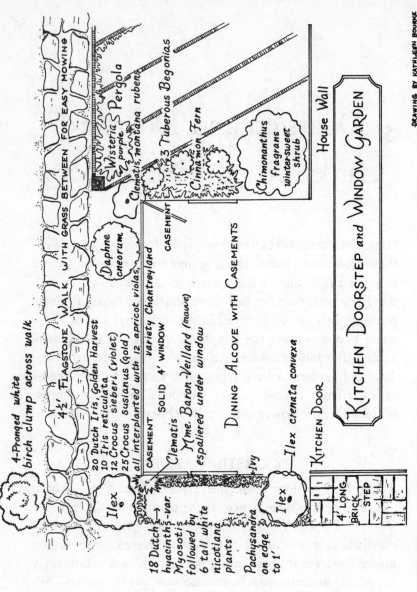

4-Pronged white birch clump across walk

4½' FLAGSTONE WALK WITH GRASS BETWEEN FOR EASY MOWING

20 Dutch Iris, Golden Harvest
10 Iris reticulata
12 Crocus sieberi (violet)
25 Crocus susianus (gold)
all interplanted with 12 apricot violas

Ilex

Daphne cneorum

Wisteria Pergola

Clematis, montana rubens

3 Tuberous Begonias

Cinnamon Fern

Chimonanthus fragrans winter-sweet shrub

CASEMENT   SOLID 4' WINDOW   variety Chantreyland

CASEMENT

CASEMENT

House Wall

Clematis Mme. Baron-Veillard (mauve) espaliered under window

DINING ALCOVE WITH CASEMENTS

Ivy

Ilex crenata convexa

18 Dutch hyacinths–var. Myosotis followed by 6 tall white nicotiana plants

Pachysandra on edge to 1'

Ilex

KITCHEN DOOR

4' LONG BRICK STEP

KITCHEN DOORSTEP and WINDOW GARDEN

DRAWING BY KATHLEEN BOURKE

26

If you round the corner of the plan, you see just under the kitchen casements a length of late-winter-into-summer color from bulbs, perennials, evergreen shrubs—a dwarf ilex at one corner, a fragrant daphne at the other—and the pink spring mountain clematis at the end. Winter iris, the very earliest crocus in purple and yellow, followed by a few plants of nasturtiums so perfect for kitchen bouquets, Dutch iris variety Golden Harvest, and yellow or apricot violas variety Chantreyland (which are more or less perennial)—all these make the kitchen door a spot worth passing by. The oil man admires the planting tremendously and since the oil tank lies beneath it he has plenty of time to enjoy it while he most carefully puts in oil and never spills a dangerous drop.

On the third side, a cinnamon fern and coral-colored tuberous begonias are pleasant to look down upon. A wintersweet shrub (*Chimonanthus fragrans,* or *C. praecox*) grows in the warm, sunny corner, with a wisteria beginning its swift and mighty ascent in front. Although, heaven knows, there is space enough for great outflung plantings, I enjoy this compact little doorstep-window arrangement as much as anything I have (except maybe the brook!). I can readily dwell upon each plant, for the breakfast casements look out on the whole thing.

The Look-Into Garden

Across the flagstone walk and just beyond my treasured four-pronged clump of white birch—which would also give *you* pleasure at a much-frequented window—is the Look-Into Garden (page 28), a planting I delight in every time I come in the kitchen way or "look into" it as I drink an encouraging cup of morning coffee. A winter honeysuckle shrub, a Japanese holly, and the most fragrant varieties of rugosa roses

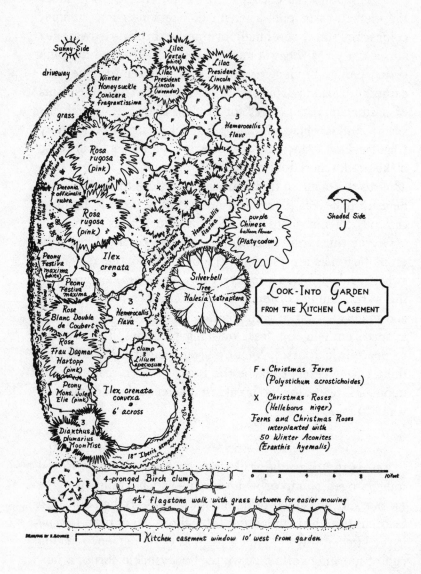

Sunny-Side

driveway

grass

Winter Honeysuckle Lonicera fragrantissima

Lilac Vestale (white)
Lilac President Lincoln (lavender)
Lilac President Lincoln
Lilac President Lincoln

midget Marigolds yellow

Rosa rugosa (pink)

Paeonia officinalis rubra

Rosa rugosa (pink)

F

F

F

F

F

3 Hemerocallis flavo

Dark blue siberian Iris followed by Phlox

Iberis

3 Hemerocallis flavo

Hemerocallis flavo

purple Chinese balloon flower (Platycodon)

Shaded Side

Peony Festiva maxima (white)

Peony Festiva maxima

Rose Blanc Double de Coubert

Rose Frau Dagmar Hartopp (pink)

midget Marigolds

Peony Mons. Jules Elie (pink)

3 Dianthus plumarius MoonMist

Ilex crenata 9

Pink limestone followed by Petunias too

3 Hemerocallis flava

Iberis

Silverbell Tree Halesia tetraptera

clump Lilium speciosum

Ilex crenata convexa 2 6' across

18" Iberis sempervirens

Look-Into Garden
FROM THE KITCHEN CASEMENT

F = Christmas Ferns
  (Polystichum acrostichoides)

X Christmas Roses
  (Helleborus niger)

Ferns and Christmas Roses
  interplanted with
  50 Winter Aconites
  (Eranthis hyemalis)

0 1 2   4   6   8   10 Feet

4-pronged Birch clump

4½' flagstone walk with grass between for easier mowing

DRAWING BY E.BOURKE

Kitchen casement window 10' west from garden

28

grow tall on the driveway side, where they are faced down by peonies and pale yellow midget marigolds, with pink dianthus as the corner.

There are lilacs at the end and a silverbell tree (*Halesia tetraptera*, or *H. carolina*) on the inside curve. These make a protective shell for a shaded planting of Christmas roses and Christmas ferns which are appropriate to each other in every way. The contrast in foliage is excellent and the two thrive under the same conditions. They are underplanted with yellow February-blooming aconites.

In early spring, pink hyacinths and white hardy candytuft make a lovely edging for them, and their color is followed by yellow daylilies, *Hemerocallis flava*, and its miniature, *H. flavina*. Finally, some single white petunias bring cool brightness at the edge of the Christmas ferns and Christmas roses. I had a hard time working out this planting to my satisfaction, but it looks fine now whether in the pale sunlight of winter or the deep shadows of summer.

The Look-Into Garden includes two other items of interest—a clump of the purple July-blooming balloon flower (platycodon) and a cluster of pink *speciosum* lilies in August, just one of each. But how I enjoy them—more I think than if there were great beds of them, for here they are so close I can easily observe their detailed perfection.

In the Look-Into Garden, as in all the close-by plantings, there is fragrance—the piercing late April-to-May sweetness of the honeysuckle shrub and the hyacinths, the spice of dianthus for late spring with a repeat through the growing season, and the summer sweetness of the lilies. Every dooryard garden is the dearer for the inclusion of a few scented plants.

At the Terrace Steps

On the brook side of the house, at both ends of the terrace, are two more doorstep gardens. When I come in the south terrace entrance (opposite page), I smell dianthus on one side and lilies-of-the-valley on both, below lilacs of unbelievable sweetness. In summer I enjoy the pale evening beauty of the lemon-yellow daylily Thistledown. There are young tree peonies here too, including the fragrant L'Esperance.

The north terrace entrance is somewhat shaded, but even so the doorstep garden (page 32) has color and also fragrance from white May hyacinths—I can never have enough of these—and white August lilies. The white "roof iris" of China, *Iris tectorum alba*, is a gay note in late May-early June. Fragrant azaleas, *arborescens* and *viscosum*, are background for the garden on one side, pale pink mountain laurel on the other, with purple-flowered periwinkle for a ground cover and the enduring green of royal ferns for summer refreshment. Additional color is provided by blue scillas and, beyond the foundation, a chartreuse mahonia.

These then are *my* doorstep gardens. You can quite easily plan for something similar, knowing that little room and less care is required (if you mulch in summer), and that the rewards are great, and also quite special. My four plans may give you ideas.

DOORYARD GARDENS

But perhaps you can have something I've never managed, a *front* dooryard garden with a wall or fence, well-contained, a whole garden close at hand for your pleasure, yet small enough for you to keep quite easily in practically perfect condition. Such a dooryard garden is a pleasant return to the

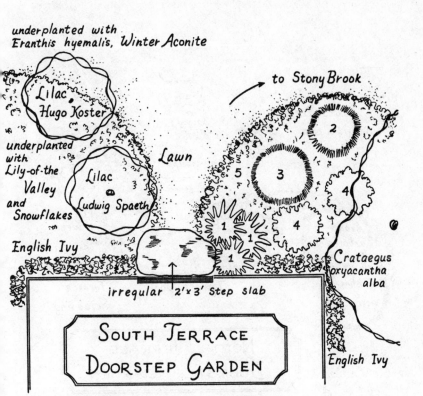

underplanted with
Eranthis hyemalis, Winter Aconite

to Stony Brook

Lilac
Hugo Koster

underplanted
with
Lily-of-the
Valley
and
Snowflakes

Lilac
Ludwig Spaeth

Lawn

English Ivy

irregular 2'x 3' Step slab

Crataegus
oxyacantha
alba

English Ivy

SOUTH TERRACE DOORSTEP GARDEN

1 - Dianthus plumarius, Apple Blossom
2 - Tree Peony, L'Esperance
3 - Tree Peony, Gessekai
4 - 2 plants, Hemerocallis, Thistledown
5 - Lily-of-the-Valley

DRAWING BY KATHLEEN BOURKE

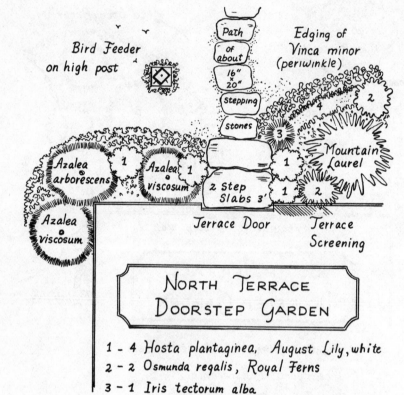

Bird Feeder
on high post

Path
of
about
16"
x
20"
Stepping
stones

Edging of
Vinca minor
(periwinkle)

2

4

3

Mountain
Laurel

Azalea
arborescens

1

Azalea
viscosum

1

1

1

2

Azalea
viscosum

2 Step
Slabs 3'

Terrace Door

Terrace
Screening

North Terrace Doorstep Garden

1 - 4 Hosta plantaginea, August Lily, white
2 - 2 Osmunda regalis, Royal Ferns
3 - 1 Iris tectorum alba
4 - 12 Dutch Hyacinths, L'Innocence, white
(followed by Tuberous Begonias)
Both sides underplanted with
Scilla siberica, Spring Beauty

DRAWING BY KATHLEEN BOURKE

32

Victorian way, I think, when people sat on front porches and had flowers out front to enjoy—and to share. In time, the front porch became passé. Entrances, alas, became formal. They shut out the world. A stern green foundation prevailed the length of the land.

Today it is again "permissible" for you to have a gay front yard, to *welcome* guests instead of *admitting* them, to share your garden with the passerby or, lacking garden space elsewhere, to develop there a garden room, but a *front* room.

Down the road from me there's a *shaded* dooryard garden in front of an old white saltbox. A New England stone fence surrounds it, interrupted by a hospitable white gate. Mountain laurel, ivy and pachysandra here are set off by various hostas and impatiens plants in melting shades of cream, lavender, pink and salmon. How I enjoy this dooryard as I walk down the road for a breath of air. And what a generous expression it gives the house with its front-yard beauty open to all.

In a Philadelphia Dooryard

In the sun, of course, a dooryard can be a riot of color and scent, and so it is in one Philadelphia garden which has delighted me for years. Here my friend Ruth Jones has worked out with *choice* plants a careful sequence of pictures set off by house and garage walls and picket fence. The plan (page 34) can only suggest the charm of this sunny dooryard garden.

Great care went initially into the preparation of the rose beds to a three-foot depth, an operation about which Ruth's husband, Jay, was less than enthusiastic when he saw subsoil piling up against the white paint of the new house. All has been forgiven, however, for the front-yard roses, so well planned for, bloom magnificently in June and intermittently

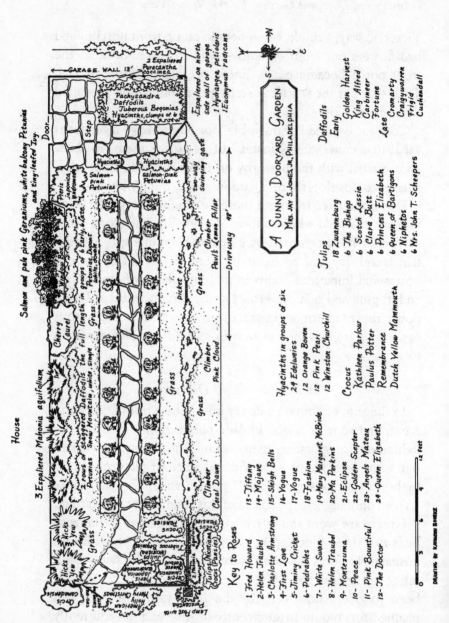

A Sunny Dooryard Garden
Mrs. Jay S. Jones, Jr., Philadelphia

34

the rest of the season. This garden is always pleasing. I have wandered through its sixteen-by-forty-eight-foot extent in all seasons. In winter, there is the atttractive design of the flagstone walk, the neat beds, the pattern of the espaliered, red-berried pyracantha against the garage wall, with the climbing hydrangea and *Euonymus radicans* giving "a charming and flawless performance in this difficult exposure." Then there are the handsome greens in yew and holly, cherry laurel and andromeda, with plants of *Mahonia aquifolium* espaliered against the wall, but some also growing naturally in one corner, and pachysandra planted along the house foundations to prevent muddy splashings.

In spring there are crocus, hyacinths, tulips, daffodils and pansies, the very beautiful Chinese redbud (*Cercis chinensis*) "far more lovely than the American counterpart" with heart-shaped leaves and lavender-pink blooms, and the cherry laurel ablaze with white candles. Indeed, I find this dooryard garden quite irresistible, even before the parade of roses, the summer frivolity of petunias and sweet-scented nicotiana, and the dramatic beauty of the tuberous begonias.

Roses Always on View

If ever there was a contradiction to the idea that rose plants are not good looking enough to have close at hand, this garden is it. Here hybrid teas and floribundas are on view and lovely in bloom, when they offer a beautiful array of soft colors, and are handsome out of bloom, for they are well-cared-for plants. Over the fence Coral Dawn, Pink Cloud and Paul's Lemon Pillar fling out their branches with charming abandon.

The color harmony of the garden emphasizes pinks, yellows, ivory, warm apricot and coral—not one note of red, which pleases me—and the window boxes are bright with salmon-pink geraniums, white petunias and tiny-leafed ivy.

This garden has always had so many lessons for me—the importance of design, the setting-off quality of flagstone and grass, the value of features—window boxes, a lamp post and the swinging gate with its two-way welcome. I didn't need to learn, of course, about picket fences; I've always loved them! Note on the plan Ruth's varietal selection in bulbs and roses; they are marvelous. Look them over. They will help you, too, with their early and late possibilities, so well thought out, and their very charming color effects for every season.

Today when the big place, and the formal garden, may present too great a hazard of work and effort, what fine possibilities there are in these small plantings. And how we grow to love them once we get in tune with the "nearer view" of doorstep and dooryard.

4. Soils, Compost
and Fertilizers

Too many of us start our gardening with seed packets. That's like concentrating on wallpaper and forgetting about the cellar. In gardens, as in houses, good foundations count, and a friable and fertile soil is the only sound basis for a beautiful garden. But to condition your soil so that it will afford a comfortable medium for the sustenance of plant roots is not always a simple matter. It need not, however, be back breaking.

First you must understand what you are after. What is meant, for example, by those terms friable and fertile, so freely scattered about in print? A friable soil has waterholding capacity. It is well aerated and easily penetrated by plant roots. Because of its humus content it is rich in active bacteria. A fertile soil is plentifully supplied with those chemical elements which are necessary to the healthy, balanced growth of plants. Bacteria present in a friable soil make the elements of fertility readily available to plants. A soil that lacks humus can be rich but still not a good growing medium because the fertile elements, failing bacterial action, are locked away and inert.

Soil must be not only of first quality but also deeply prepared, at least twelve or fifteen inches for perennial borders.

Then, unless you are certain drainage is good, as on a sloping site, dig a bit deeper and place a six-inch layer of stones and debris in the bottom for drainage purposes. Next, take pains to improve the soil. The first year, if most of your garden budget goes in this direction, it is all to the good. If you plant first and consider the soil second, you will be eternally frustrated by losses due to rot from standing water or fatigued by more cultivating than a better prepared soil would require.

LIME

After spading, consider the advisability of a soil test. But do not imitate the routine practice of many gardeners who follow digging with liming. The indiscriminate use of lime is dangerous policy since lime is neither cure-all nor fertilizer. Lime has a lightening effect on heavy clay soils and it is the principal means of raising the pH (sweetening) of the soil. Sometimes the pH of a soil is just fine as it is and changing it means doing something you must later undo. Incidentally pH is a term describing the sweet-sour condition of the soil, the way Fahrenheit readings indicate hot-cold degrees of temperature.

Most perennials thrive in a fairly neutral or pH 7 soil with toleration for slight variations either way. You can determine the pH of your own particular plot only by test. This you can manage yourself by means of a simple chemical home testing kit or you can send a soil sample to your county agent. Without charge, or for a small fee, he will make the necessary analysis and recommendation.

The sandy or clayey consistency of soil and its humus content are further determining factors. So don't follow blindly any general advice about adding so many pounds of lime per square foot of flower bed. This is no kindness to your perennials.

Generally speaking apply lime (1) to sweeten sour soils (2) to produce a definitely alkaline condition, reading above pH 7, for plants like delphinium, gypsophila and pink which seem to prefer a sweet growing medium (3) to correct overrich conditions due to too frequent applications of manure and (4) to exert a slightly disinfecting action where soil-borne diseases have been prevalent and where nematodes frequently attack peonies and chrysanthemums.

Lime the soil when it is necessary at least two weeks ahead of fertilizing, never at the same time since lime tends to free food elements faster than perennials can assimilate them. This results in waste. Late autumn is propitious for liming since other garden work slows down then and fertilizing is over for the season.

HUMUS

Next, consider the consistency of the soil and its humus content. A garden cannot be made by scratching the earth and applying fertilizer. Foods are important, to be sure, but they are, as I have pointed out, beneficial only when their medium of operation is a soil rich in humus. Humus is partially decomposed organic or once-living matter. It improves a clayey soil by opening it up and making it porous. It corrects a thin sandy one by giving it bulk and some capacity for holding water. But the greatest value of humus lies in its supply of bateria which, operating in the soil, make available to plant roots elements otherwise useless.

For gardens not yet on a self-running basis (without a compost pit or heap), either commercially available humus or peat moss is excellent. Peat moss corrects the mechanical ills of the soil and increases bacterial action. It supplies soil sponges for retaining water. In fact, it holds about ten times its dry weight in moisture. When beds are newly dug, enough peat moss should be added by bulk to give the soil a crumbly consistency if a handful of it is squeezed.

Other sources of humus are mushroom compost and the readily available and excellent shredded and pulverized manures. Well-rotted, that means two-year-old, horse or cow manure from a farm is still perhaps the best soil conditioner there is, though of slight fertilizing value. Leaf mold, of course, is fine. In time, however, a garden should become self-sufficient and produce a large quantity of its own humus through the conservation of leaves and other vegetable material collected and rotted down via the compost heap or pit. Personally, I could not manage a garden without at least one and better three compost pits.

COMPOST

I prefer pits to heaps because there are few out-of-sight spots in my garden. My compost pits are, therefore, dug three by six by four feet deep and the sides lined with old porch floor boards. Into their roomy depths go in the course of summer and fall most of the garden debris—grass clippings, leaves, vegetable tops (but not corn stalks) and faded bouquets. A sprinkling of lime or ordinary garden fertilizer, to hasten decomposition, and a thin layer of soil are more or less systematically cast over each twelve-inch layer of refuse until the top of the pit is reached.

The surface then is not flattened off, but hollowed a little to catch the rain water. This too hastens decomposition. In addition, the pit is soaked monthly through the summer for a whole day by a full-tilt hose. With some two or three turnings in the course of the season on days when other work is almost caught up, this material is thoroughly mingled. Within a twelve- to eighteen-month period most of it has reached that pleasant, crumbly condition so dear to the experienced gardener's heart. By keeping two pits going, there is always one about ready for use and one on the way. Three, of course, with one just for leaves, is pure luxury.

Gardeners who work on a small scale will find that even the behind-a-shrub compost heap, small though it be, has value. With a spreading spirea as a screen, perhaps, scoop out a wide circle of soil, six to twelve inches deep. Around this stake a retentive ten- to twelve-foot strip of woven wire and into the area throw the garden refuse, except, of course, infected or pest-carrying stalks. Here, too, time will produce several wheelbarrow loads of humus.

BASIC PLANT NUTRIENTS

To keep your garden richly supplied with basic plant nutrients you need to know something of its requirements. Plants must have nitrogen to promote leaf and stem strength and to stimulate growth generally. When there is too much, they grow prodigiously, but in spindly fashion and are poor flower producers. Witness the too-thin delphinium plants with small florets of sickly bloom or the sappy growth of overfed phlox. Obviously, however, plants emphasizing leaf growth, like baptisia, can do with a lot of nitrogen.

Phosphorus is for roots. It also gives a steady push to flower and seed production. With too little phosphorus, foliage lacks color. With too much, it is sappy, lacking fiber, and weak so that plants require a lot of staking.

Potash, the third essential element, is the antitoxin among plant foods. It wards off disease, stabilizes growth, and intensifies color. A plant suffering from a lack of it is dull and sickly looking. But if it has too much, it may make false growth, which afterwards will fall over.

The amounts of these three basic elements are marked on the bags and cartons of the various trade-marked brands of complete plant foods in numbered series like 5-8-5, 4-12-4, 6-7-3, 5-10-5 and so forth. The first number always represents the proportion of nitrogen content, the second the phosphate, and the third the potash. In addition, mention may be made of the presence of certain "trace elements"—iron, boron, manganese and others,—which in small quantities are also necessary to healthy plant life.

All-Purpose Foods

When buying a commercial plant food, read the label carefully and try to select one on which it is plainly indicated that some of the nitrogen is from organic or once-living material. These organic elements will be less quickly available and hence have a more lasting value than those which the greedy plant can consume all at once. For regular use I am partial to a 6-8-5 plant food with not less than sixty percent of the nitrogen derived from organic sources, but I have, too, a purely chemical 4-12-4 mix for spring and summer stimulation. With this, plants need in fall some rotted manure or organic bone meal as supplementary food.

As a general thing apply commercial plant foods to perennials about April 15 and again on May 15 in sufficient quantity slightly to obscure the soil. Do this just before you cultivate. After you have worked food in well, water deeply, unless you are lucky enough to catch a rain.

Avoid mixing plant foods with the soil in which seeds are to be sown. Also, if seedlings are transplanted, and not just thinned out, wait until growth has commenced before applying fertilizer. These all-purpose foods often act faster than such young plants can tolerate.

Manures

Special feeding and stimulation does not, of course, take the place of proper soil preparation before planting. If you live in the country and have natural manures available, your procedure can include less buying. Poultry manure is a fertile humus material. Before use, compost it for six months under cover of old burlap bags but with the sides of the stack exposed. A good plan is to make alternate layers of four inches of the manure and one inch of commercial superphosphate. The urea will thus be absorbed and the superphosphate cause quick rotting.

When a horse or cow manure is available, pile it in the open without cover for at least one year. Two years are better. Then dig it into the flower beds when they are first prepared and supplement with a top dressing of some complete fertilizer since manure is, as I have said, a soil conditioner rather than a plant food.

With some such soil-building program, your garden will grow on the finest of foundations. It will require of you a minimum of upkeep. It will even produce that beauty your optimism and the seed catalogues have led you to expect.

5. Comforts of
Moisture and Mulch

When your perennials have been planted in carefully prepared soil, they can stand well the heat and drought of summer, especially if cultivation is constant and what the old
hands call a "dust mulch" is maintained. A dust mulch consists
of a fine loose condition of the top inch or so of soil. When
this is worked up regularly, particularly after each rain, weeds,
discouraged in infancy, do not mature to spoil the garden's
looks and feed upon its resources. Furthermore, a pleasantly
cool and moist condition is maintained around the roots.

But how many of us have time or vigor to keep a dust
mulch in operation? More generally useful, therefore, is the
applied mulch through which weeds seldom intrude and from
which soil moisture does not evaporate. A number of good
mulching materials may be purchased. You will do well to
consider coarse wood chips. This material, fine enough for
water to pass directly through, is still so tough it disintegrates
slowly—yet it effectively throttles weeds. If your soil is
heavy, spread it an inch deep. Allow two inches on sandy
soils. Buckwheat hulls are another possibility, and this is the
mulch I am now using most freely—a dozen fifty-pound bags
of it last year. I like its good looks and light aeration and it

does not disintegrate too fast. Some always remains of last year's spreading for next year's base.

Peat moss is also good for mulching. The Fern Garden took ten bales of this for the initial spreading. The horticultural grade of peat is the kind I like for its just-right degree of coarseness. If a two-inch layer of this is spread in mid-June over the entire garden just after it has been well cultivated and watered, how exquisitely neat it stays through the summer heat and how very comfortable it appears to feel. The gardener is comfortable too, for you have then only the most occasional weed to pull and in the heat you can contentedly relax in the shade without being reproached by the terrible urgency of an unkempt border.

This peat moss may in fall or spring be worked into the soil. It thus adds beneficially to the organic content there. If your soil is very heavy, add sand to "cut" it—in proportions of six peat moss to one of sand. But if a very thick layer of peat moss has been used and the expense has been noticeable, the mulch is not worked in at all but scraped up and stored in baskets for next summer's spreading.

In any case, before applying peat moss to your borders, *moisten it thoroughly. Dry peat moss spread on dry soil can be a detriment unless there is an immediate heavy rainfall.* After ripping off the top and bottom strip of burlap and removing much of the packing, stand a new bale outside where rain will reach it. Or place a slow-running hose in the center and let it go until the peat moss has absorbed as much moisture as possible. Since a standard bale contains eighteen to twenty-two bushels, you can obtain from it an inch-deep mulch for two hundred and fifty to three hundred square feet of bed. I think so well of all of these mulching materials and want so much of them that I regularly put "mulches" on my Christmas list along with my annual request for a load of manure. The latter is my favorite present, but, alas, one I have been able to achieve but once, my family not considering it suitable for greetings of the season.

Some mulches can also be produced right in the garden. Fairly fine leaf mold from your compost pit does not look so well as peat moss, perhaps, but it does the job and is also reasonably nutritious, which peat moss is not. Grass clippings, if applied gradually, a thin layer at a time with opportunity to dry thoroughly before additions are made, are also suitable.

WATERING

Although mulching conserves mositure there still are times of prolonged drought in summer which necessitate extra watering. When these occur, be thorough and don't settle for less than a *deep* soaking for everything. Actually summer rains may not amount to enough to moisten more than the surface. I know. I have kept hoses going right through showers.

Even if your husband adores it and it soothes and quiets him in hot weather, don't give him the hose to play with in the evening. Nothing is worse for a garden than a regular evening sprinkle. It encourages surface instead of deep rooting of perennials, and foliage that is wet at night (with no sun to dry it off) is an out-and-out invitation to a number of blights and diseases. Mornings and late afternoons are the best times to water, but not nearer than two hours to sunset. Blazing midday and early afternoon are not good. But if you are doing the job thoroughly it will not matter if the sun shines on the foliage at the same time that the sprinkler is running.

The best way to soak roots deeply, of course, is not to use a sprinkler but to draw a slow-running hose among peonies or phlox or into the midst of the border. If the nozzle is laid on a narrow board this will prevent washing of the soil. Let the water run about an hour in each area. If you examine the soil in half an hour or so, you will be surprised to see how little of it has been reached. At least six inches deep is your goal.

A porous canvas tube called a soil soaker makes deep, thorough watering a less exacting task than the nozzle-on-board system. This soaker, which can be attached to your hose, comes in twelve- to fifty-foot lengths. Select a length nearest that of your longest bed. Use of this device in extensive sections in a small garden is difficult because water backs up in the soaker if you have to bend it.

Sometimes, of course, you will need to use a rotating sprinkler which projects a fine mist over a long distance. This overhead method, taking the place of rainfall, covers a wide section of garden without puddling soil and without requiring much attention from you. And it does afford great refreshment to plant tops on a hot day.

Incidentally, if the autumn tends to be dry, give your garden a thorough final soaking in late October or early November. Then plant roots will go into the winter plump and healthy. Plants left thirsty in autumn are always likely to winterkill.

WINTER COVERING

Winter protection is the final matter of plant contentment to be considered. Don't overdo it. In many locations, especially where gardens are hedged in considerably, very little is

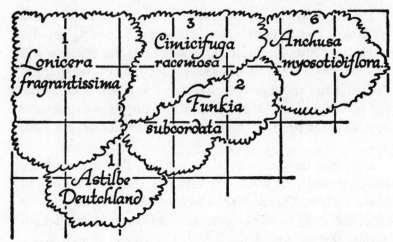

FOR A SHADY CORNER

needed. Indeed, for some years now I have not covered my garden at all and my losses seem slight. This has been true both in Philadelphia and Connecticut, though here, of course, I am near Long Island Sound, and nearness to water always mitigates the cold.

The aim in covering or mulching at this season, is, of course, to prevent that alternate freezing and thawing of the soil which a fluctuating winter and early spring climate induces. The summer mulch is used to conserve moisture and insulate the soil against extreme heat but the winter mulch is applied to keep the cold in and the frozen condition constant. Persisting snow is a natural mulch. So, too, are leaves. And this is the one for most of us to rely on unless the luxury of a two- to three-inch winter layer of peat moss is possible. Peat moss, I may say, certainly does look well for on-view beds near the house.

Many leaves naturally collect, however, and catch among

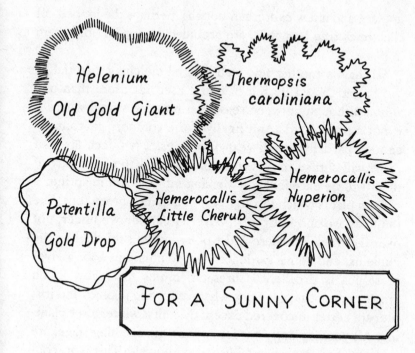

Helenium
Old Gold Giant

Thermopsis
caroliniana

Potentilla
Gold Drop

Hemerocallis
Little Cherub

Hemerocallis
Hyperion

FOR A SUNNY CORNER

K.B.

the crowns of the plants in the perennial border (the tall tops are, of course, cut down before mulching). But more leaves usually have to be added to get a uniform distribution. Any leaves will do except those of the poplars and Norway maples which mat down like soggy rags and exclude all air from the plants while pressing dampness down upon them all winter long. Leaves of oak, birch, hickory, beech, linden and the hardwood maples are fine. Indeed, any leaves which curl when they fall will do, while those which lie flat will not. Leaves may be collected in baskets or piled in a corner of the yard until needed in mid-December or later if a hard freeze has not occurred by that time. Then they are spread in place and a few evergreen boughs, perhaps the lopped-off Christmas tree branches, are arranged on top to hold them in place.

Salt hay is another fine well-aerated mulching material. It can be purchased by the bale and used for more than one winter although between seasons it must be stored where it is not a fire hazard. And finally if the compost pit contains enough partially rotted year-old leaves, a two-inch layer of these will suffice for a winter blanket and the finer part of them will be excellent for working into the soil in spring.

With plants which through winter maintain green tops, like the foxglove and hollyhock, coverings are drawn under, not over the tops. For these and woolly-leaved subjects like the mulleins, and some gardeners say delphiniums too, a layer of stones is excellent. Chrysanthemums that show green crowns require no covering whatever, while peonies and iris, too, are better uncovered except their first winter after planting. All young plants, not far beyond the seedling stage, are mulched earlier than established perennials. This is to conserve autumn soil warmth and so prolong their growing stage. Early November is usually not too soon to protect them.

In spring the greater part of the mulch is removed just as the forsythias bloom while the final amount is lifted as the buds appear on the maple trees. No exact dates can be set since the end of winter differs not only with localities but from year to year. Late in March is the time most of us have a winter-underwear feeling about mulches. Then it is time to poke underneath leaves or hay and see what goes on. Very likely coverings can be loosened a little to aerate the awakening plants. Mulches left too long in place in spring force abnormal growth but, by the same token, removing protection too early may expose the new growth to frostbite.

6. Supports for Giants and Spreaders

Good looks in a garden depend to a great extent on tidiness. This is particularly true of small plots. A handsome effect is well-nigh impossible if scattered about are supine plants which should be perpendicular rather than prone.

To maintain uprightness through the border I subscribe definitely to a far-sighted program. This means only the occasional use of certain loose-growing subjects like the lovely *Salvia azurea* which invariably needs special attention. Penstemons, bergamot and most physostegias are other rampant flounderers. Before banishing these, however, you will be wise to consider whether this loose growth is an inherent characteristic, as it certainly is of these, or is a weak condition due to a soil lack which should be remedied at the source with applications of phosphorus in the form of bone meal in the fall and superphosphate in the spring.

Many plants require support against wind and summer rain. This need brings the forehanded gardener at spring ordering time to a most fascinating collection of gadgetry. When I bring my box out on Stake Day I find I have a considerable variety of supports acquired over a period of years according to the needs of individual plant groups as I became aware of them.

The newer supports are quite different from the stout broom or mop handles which once sufficed. When these were plunged into the center of hangdog growers and the foliage was drawn up and bunched together with heavy white cord, it is doubtful that anyone got satisfaction from the process. Certainly not the plants. They seemed in their unnatural state to be suffering continuous indignity, while the beauty-loving gardener knew something was wrong, even if no other method of dealing with floppy plants came to mind. (If you should unavoidably have to deal with such plants, gather the stems loosely near the base and fasten to a short, stout stake; this method will at least allow the tops of the plants to arch with some degree of grace.)

The Natural Look with Twigs

Today we respect the natural tendencies of growth. When the garden abounds in platycodon, veronica, coreopsis, gaillardia, oriental poppies and achillea, twiggy branches are early set among them so that, as the plants develop, they arrange themselves naturally over their supports and these are eventually hidden. You can have a convenient source of just the right kind of twiggy branches if you will plant, for the purpose, in some out-of-the-way corner a couple of bushes of California privet and allow them to grow unpruned.

When twigs do not suffice, you must buy various plant supports and some "ties" of one kind or another too. Once it seemed to me that staking and tying involved so many operations at once that I needed an extra hand. All this is now simplified.

Bamboo and Wire

For single-stemmed plants I use assorted lengths of bamboo and wire, not held in place by string or tape but by flexible wire tapes or twistems designed like pipe-cleaners. These are as easy to fasten securely as a bobby pin and they provide enough "give" to prevent breaking.

Natural-color bamboo is less expensive than that dyed green, but the green ones are worth the difference because they show less. Galvanized iron wire one-eighth inch in diameter and in two- to six-foot lengths I like even better because it is narrow yet very strong. When there are many separate stems as in mature meadowrue or delphinium, I fasten a separate wire support to each. This is a beautifully neat and strong arrangement.

Commercial Gadgets

Steel plant props are now available in sixteen- to seventy-eight-inch lengths with a little twist at one end to hold the stem. These are most convenient for everything from a tulip to a hollyhock, the steel being of weights commensurate with the lengths.

Then there is a contraption designed for bunchy plants like hardy asters, oriental poppies, dahlias, sunflowers, also delphiniums. It consists of a seven-eighths-inch square, green, wooden stake—three, four, or five feet long—and an adjustable self-locking, thirteen-inch wire ring, which can be slid up the stake as the spreading plant grows. This has its uses but is hard to place inconspicuously.

For peonies, and the more rampant chrysanthemums, I like the double-ring peony support of tripod type. Some gardeners use this also for large delphinium and oriental poppy clumps. Thrust among the plants early, it is soon covered by new growth. Two kinds of double-ring supports have been available, one with the top ring adjustable. I prefer the type with both rings stationary because it wears better. Mine now have eight years of double duty to their credit. In April they are thrust deeply around each clump of peonies. In late June, they are transferred for the summer to those chrysanthemums destined for prolific autumn display. With either plant, at maturity, these supports are blessedly invisible.

And that is the aim of proper plant supporting—invisibility. If visitors to my garden ever remark, "What interesting supports you are using," or, "How carefully you stake your plants," I know that in that season I have done an inept job.

7. Guides to Garden Health

Successful coping with pests and disease seems to be a necessary though completely unappealing aspect of gardening. But you can mitigate the pain considerably, I have discovered, by growing only the sturdier plant varieties and also by careful garden sanitation. This means keeping a clean garden, burning disease-ridden stalks and yellow leaves, and *not planting so thickly that you check a free circulation of cleansing air.*

Even the not-too-serious gardeners, however, usually have some pet perennials on which they are willing to lavish a certain amount of extra effort, providing, of course, there are rewards. With these plants in mind—and I think particularly of chrysanthemums, columbine, peonies, phlox, bearded iris and delphinium—some discussion, admittedly superficial, seems now in order as to the general problems which may confront, but should not overwhelm, you.

Problems are really of four kinds. There are the "psychological" problems, due to too much or too little water, as when in drought stems harden and later cannot benefit from copious watering. Or soil is sweet or alkaline and a plant needs it slightly acid, as most of them do; or soil is sour or acid, and the need, as with delphinium, is for lime. Or, as I have said, plants suffer from crowding.

55

INSECT PESTS

Then there are all the bugs. Some suck, some chew. Sucking insects weaken or destroy by piercing plant tissues with their beaks and drawing from them the vital juices. General debility and loss of color follow an attack. The most common insect in this class is the aphid, black groups of which are all too familiar on the succulent shoots of chrysanthemums, while lighter ones cluster on the undersides of columbine foliage. Any time after growth commences in spring, the black, green, white or red aphids may make an appearance. Insecticidal soap or pyrethrum sprays, alone or in combination, seal their doom.

The red spider and other mites likewise debilitate plants by sucking. And they are almost invisible without a magnifying glass. However, mites will proclaim their presence if you know what to look for—mealiness and brittleness of leaves with tiny webs underneath; and finally, a general yellowing of foliage. Attacks can occur as soon as leaves begin to develop and are most persistent when air is hot and ground is dry. A good hose drenching helps to *some* extent because it dampens the atmosphere and mites do not thrive when it is cool and moist. Phlox, hollyhocks, delphinium and the hardy evergreen candytuft (iberis) are favorite abodes. You may have to take *special* measures—such as applications of insecticidal soaps—to control mites, but remember, their presence in life-threatening numbers almost always indicates a plant stressed by lack of adequate soil moisture.

Other insects may harm by chewing even to the point of skeletonizing foliage. They are destroyed when they eat foliage that is covered with something poisonous to them. Japanese beetles are the worst, and you can hardly protect flowers from them, only leaves, since an opening blossom presents a continually *fresh* surface for attack. When plants such as hollyhocks need protection, spray with one of the beetle preparations at emerging time (June 20 in Philadelphia and 30 in New York) and keep on spraying as you have to, to save your plants. Or omit hollyhocks for a few years. Japanese beetles eventually leave a locality, you know. Although I never have many here now, time was in Philadelphia—but over that era of my gardening, let me draw a veil.

Borers or caterpillars which work inside stems are likewise chewers and very hard to deal with. Sometimes they can be caught working and destroyed on the spot. Their favorite eating place, the bearded iris, can be protected by letting organic litter accumulate amongst the leaves and over the rhizomes in late summer and early fall. This is where the moth responsible for them lays her eggs. Before the first hard freeze, remove the litter and destroy it; do not put this in your compost pile. If borers are found at the time of digging and transplanting iris rhizomes, clean them well, then dust generously with diatomaceous earth. In the larval stage these appear as leaf miners which can be destroyed by squeezing them between your fingers, presuming you have the stomach for this sort of garden combat.

Occasionally trouble originates in the soil, as when cutworms attack the columbines or other seedlings just after you have proudly set them out. And slugs, which are slimy snails without shells, may feed at night on your hollyhocks, leaving riddled leaves as evidence. Slugs can be controlled by setting out shallow trays of stale beer or preferably a non-alcoholic malt beverage containing lager yeast; the smell lures them into the liquid and they drown. Scattering diatomaceous earth around slug-infested plants also works as a deterrent, as well as any fairly rough mulch material such as bark chips.

Ants may cause trouble, not on peony buds, from which they disappear when the flower opens, but in flower beds where their busy hills are objectionable. Pouring boiling water into their busy hills is an effective and environmentally safe way to deter ants. The grubs that become Japanese beetles can be controlled by applications of milky spore disease, *Bacillus popilliae,* or BP for short. Indirectly this treatment deters moles by destroying the grubs on which they feed.

SOME PLANT DISEASES

It would be pleasant if at this point I could end my homily on sorrow with the assurance that not all gardens get all the pests, nor even some of them, every year. Which is, indeed, a comforting as well as a true thought. I must add, however, that there are fungus disease troubles which must also be dealt with. Three kinds are most common—mildew, leaf blights of many kinds, and rusts.

Mildew sometimes covers, with a white powdery coating, plants of peony, phlox, chrysanthemum and delphinium when July and August days are damp and muggy. This may be treated by spraying at any time trouble appears with a mixture of baking soda and water (one tablespoon to one gallon), or by use of a natural garden fungicide. Crowded, damp or sunless plantings, where the atmosphere is close, are the most prone to attack, or those gardens which are persistenly sprinkled at dusk so that foliage goes into the night wet. Cut down and destroy all plant tops in fall as a control measure.

Various leaf blights and spots may mar, curl and disfigure foliage. Peonies on which buds blacken and fail to open are affected by a fungus known as botrytis blight. Also spray these plants from the time the spring points emerge until the foliage is about one foot high. Use a spray of Bordeaux mixture for peonies, likewise against the devastating rust that attacks hollyhocks.

EQUIPMENT

Two pieces of equipment are necessary for garden doctoring: a duster and a sprayer, small or large, according to the number of plants to be tended. When remedies for plant ills are available as dusts, I prefer these to sprays. I have something called a Midget Duster which is not only efficient but is as much fun to operate as a child's mechanical toy. I keep it filled with an all-purpose dust all the time for quick and limited attacks. It seems to me far simpler to transfer a dry material from package to dust gun than to go through the measuring and diluting process for sprays, and then afterwards to wash and dry your sprayer.

The "spraying school" maintains, however, that you get a more thorough coverage with a spray and also that a spray sticks longer, especially if it contains (or you add) some good prepared spreader-sticker compound or just common soap or detergent. Even though I personally prefer dusts, I concede the merit of sprays. So here is a formula for an all-purpose spray that you can make up at home, with plant food added for superconvenience. For the most part you can rely on this spray—just as you can rely on an all-purpose dust— to keep your perennials trouble-free.

ALL-PURPOSE SPRAY PLUS PLANT FOOD

1 gallon water
1 tablespoon insecticidal soap
1 tablespoon baking powder
2 tablespoons liquid seaweed or
    fish emulsion

Mix ingredients well and apply as needed, *regularly* if you wish, say twice a month. The soap acts as a spreader, particularly if water is hard. Insecticidal soap sprays, if applied thoroughly to all surfaces, especially leaf undersides, and on a weekly basis, will rout most garden insect problems without any particular threat to beneficial insects or to the gardener or other human visitors. Baking powder (or the use of a commercial product such as Safer Garden Fungicide) takes care of disease troubles.

If you add to this all-purpose spray a portion of fertilizer such as liquid seaweed or fish emulsion, you will be doing your plants an extra favor every time you protect them.

However, you can save yourself a lot of trouble by being sensible in your choice of plant material. If you find that delphiniums are one long headache or that phlox blight more than they bloom and you are tired to death of their temperamental demands, for heaven's sake, throw them out. Life is too short to let gardening be more chore than fun. Emphasize more robust material so you can have a fan in your hand part of the summer instead of a duster or spray gun. P.S. The summer phlox Bright Eyes is remarkably resistant to mildew.

Having thus handed over to you the fruits of my rarely bitter experience, I won't here name the few plants I do not intend to grow again. But I will suggest that you consider this list of kinds which for me have been singularly free from

the common plant troubles. Fill your garden with the likes
of these if abundant bloom from healthy plants is for you an
important gardening goal.

PLANTS THAT TAKE CARE OF THEMSELVES

Astilbe (Spiraea)
Baptisia (False indigo)
Chrysanthemum maximum (Shasta daisy)
Convallaria (Lily-of-the-valley)
Coreopsis
Delphinium (only the Chinese type)
Dianthus (Pinks)
Dicentra (Bleedingheart)
Dictamnus (Gas plant)
Doronicum (Leopardbane)
Eupatorium
Gaillardia (Blanket flower)
Gypsophila (Babysbreath)
Helenium (Helen's flower)
Heliopsis (Orange sunflower)
Helleborus niger (Christmas rose)
Hemerocallis (Daylily)
Heuchera (Coralbells)
Hosta or *Funkia* (August lilies and their relatives)
Iris sibirica (Siberian iris)
Linum perenne (Flax)
Monarda (Beebalm)
Papaver orientale (Oriental poppy)
Phlox subulata
Physostegia (False dragonhead)
Polemonium reptans (Jacob's ladder)

Primula (Primrose)
Pyrethrum
Salvia azurea
Thalictrum (Meadowrue)
Thermopsis
Veronica
Viola (Violet)

All of the self-help plants are not distinguished or even refined growers but they are sturdy. Many, however, such as the bleedinghearts, are the loveliest possible garden flowers, while such perennials as baptisia, gas plant and hosta have an enduringly fine plant form with consistent attractiveness from spring to fall. Peonies, hybrid delphinium, bearded iris and phlox are not included although I consider these first when I plan a border. For reasons which you may happily never discover for yourself, I omit them from this list of essentially reliable plants. I also see no reason to prejudice you against plants that, under your conditions, might easily be the joy of your garden.

8. Means of Multiplication

When the plan for your perennial garden has reached the completed drawn-to-scale on-paper stage, where will you find your plants? At the risk of sounding cynical I advise you to depend very little on the bounty of friends and neighbors. Don't mind, indeed, looking the gift horse very searchingly in the mouth since all too often the given plant turns out to be magenta phlox, orange daylily, fried-egg iris or the all-encompassing Golden Glow (rudbeckia). Only rarely is it a fine strain of columbine seedlings or divisions from a pale and scented hemerocallis. As a particular gardener, even if a new one, you want only choice perennials and of these no one ever seems to have many to give away.

BY PURCHASE

Next, about buying. If a local nursery can supply you with well-developed clumps—not barely started seedlings or minute divisions—make your selections there. But you will find few if any local nurseries that can hold a candle to the number and variety of plant selections offered by a good mail-order nursery. In any case, when you buy, be certain you are getting the varieties you desire. Nothing so upsets a well-laid scheme as the planting of the loud yellow basket-of-gold, *Alyssum saxatile compactum,* when it was the lemon-yellow *A. saxatile citrinum* you ordered, or the placing of a salmon pink phlox where you wanted a delicate rose variety. (A list of Sources of Plants is given on page 295.)

At the start, you will do well to purchase fine varieties of iris, daylily, hybrid delphinium, peony, chrysanthemum, hardy aster, oriental poppy, helenium, babysbreath, gas plant, baptisia, anemone, aconite, hardy candytuft and hellebore, also plants of bleedingheart and mertensia.

You do not, however, need quantities of these. Three or more, depending on space, will suffice of the delphinium, iris, anemone, gas plant, mertensia and aconite. One each is enough of the named varieties of chrysanthemum, aster, most daisies, babysbreath and bleedingheart, since all of these soon lend themselves to simple means of home propagation. And, of course, with the more expensive kinds of peony and oriental poppy, one each is plenty unless you are familiar with the variety.

Until I learned the danger of blind ordering, I sometimes used to be inundated with twelve plants of something rampant like helenium when with a little patience I could have had my twelve by the second year from one bought plant. Once I purchased nine *Artemisia lactiflora,* "Hawthorne-scented, five feet, exquisite combined with buddleia and hardy asters" and found myself in possession of an enormous crop of something very near a weed. I do not mean, of course, for you to be a one-of-each buyer or planter. Catalogues sensibly encourage selection by threes. From an economical and practical point of view, however, your larger purchases should be limited to plants hard to propagate at home such as delphinium in some places, or slow like the peony or gas plant, or scarce like hellebores.

BY DIVISION

Meanwhile purchased or "gift" stock, or desirable plants that a neighbor is willing to share, can be increased in three ways— by division, by stem cuttings or by root cuttings—and in some cases by saved seed.

After heleniums, shasta daisies and most chrysanthemums have grown in your garden for only a year you can lift the plants with a spading fork, in spring, and carefully pull, pry, or cut them into a number of divisions. These, set out separately, will by summer or fall give you new plants of a size equal to the parents. Phlox, iris and columbine can be divided by the third year.

When you lift some plants a hard woody center will appear. Discard this, resetting only the younger sections. But don't make the divisions too small or the next year your garden will have a very sparse and meager look. Experience will reveal each plant's rate of development. You will discover that a well-grown phlox can usually be separated into thirds while very small piece of rooted chrysanthemum has the capacity for equaling its mature parent within the one growing season.

And you will find that spring- and summer-flowering plants like iris, phlox, columbine and primrose are best divided after a rain in late August or September. Deal with them as soon as the heat has sufficiently waned for you to attack the business cheerfully but while at least a month or more of growing weather remains before frost. This allows divided plants to anchor themselves in their new locations. Plan spring division for chrysanthemums, hardy asters, aconites and other fall-flowering plants. Some perennials like the peony, gypsophila, bleedingheart, lupine, gas plant, anemone and Christmas rose you will not disturb for years and years since these flourish only after they have been thoroughly acclimated to your garden.

BY CUTTINGS

Another method of increase is by cuttings—stem or root. In early summer, when the second growth of rockcress, hardy candytuft, phlox or pinks is well advanced, just go through the plantings with a razor blade. Exactly beneath the point where a leaf emerges, cut the stems off. Leave several eyes or points of growth, of course, below the cut so that the older plant can sprout again. This treatment does not harm developed perennials. It only makes them thick and branching.

Next, from the cut sections you have taken, remove the lower leaves and any incipient flowers at the top. Then insert the bare stems an inch or so of their approximately three-inch lengths in a box of moist sand set in the shade or in a shaded cold frame. In this way you can quickly and easily obtain a large crop of one variety. I have had Miss Lingard phlox root in less than three weeks in August and with almost no attention from me. If you want to obtain economically an edging of one kind, like hardy candytuft, for instance, try this method of increase after your three or more purchased plants are established.

2 Rosa hugonis		3 Thermopsis caroliniana	
5 Coreopsis			
4 Chrysanthemum Eugene Wander	4 Trollius Lemon Queen	1 Hemerocallis Patricia	1 Hemerocallis Cinnabar
		3 Alyssum saxatile	

A GOLDEN GROUP

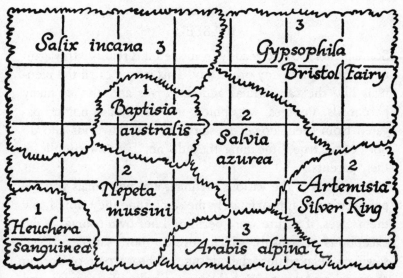

Salix incana 3		3 Gypsophila Bristol Fairy	
1 Baptisia australis	2 Salvia azurea		
2 Nepeta mussini		2 Artemisia Silver King	
1 Heuchera sanguinea	3 Arabis alpina		

A SILVER GROUP

Root Cuttings

The root cutting is a good way to extend your stock of bleedinghearts, phlox, sea lavender, babysbreath, anemone and oriental poppy. In late August or September lift the plant you wish to propagate and select roots of approximately lead pencil size. Cut these into three-inch pieces and lay the sections horizontally in rows in a cold frame. Space them about three inches apart and firm over them a one- to two-inch layer of sand or sand and peat moss mixed. Leave the frame open until after the freezing weather. Then close and shade it until warm middays occur in February. Begin to ventilate for progressively longer periods as the spring season advances. Water from April on as the soil requires it. By May you will have a fine lusty crop of complete plants to move to permanent quarters.

BY SEED

Some plants grow so readily from seed it is really extravagant to obtain them in any other way. This is true of all the biennials like the campanulas and foxgloves and also of many perennials. Peonies, iris, phlox and daylily are not propagated from seed, however, since these are hybrids and do not "come true," meaning they do not faithfully duplicate their parents.

Sow seeds of the various biennials and perennials you are propagating at approximately the same time they would sow themselves, if nature were permitted her own course. Make exceptions of pansies, which develop more satisfactorily if sowing is delayed until the midsummer heat is past, of Korean chrysanthemums, which behave practically like annuals, and of delphinium. Of these three you want fresh seed and unless you are using your own, it cannot be purchased before late July. As for the rest, sow the spring-flowering arabis, alyssum, columbine, iberis and primrose preferably in May and June; the early summer lupines, foxgloves, coralbells, campanulas, meadowrue, thermopsis and pyrethrum before the end of July; and the aconite, gaillardia, platycodon, salvia, scabiosa, shasta daisy, stokesia and other summer- and fall-blooming perennials between mid-July and mid-August.

Cold Frame or Open Bed

Make your sowings either in a cold frame or in the open near a hedge or wall. Keep in mind that your success depends on a *constant* supply of moisture, protection from wind and strong sunshine and a loose soil which will neither bake out nor drain rapidly. Prepare the top inch of soil with particular care. Finely pulverized humus or compost will improve texture; sand should be liberally added if the soil is heavy.

Sow the seeds thinly and evenly and press them lightly into the soil. Then water gently. I use the house-plant syringe or my quart can sprayer for this purpose. Finally cover with a thin layer of soil and never for a minute thereafter neglect the need for even moisture. Sowings are easily protected from glare and drying wind, and also from drowning in a heavy rain, by a lath shade, old window shade or length of cheese-cloth supported by sturdy plant stakes.

Meanwhile prepare a second bed or another cold frame section to receive the seedlings as soon as they are of a size to handle conveniently. Use plenty of humus in this second bed but no chemical fertilizers. Space the plants according to their natures from three inches for iberis to nine inches for foxgloves. Provide protection from the sun for the first week after transplanting and cultivate to eliminate weeds

carefully by hand. Many perennials, certainly, may be propagated in several ways depending on your preference and
convenience.

A Gem of Simplicity

Of course, you must have a cold frame. Even if your garden
is small, gardening without one is like cooking without elec-
tric appliances. You can do it, but it's more work and less
fun. In its basic form a cold frame is simply a box without
top and bottom. For bottom it has the soil; for top, a piece
of glass. In a sunny spot this wooden frame is inserted into
the ground so that the front rests about ten inches above soil
level and the rear twenty. Thus a sloping top surface is provided to catch sunshine. For cold protection the box is banked
with several inches of soil on the outside and, in extreme
weather, burlap bags or a piece of blanket or carpet are
thrown over the glass at night to keep in the warmth the sun
afforded during the day.

My first cold frame was simply a wooden grocery box inserted into the soil near the kitchen door where the sun could
warm it quickly and I could examine it constantly. (In my
early days of gardening I was certainly one to watch the pot
until I wonder it ever boiled.)

Anyway it was amazing the crops I grew in there, using a
cheap adjustable window screen as a sun shade in the heat.
Late in March I'd start a crop of Chinese larkspur along with
one of the slow annuals like petunias. When these were
moved in May, I put in cuttings of Miss Lingard phlox followed by a sowing of Mrs. Scott Elliott columbines which
remained until the next spring. Thus that little makeshift
structure was put to use every month of the year.

Bigger and Better

Later I worked on a little larger scale with a triple cold frame, the tops made from casements taken from the children's torn-down playhouse and the sides from creosoted floor boards from the same source. The only new materials used were two-by-four posts cut into lengths to form strong corners. Slatted covers, made from a bundle of lath, gave excellent protection to summer sowings. The end sections of this frame measured eighteen by thirty-six inches; the middle was only ten inches wide. Today, there is available a convenient aluminum frame with clear plastic wire-reinforced lid. It can readily be lifted up and set wherever you need it.

I have never owned a so-called regulation cold frame made of three by six standard sash. I hope I never shall. These are ungainly for a woman to handle and also not nearly so convenient as several small frames in which different-length operations can be carried on at the same time.

Unstinted Service

Besides a spot for plant propagation, frames also offer safe winter quarters for tender plants like spoon chrysanthemums or gerberas which are moved there after they stop flowering. Cuttings and seedlings still too small for outside wintering can likewise be stored there during the cold months. And I like an extra frame too for a permanent crop. I particularly enjoy a small duplex built in a sun-drenched corner by the sturdy steps. Here I have a planting of *Iris stylosa* and sweet violets—very nice for midwinter and early spring picking.

Without a cold frame you can still raise many perennials from seed or cutting. A somewhat raised bed in a light but not sunny, protected spot outdoors near a faucet or within reach of the hose will do. Or a box of well-prepared soil makes a nice nursery. After sowing, cover with a piece of burlap to keep the soil from drying out. Water right through this until germination occurs. But at the sign of the first green shoot, whisk away the burlap, for plants have been known to get their young necks broken when they poked them through burlap weave. You cannot regulate conditions so well in the open and, of course, you cannot sow early or protect plants late.

So do have a cold frame, even a makeshift one like my own early love.

9. Iris, Indispensable
and Irresistible

In the temperate zone, the iris or fleur-de-lis, Ruskin's flower of chivalry, "with a sword for its leaf and a lily for its heart," is a cherished perennial. Alone in spacious hobby gardens it makes a magnificent spring and early summer picture with long drifts of translucent white passing into cream and yellow and pink, lavender, purple and red terminating in masses of seashell and sunset blends. Indeed, iris is so dear to most of us that even when our space is limited we devote some of the border area behind edging plants and early bulbs to iris. Here we set out a colorful array of intermediate and tall bearded varieties for May and June and perhaps autumn bloom and are pleased to give them important placement because their foliage has such fine enduring quality.

Lacking a border, we find iris excellent in small but bold plantings (each devoted to one variety) beside a door, a flight of steps, below a window or beside a terrace. In my Fern Garden, I plant clumps of the purple species, *Iris versicolor*, for flowering amidst the green there, the lance leaves supplying a fine continuing contrast in foliage form to the fern fronds. A visit to an iris garden in May and June sends us home reeling, our minds aglow with color combinations we must have in melting pinks, cerulean blues, pale yellows, delicate whites—at least they are the ones that lead me on!

THE SMALLER IRISES

Actually, however, May is much too late for me to start my iris story. I want to commence in December with the species *Iris stylosa* or *unguicularis* which is established in one section of a cold frame. Early in winter after it has been lightly touched by frost, this so-called Algerian iris produces exquisite flowers "of real sky blue—not the deep blue of summer, but the brilliant paler blue of a frosty January." *Stylosa* may not flower the first season it is set out, but it produces winter bouquets the second or third as it gets to feeling at home in the coarse sandy or gravelly soil I have provided. Of course, it cannot conveniently be moved in and out of the cold frame but must occupy a section permanently.

In my sunny Kitchen Doorstep Garden, *stylosa* is followed—sometimes in February (in some years, even with snow) but certainly in March—by *I. reticulata*. The netted iris is a bulbous type, like the English and Spanish, a dwarf, fragrant, purple with gold markings and four-angled stems, just the plant for all of us who try for winter bloom.

In April appears a bright amethyst patch of the crested little species, *I. cristata*. Under an apple tree with White Lady narcissus, this little charmer has been one of the first delights of spring. A moist soil, rich in humus, and a lightly shaded location constitute its happy life. Perhaps in your rock garden, you too can find just the spot for it.

I must also have a few plants of *I. tectorum*, the roof iris, which in China blooms purple and white on thatched roofs like flowers on a lady's hat. These twelve-inch plants, in the white variety *alba*, are pleasing when alternately grouped with lavender *Phlox divaricata*. They make nice specimen groups too. Since *alba* is relatively expensive, you may want to feature just a plant or so of it. I have it along the path at the edge of the North Terrace Doorstep Garden. Here where I pass so often, I enjoy every lovely cluster of May-into-June flowers. The blue one costs less and is also attractive. Shade and soil from the compost pit also delight tectorum.

Iris gracilipes blooms about the same time as *I. tectorum*, and is a lovely tiny gem of a plant. Also in lavender or white, and just eight to ten inches tall, *I. gracilipes* is pretty for a rock garden or informal border edging with its excellent foliage.

Blooming in many gardens at about the same time is the dwarf *I. pumila*, but not in mine. This is an iris I definitely cannot abide. It looks all wrong to me, those big blooms and those little plants, ugly, somehow, the way many story-book dwarfs are ugly and physically not well composed. No, indeed, no *I. pumila* for me, let the catalogue color plates bleat as they will.

The table irises are another story. They are true miniatures of the tall bearded varieties, a charming addition to the iris clan. They are so called for their value as table decoration, and flower arrangers find them delightful and somewhat easier to handle than their big handsome relatives. Except for rather large arrangements, the tall beardeds seem more appropriate and useful in the garden than in the house. Varieties of table iris you will be pleased with for bouquets include Kinglet, Peewee, Tom Tit, Two for Tea, Warbler.

BEARDED IRIS

The most important iris is, of course, the bearded type, the earliest of which blooms for me about mid-May. In this group, do consider the intermediates which I find so attractive to flank the taller kinds in the border. Of sturdy constitution, they grow from sixteen to twenty-eight inches tall and are, indeed, intermediate in size of flower and height. Some kinds, like Autumn King and Autumn Haze, tend to repeat their pleasing performance in the fall. A few, like Autumn Queen, often flower intermittently through the summer. But do not count on this later blooming as a certainty, although it does sometimes occur on varieties sold as fall-flowering. It is in May that you will find such intermediates as the white Cosette, golden Crysora, yellow Nymph, Ruby Glow, and Andalusian Blue ideal and dependable companions for tulips, or even substitutes for them—just the perennial, in fact, to fill in a possible lull following narcissus.

The taller bearded iris have in recent years undergone a transformation which makes the varieties of today a far and joyful cry from the muddy purples and blurred yellows of the plants we knew in childhood as "flags." Selecting a limited group, however, is a complicated business, for varieties now number in the thousands with a flowering period from mid-May well into June, and heights varying from thirty to fifty inches.

But you must be self-controlled with iris or your garden becomes a melee. Certainly in the mixed border, repeated groups of just a few varieties give a far lovelier effect than a confusion of numerous kinds, fine as each may be. In fact, one kind—perhaps a pale blue, a white or light yellow—might provide a theme. I grow only the "selfs" or varieties of one color. I think bicolors, blends and even the "stitched" plicatas incline to spotty effects, and my cut-flower arrangements are never sufficiently subtle for me to struggle with these dual shadings.

In a border, I often plant bearded iris in large clumps, with specimen plants of hemerocallis or peonies or phlox to interrupt and separate the iris colonies. This gives a pleasant effect in bloom, and later the whole line remains unfalteringly green. Through the summer I occasionally trim back the daylilies and remove some side shoots from the peonies to keep them from shading the iris.

If your garden is quite small, three plants of bearded iris are enough for each colony. Where space permits, use large groups of one kind. Seek attractive companions among daylilies, oriental poppies and columbines, and for minor harmonies use pinks, coralbells and flax. Try the white iris, Cliffs of Dover, the pale yellow Moonlight Sonata with the silvery pink and fragrant peony, Mons. Jules Elie; or an early-midseason association of the pink Cherie, blue Jane Phillips and yellow-tinged cream Desert Song. A lovely midseason group includes the flaming-pink Happy Birthday, clear blue Great Lakes, milk-white Tranquility and yellow-and-white Truly Yours to bring out the yellow tones in Happy Birthday. With a dark iris like The Red Douglas, use blue lupines and white meadowrue.

Perhaps you will prefer tall bearded iris separately in bold clumps of one color. In the intersection of garden paths, five to seven plants of one of the blends like Copper Lustre would be handsome, or a flight of steps might be graced by the Carrara whiteness of Spanish Peaks. The darker golden copper Prairie Sunset or deep violet Midnight Blue, or any other dark kind looks well along a white fence. Light varieties like the white Lady Boscawen, pale shrimp-colored Cathedral Bells or bold Orange Gem are well set off by a background of evergreens, a house wall or stone wall.

Plans for Iris Gardens

If you have a rather small layout but wish to feature iris, arrange it so as to simulate depth. I once saw in an almost square plot, with a paved circular center, iris set in skillful gradations in deep triangular corner beds to give perspective. The whites and yellows were planted in the foreground. These have, of course, the strongest visual value. The blues and pinks were behind them with the deeper violets like Midnight Blue giving an effect of distance in the background. Extremely dark or "black" varieties and the coppery blends were wisely omitted here. These require lighter varieties among them to set them off and even then may not be so telling as the lovely blues or glowing yellows.

Another good way to lay out an iris garden, large or small, is with elliptical beds with broad paths of grass bisecting an oblong surrounded by some evergreen hedge, or better still a low stone wall made broad enough to sit on. Then plan grass strips between the beds wide enough for convenient mowing, say thirty inches or so.

I saw a fine layout of this type at the Brooklyn Botanic Garden. If you live near it, you will find it well worth studying both for design and varieties since these are numerous and include the finer new ones. The foreground ellipsis is all white, but in mixed varieties (in a small garden just one variety would be better). Then come ellipses of yellows, pale, deep and bicolored; next the blues both pale and deep, and farthest back the copper blends and dark purples, of which a little goes a great way with me.

Tweed-Suit Test for Bicolors and Blends

When you want to work out pleasing groupings with a bicolor or blended iris, do the way you* do when selecting a blouse for a tweed-mixture suit, where you want contrast and not a match. If the tweed is violet with a blue thread, you pick out a blue blouse of the same shade, but if there is a pale yellow line through the tweed, you wear a cream or pale yellow blouse or sweater. In each case you emphasize the secondary tone.

This method works particularly well with pink iris. These are "shrimp" or "flamingo" pinks (meaning they have yellow tones, as in Pink Cameo, Happy Birthday or Cherie) or rose pinks (meaning there are blue tones, as in China Maid or Pink Sensation). Mary Randall is a deep rose color. Pale yellow iris look well with the flamingo pinks; blues and lavenders look well with the blue-pinks, following the tweed-suit plan. (With pink and rose-colored peonies, use mostly blue-pinks; avoid the flamingo-pinks, which kill the peony colors.)

When it comes to the red-browns and the brown-reds, use them alone or with a tint your eye can extract—with golden brown Argus Pheasant, use cream-colored Desert Song or lemon-cream Amandine perhaps; the same two with the apricot-tan Cascade Splendor; or, with the golden brown Tobacco Road, the deep yellow Foxfire would be striking. Good color harmonies with the strong iris really take doing. The marvelous color-illustrated catalogues of iris specialists can help a lot. (See the Sources list on page 295). But you should

---

*In this case "you" is addressed to women, but only because the suit-blouse analogy gave me an easy way to explain myself. Men gardeners can readily use this test by visualizing similar "tweed color" combinations in their clothing.

see plants in bloom or try out a few together before getting too ambitious about big plantings of strong colors.

Personally, strong colors scare me to death, and I usually follow meekly along the pastel path of whites, blues, pinks and pale yellows—no deep purples, no blacks, no strong blends. What I come out with can probably be described in terms of clothes as "negative good taste," safe but not brilliant! Anyhow, I get tremendous pleasure from a planting of Cahokia (melting blue), Limelight (pale yellow), Happy Birthday (flamingo-pink) and Cliffs of Dover (pure white, ruffled, with a yellow beard). When you can't go all out for iris or peonies or any other plant because of space or *time*, settle for just one small and perfect planting of it.

Culture of Bearded Iris

These bearded iris have two definite requirements—drainage and plenty of sunshine. They are a joy even if you suffer with a cement-mix of stoney soil and they seem to thrive in alkaline, neutral or slightly acid loam of average fertility. For extra food, use a light sprinkling of bone meal in fall and of pulverized sheep manure or a balanced fertilizer in spring. Be sure to plant the rhizomes with the top of the fleshy roots but half an inch or so under the surface of the soil. Here they can bask in the sun. If set deeper, they will either refuse to bloom, die of discouragement or energetically work their way up to their favorite position.

And don't attempt to cultivate iris in the usual way. Roots lie too near the surface for safe hoeing. Weed the plants by hand instead. And clean them up in spring as early and as thoroughly as possible. Then remove all old leaves and debris to prevent attacks of the familiar iris borer which winters over in eggs deposited by a moth the previous fall. The borer first punctures the foliage and then slowly works its way down into the rhizome. Decay and rot mark its travels although rot may occur from other causes as well, winter injury being one.

Borer Trouble

If your plants have revealed zigzag edges and lines of slime, if flower stalks have toppled over and there have been many yellow leaves and if, on pulling these out, you have easily yanked out pieces of decayed evil-smelling rhizome as well, you know to your sorrow just what I mean by borer trouble. Now besides Dutch-housekeeping sanitary measures, this is what you can do. Early in March or when plants are about six inches high, apply a protective film of insecticidal soap or pyrethrum to the foliage. Spray a second time and a third if rain washes away the coating before the flower buds show color. And if you see a punctured leaf and signs of borer activity, cut the foliage off below the point of attack and destroy it. Or try to slay the invader by squeezing the leaves between two fingers—an extremely effective if unpleasant procedure.

Sometimes without the borer, leaf tips wither and brown and appear water-soaked at the base. When rhizome rot is thus in evidence, lift the plants and cut out any soft portions with a sharp knife. Let the rhizomes dry in the sun for a day or so, then coat them generously with diatomaceous earth and replant in a new location if possible or in fresh soil in their former place.

Time to Separate

The best time for such rhizome surgery and for the separating of overthick bearded iris is between July and September. Wait, however, until in their third or fourth year plants are falling off in quality of bloom—and then lift only *healthy* clumps. Trim the fan tops halfway back, pull the plants apart and reset the small outside divisions shallowly and at twelve-inch distances. Face all the rhizomes the same way and plant in rows, not circles around a hole, since this center space never fills in properly.

The first winter after planting, mulch lightly but afterwards omit this protection unless you live in a sub-zero section. In spring, however, go over the plantings early to press back into the soil any frost-heaved plants. Although established iris are quite drought tolerant, newly set plantings will need watering during dry spells until the roots take hold. Sometimes, too, brown leaf tips on older plants in times of drought indicate the need for a thorough soaking. Finally, make it a routine matter to relieve plants promptly of the stems of faded flowers at the ground line. This helps to let into each clump more health-giving sun and air.

SIBERIAN IRIS

How I treasure the tall and dignified Siberians. If you have known only the familiar bearded iris, do now make the acquaintance of this beardless type which flowers from late May to mid-June. It develops strong clumps two to four feet tall with slender, grassy foliage and a quantity of individual stems each carrying a half dozen or so delicate white, lavender or violet blooms, which usually appear just before the later tall bearded varieties.

Because these Siberians present the dual blessing of flower quality and extreme ease of culture, they are just the plants for every one of you whose time is at a premium. I have grown the older varieties like Perry's Blue and Snowcrest for

years and years, in a richly prepared border as well as in the
less mellow shrubbery borders, and in both places they provide quantities of bouquets. Although there was, of course,
a difference in flower quality, both plantings required little
beyond a few deep soakings prior to blooming, if the season
was dry, the clipping off of faded flower stems and the division
of roots once in four years. Bone meal and pulverized manure
are good soil conditioners for these completely pest-free and
disease-free perennials. And after the first winter, you do not
even have to bother with a cold-weather covering.

Their garden uses are, indeed, multiple. When you plant
Siberians, space several single divisions three to four inches
apart to form a clump. Even one of each color will afford
quantities of cut flowers. You can naturalize Perry's Blue
delightfully or fit Red Emperor or the mauve Helen Astor
into the landscape design as a facing-down plant for shrubs
or along a low porch to conceal foundations.

In the border, varieties like Alaska, Snowcrest or the
newer, more expensive Snow Wheel form strong, pleasing
white accents. Siberians look well, too, in separate beds where
after flowering their foliage continues excellently green. Or
they may be combined with other perennials. The clear blue
Gatineau is handsome with such early daylilies as the yellow
Flava or Tangerine, while the dark, pansy-purple Caesar's
Brother or paler blue Summer Sky is an ideal companion for
the crimson-flecked, fragrant, white Festiva Maxima peony.

If you want to cut down on upkeep, select a favorite Siberian variety and have just one big clump to enjoy from a
window. This is also the way I enjoy my single planting of
Iris spuria, another delightful beardless type but taller, to five
feet, a fine bold accent plant. Mine is *I. ochroleuca* Golden
Nugget (when I have only a little of something it is usually

yellow), and its companion is clematis Ramona, a great blue single variety growing on a nearby post of the wisteria arbor.

A little farther along the arbor path is a clump of Dutch iris Golden Harvest with an underplanting of the apricot viola Chantreyland. I always buy violas in spring to carry out various pictures as an underplanting. This is a charming combination that gives pleasure for weeks to all who pass by on the way to the kitchen door. Spanish and English iris—Dutch is a type of Spanish—grow from bulbs, not rhizomes like the others.

JAPANESE IRIS

From mid-June until mid-July after the pageantry of the tall bearded iris has subsided a completely different type, *Iris kaempferi*, or Japanese iris, now called oriental, comes into beauty. Blooming for the most part after the first delphiniums and before summer phlox, the large flowers—six to ten inches across—bring strong color to the border while for cutting they are unbelievably beautiful. Especially to those who are adept at arrangements in the oriental manner is the kaempferi iris challenging material.

Plants vary in height from thirty to fifty inches, a matter more of moisture and fertility than of variety, although Gold Bound is always shorter. The singles show three large and three small petals. Then there are doubles and triples with six or more petals or petal-like forms. Colors run from luscious deep, deep purple through burgundy and pink shades to soft blues and white with striking yellow markings. Indeed, I cannot recall seeing any variety I could dislike.

Success with this *I. kaempferi* is dependent on three factors: a well-drained site, a soil rich in organic matter, and, above all—and this is the real key to success—abundant moisture, especially during the growing season.

Many gardeners would also advise acidity, declaring that flowering noticeably improved after aluminum sulphate, sulphur, or acid peat moss was liberally worked into the soil around their plants. If you have a pool or stream, by all means plant oriental iris beside it, not only because the reflection doubles the beauty of the iris but also because plenty of water keeps it culturally content. But make certain the situation is not wet in winter; here in the north plants sometimes suffer injury under such conditions. In the Fern-Garden Finale plan (page 192), you can see how I use Japanese iris with astilbe and ferns.

If you include this iris in occasional sentinel clumps through the border, you will find the yellow lupinlike *Thermopsis caroliniana* a pleasing companion. I have also liked white oriental iris varieties and blues with yellow meadowrue, *Thalictrum glaucum*, Bristol Fairy babysbreath, regal lilies and deep purple petunias. And many daylilies bloom handsomely with the Japanese iris. To make certain of fine flowering in the border all through the spring and up to blooming time, let the slow-running hose rest for several hours weekly among the plants unless, of course, there is a heavy rainfall.

Each year notice the quality of the blossoms. If with good culture these tend to get smaller and stems shorter, you had better decide upon division. This is usually advisable every three or four years, preferably just after flowering in July although any time before October is safe, if a later date is more convenient for you. Separate each large clump into two or three sections, not into single pieces, or you will lack flowers completely for the next year or so. Water well following division to stimulate strong rooting before frost.

From winter *stylosa* to midsummer *kaempferi* is a long and entrancing iris season; not too long, however, for us who have tried iris values in the garden over many years and never found them disappointing. Omit the odd little species if you will, but consider indispensable both the intermediate and tall bearded varieties, the Siberian and the oriental types, which bloom in about that order. For iris not only afford the border weeks of rich, pure color but their foliage gives strength to the garden composition throughout the entire growing season.

A CHART OF TALL, DELECTABLE IRIS

(E—Early, Mid-May; M—Midseason, May 23; ML—Midseason to Late, May 27; L—Late Iris, May 31)

Variety	Color Note	Height in Inches	Season
WHITE			
Carissima	Ruffled pure white	38	M
Cliffs of Dover	Ruffled with yellow beard	36	M
Late Snow	Very useful, with yellow beard	42	L
Spanish Peaks	All white	38	ML
Tranquility	Glistening milk-white	38	ML
LAVENDER TO "BLUE"			
Blue Rhythm	Silvery, medium shade	38	ML
Blue Sapphire	Silvery, ruffled	40	E
Great Lakes	Clear blue	40	M
Jane Phillips	Similar, but earlier (my favorite blue)	34	EM
Sylvia Murray	Pale and fragrant	38	EM
DARK BLUE TO PURPLE TO BLACK			
Black Forest	Blue-black, fragrant, floriferous	33	M
Chivalry	Dark blue	36	ML
Sable	Claret-toned "black"	37	EM
Top Hat	Tall, large, deep purple	40	ML
Violet Harmony	Lavender-violet	38	EM

Variety	Color Note	Height in Inches	Season
	PINK AND ROSE		
Cherie	Ruffled "flamingo" pink	34	EM
Happy Birthday	My favorite flamingo	36	M
Mary Randall	Deep rose-pink	36	M
Pink Cameo	Flamingo with tangerine heart	34	EM
Pink Ruffles	Lilac-pink, very floriferous	27	M
Pink Sensation	True delicate pink, tangerine beard	33	E
	"RED"		
Elmohr	Huge, rich, mulberry	36	ML
The Red Douglas	Dark shade	38	ML
Pacemaker	Nearest to red self	36	EM
Sunset Blaze	Rust-red, brilliant	40	EM
	LIGHT YELLOW		
Amandine	Lemon-cream, fragrant	36	ML
Desert Song	Cream, yellow-tinged	40	EM
Limelight	Lemon-yellow with chartreuse tones	38	ML
Moonlight Sonata	Soft pale shade, notched petals	35	L
Truly Yours	Lacy yellow and white bicolor	40	L
	GOLD TO ORANGE		
Cloth of Gold	Deep yellow self, orange beard	38	M
Foxfire	Glowing yellow with lighter areas	40	M
Melody Lane	Golden apricot, orange beard	36	E
Ola Kala	Ruffled bright gold self	38	M
Orange Gem	Orange self, orange beard	40	M
Summertime	Dark yellow, lighter falls	40	ML
	BUFF TO BROWN TO COPPER BLENDS		
Argus Pheasant	Golden brown	38	EM
Cascade Splendor	Apricot to tan	38	L
Solid Mahogany	Dark red-brown	38	M
Temple Bells	Peach-yellow-orange blend	36	ML
Tobacco Road	Golden brown	34	M

10. Peonies Attract Everyone

Peonies are essential. They are part of your permanent planting whether you have a perennial border or what I think of as a "planted place," that is, a property with areas of shrubs and flowers but perhaps no formal planting of perennials. Wherever I have had a garden I have had peonies, and my thinking usually starts with them for I realize that once they are in, they are in for keeps. Peonies can provide a charming basic structure for a flower garden.

In Philadelphia, I had a hedge of white peonies. When, late in May, it came into bloom along the far boundary of the garden I viewed it with the deepest satisfaction. Before that garden was mine, those handsome white flowers, red-flecked and fragrant, gave pleasure to the people who loved the place before me, and I do not doubt that when it passed into other hands, those peonies continued year after year to dispense sweetness on the May breeze. For peonies are plants with a delightful present and a long future.

A good way to learn about peonies is to obtain several catalogues from firms specializing in them. (Some are mentioned in "Sources of Plants" list on page 295.) Here you can study the descriptions according to color, season and type.

At the end of the chapter are lists of herbaceous peonies presented in order of blooming time. However, the woody Japanese tree peonies which actually bloom ahead of the herbaceous types are such a different story they are considered separately in Chapter 11.

This is the way the sequence works out with approximate dates for Philadelphia–New York.

PEONY BLOOM SEQUENCE

May 10-30 Japanese tree peonies (*Paeonia suffruticosa*) "New" Herbaceous Hybrids (including *P. tenuifolia, officinalis,* and *lactiflora,* also listed as *albiflora*)

May 20-30 Lutea tree peonies (*P. suffruticosa* x *lutea*)

May 25 on Early Chinese peonies (*P. lactiflora* hybrids)

May 30 on Midseason Chinese peonies

All other singles, doubles and Japanese (crested) fit into this same schedule.

The familiar Chinese doubles in early, midseason and late varieties offer a wealth of exquisite form, color and sometimes fragrance, too. If you want a half-dozen *scented* moderate-priced and outstanding kinds of these to cover the full season, consider first two earlies—the white Festiva Maxima, a variety more than a century old yet which still holds its own, and the silvery rose Mons. Jules Elie with bomb-shaped flowers. For midseason, Georgiana Shaylor is a fine rose-pink, and Walter Faxon a handsome pure rose. Let the procession end with two whites, Siloam and the rather dwarf ivory Mrs. Frank Beach.

The "herbaceous hybrids," which bloom two to three weeks before our favorite Chinese doubles, are becoming popular. Although some in this group like Lemoine's famous old ones, Avante Garde and Le Printemps, are not much more expensive than other peonies, many of the handsome new ones like the exquisite Claire de Lune still cost a great deal. However, as production increases, prices will come down.

Among singles there are two outstanding groups. The Japanese or anemone types, with thick golden petaloids forming a high crested center, include three very beautiful varieties— the white Christine, rose-pink Tokio and glowing red Nippon Brilliant. The other class of singles has a less prominent center and is lovely in varieties like the shell-pink Helen, pure white LeJour, rich red President Lincoln and yellow-tinted, white Gold Standard. Singles make fine, long-lasting cut flowers. Take them just as the buds crack.

Garden Values and Companions

Peonies in the garden have many values. If their primary use is for bouquets, one plant each of an early, midseason and late variety in favorite colors, plus one or two of the early species, may be set out in a cutting row. These will flower from early May through June. For boundaries or low hedges one variety looks best, unless the line is long. Then it may be composed of groups of different colors but all blooming at the same season. For example, an early-flowering boundary could be made of white, blush and rose with groups of Duchesse de Nemours, Judge Berry and Mons. Jules Elie, or a one-color effect for midseason obtained from the very handsome red Philippe Rivoire, or gleaming white Kelway's Glorious.

In the perennial border, peonies make fine accents and
with their excellent foliage look well there throughout the
season. I like the singles for the border perhaps better than
the doubles because they are less massive when in bloom and
the flowers are light enough to hold up proud heads unass-
isted after a driving spring rain. The white Christine, for
example, is stunning with a tall yellow iris like Truly Yours
behind it and clusters of forget-me-not anchusa for foreground. The single pink Mischief is charming with iris Jane
Phillips and the low, lavender European columbine, *Aquilegia
vulgaris.*

The double pink peony Sarah Bernhardt in the border is
well accompanied by a tall *Iris sibirica* such as the bright blue
Gatineau, with low *Nepeta mussini* before it. If the pink New
Dawn climbing rose grows in the garden, try this group in
front of it for June beauty. With the creamy yellow peony
Primevere, plant the blue bearded iris Great Lakes and oriental poppy Mrs. Perry. This results in pure enchantment if
a deep blue carpet of Jersey Gem viola is laid before it. Broad
masses of blue baptisia, yellow thermopsis and the white and
fragrant garden heliotrope, *Valeriana officinalis*, also form
pleasing backgrounds for peonies.

Peonies in the bounteous period of spring flowering may
thus be used in innumerable beautiful combinations, but they
also look well in beds by themselves. And these can be prominently placed since their foliage—from its rosy April point
to final September green—is always of handsome quality. If
you plant these perennials near the house, however, by all
means select varieties with the added blessing of fragrance.
Scent is an important criterion in considering peonies for
cutting, too. Pale varieties are especially good to select for

cutting since many hold their pastel tones only when cut in the bud and brought indoors.

Planting and Care

Well-rooted two-year-old roots possessing three to five eyes are the only reliable kind to buy and mid-September to early October the best time to plant. A rich, well-drained soil is essential, as is a location in full sun for half the day or longer, except for the pale pinks which retain their colors better in very light shade. Dig the beds deeply, two feet if you can manage it, for this quite permanent planting. Mix in manure liberally but beyond the immediate range of roots. Let an area of loose sweet soil, either clayey or sandy, surround the crowns and the existing root system. Manure—so important to perennial vigor—is thus kept from direct contact because it seems to be connected with the presence of botrytis blight. Leaf mold is a good thing to combine with the soil around each crown.

When you set out peonies, place the growing points, pink buds, called "eyes," protruding from the roots, just below the soil surface so that the buds will be but two inches deep in a firm clay loam and certainly no more than three inches in very light soil. Reserve three to five feet for the full development of each plant. (You can use the space between for a planting of early narcissus.) If you cannot allow two safe weeks between soil preparation and planting, soak the new bed thoroughly to hasten settling. Sinking is dangerous afterwards since it results in the burial of crowns which should remain near the surface.

Take all possible care with this planting operation. Hollow out sufficiently large holes for each clump and work the soil firmly around the roots so as to leave no air pockets. Finally tramp the soil down well and water deeply. Remember you are not planting a perennial which is to be reset in a year or so but one which is to dwell in the same place for five to ten years or more.

When in the course of time it is necessary to divide the root clump, choose a new location or else remove the exhausted soil in the present one and replace it with fresh before resetting the stock. Separate clumps with a sharp knife into strong natural divisions containing at least three growing points. Don't hesitate to discard very old material since this seldom yields worthwhile stock.

In October, as a sanitary measure, cut off all peony foliage and stems and burn them. Then work a trowelful of bone meal into the soil around each crown. Except for the first year, provide no winter covering.

In the spring, as new growth appears, spray with Bordeaux mixture every ten days from the time the shoots are a few inches high until buds appear. This spraying or dusting seems to be a reliable check for the blight which results in the drying up or blasting of buds. *Many plantings, of course, are never so affected.* A trowelful of wood ashes and of sheep manure at this time supplements the autumn feeding of bone meal and, in all, affords for an average-size plant a very square meal indeed. Peonies of great size or peonies which are being reconditioned can do with three times as much food. Or if a complete fertilizer is being used in the garden, the peonies can be given this in spring. In any case it is doubtful if there ever was an overfed peony plant.

Disbudding is another spring chore. If you want large-sized flowers for cutting, remove the two side buds as each group of three forms. If the flowers are to stay on your plants, as mine are, don't disbud at all and the flowering period will last longer and be more effective too.

By all means put supports in place early. I always thrust the double-ring tripod around the double peonies when growth first appears. Otherwise I find myself so overwhelmed with the spring rush that suddenly the peonies are in full and heavy bloom and handling them then is a terrific chore involving not me alone but two of us. Incidentally, don't worry about ants on the buds. They are after the honey exuding there and do no harm at all.

Why They Don't Bloom

Perhaps you are not nearly so keen as I am on peonies because for you they have been plants which simply will not bloom. Don't give them up on this account. There is probably a simple reason for this condition which you are sure to be able to remedy.

If plants are in deep shade or growing where they must compete for food and moisture with tree and shrub roots, by all means transplant them to an open, sunny location where very likely they will start to bloom after a year's residence. If you suspect that they have been planted deeper than the allowed two inches, reset them. If they are very old plants in a starved condition, you might try to revive them with generous spring and autumn doses of plant food, but replacing them with a few stalwart new plants will give you a lot more satisfaction.

If buds drop prematurely and stems discolor or rot off at the base, or if buds turn brown while small, suspect botrytis blight and spray accordingly. Then in fall, cut stalks at ground level and destroy them. A further precaution would be to remove carefully the soil from around the crowns to a depth of two to three inches and to replace it with new. And then to prevent the spread of trouble in the spring, cut off and drop into a paper bag all imperfect buds as well as any open flowers before they shatter. Then destroy it.

Sometimes failing plants reveal, on examination of roots, galls or knots which pathologists say are caused by nematodes. If such roots are dug up and immersed for thirty minutes in water heated to one hundred and twenty degrees Fahrenheit, they may be saved. Crown and root rot can be similarly checked; sterilized plants are reset in fresh soil and preferably in a new location. Only I confess if I had to do all this I'd just throw the plants out and either get a few new ones or conclude there were other perennials for me.

Finally your peonies may not bloom because they are too small and young. The first year after they have been planted, flowering is always meager. If the divisions you set out included less than three eyes, there may be no bloom for a year or two. Quite obviously then, your only remedy is an attitude of patient anticipation. But when they are in full swing and healthy, you will find they have been well worth awaiting, for they are handsome plants, indeed, in or out of bloom, and there is never a shabby spring-to-autumn-moment on the peony calendar.

PEONIES OF GREAT BEAUTY AND EASY CULTURE
"New" Herbaceous Hybrids—May 10-30
(Crosses of many species)

Alexander Woollcott	Crimson	Semidouble
Carina	Scarlet	Semidouble
Chocolate Soldier	Maroon to black	Double
Laura Magnuson	Delicate light rose pink	Semidouble
Le Printemps	Creamy yellow	Single
Moonrise	Yellow-shaded white	Semidouble
Nadia	Bright cherry	Wide-open blooms
Nathalie	Salmon-rose	Semidouble
Red Charm	Ruby red	Double bomb type
Salmon Beauty	Salmon-pink	Double

"JAPANESE" HERBACEOUS PEONIES
(With Thick Petaloid Centers)

Anna-no-sode	Rose-pink, yellow-centered	Midseason
Carrara	White; yellow-edged white center	Midseason
Gay Paree	Pink and white	Midseason
Elma	Pink-white anemone type, yellow-centered	Early
Isani-Gidui	White-buff petaloids	Midseason
Largo	Pink; yellow-tipped white staminoides	Midseason
Lilac Time	Deep lilac with self center	Midseason (Expensive)
Mrs. Wilder Bancroft	Dark red, yellow-tipped red staminoides	Early
Nippon Beauty	Red, yellow-edged petaloids	Late
Nippon Gold	Crinkled pink with golden center	Late
Westerner	Light pink, cup-shaped	Midseason

FAMILIAR "CHINESE" DOUBLES

(Paeonia lactiflora hybrids; F, fragrant; VF, very fragrant;
RF, notable rose fragrance)*

EARLY—EARLY MIDSEASON, MAY 25 ON

Festiva Maxima	White, flecked red; well over 100 years old	F
Kelway's Glorious	Iridescent white; highest rated of all	RF
Mons. Jules Elie	Large deep pink; "bomb" type	VF
Mrs. Franklin Roosevelt	Deep, cup-shaped pink	VF
Therese	Very large pink to lilac-white	VF

MIDSEASON—LATE MIDSEASON, MAY 30 ON

Baroness Shroeder	Blush to white	F
Dr. J. H. Neeley	Very tall white	VF
Ella Christiansen	Very large, deep pink	F
Flower Girl	Blush to white, on low plant	RF
Georgiana Shaylor	Rose-pink, floriferous	F
Irwin Altman	Attractive light red, pleasing form	VF
Mary Brand	Large bright crimson-red	F
Philippe Rivoire	Small, deep red, lovely form	F
Primevere	White outer petals, cream-yellow "bomb" type	VF
Victory Chateau Thierry	Prolific large bright pink, low plant	F
Walter Faxon	Bright rose, medium height	F

LATE—VERY LATE, JUNE 5 ON

Auten's Pride	Pink with lilac tint, large, dependable	RF
Blanche King	Deep pink, perfect form	F
Mrs. Frank Beach	Rather dwarf, ivory, flat laciniated petals	F
Myrtle Gentry	Flesh-pink to white	RF
Siloam	Large white, never balls	RF

SINGLE HERBACEOUS PEONIES

(With Prominent Yellow Stamens)

Arcturus	Red	Midseason
Helen	Shell Pink	Midseason
Krinkled White	White	Late
Le Jour (semidouble)	White	Early
Mischief	Pink	Late
Pico	Blush	Early
President Lincoln	Dark Red	Late
Sea Shell	Deep Pink	Midseason

BLOOM SEQUENCE OF IRIS WITH PEONIES

Early peonies bloom with midseason iris, beginning about May 23.
Early-midseason peonies bloom with medium-late iris, beginning
   about May 27.
Midseason peonies bloom with late iris, beginning about May 31.
Late peonies bloom with those iris of very long season, still in
   bloom in June.

11. Those Elegant
Tree Peonies

Tree peonies are garden aristocrats, expensive and worth it. Like antiques in your house, established tree peonies in the garden are a delight which continues not for seasons alone nor for years but actually for generations. In some Philadelphia gardens which date back to the Revolution are tree peonies known to be a century old. Others are upstarts, tracing their origins only to the Centennial Exposition of 1876. All, like true philosophers, have gained in beauty with age and have refused to succumb to the rigors of time.

The tree peony is so called because, unlike the familiar herbaceous varieties, it retains a woody framework through the winter. Actually it is a shrub rather than a perennial, but its value in the garden is similar to that of perennials. In maturity, it usually grows three to four feet tall with a spread of about the same distance, but it may reach seven to eight feet. Blooms are five to twelve inches across; twenty-five to 125 may appear on each well-developed plant. There are records of specimens that have borne 400 blooms but no such abundance is necessary for a handsome showing. If in your garden two dozen or so flowers appear on a single specimen, I am sure you will be well content.

These unusual plants are arresting in appearance. In fact,

they are inevitable conversation pieces, as attractive to every visitor as they were to the explorer Farrar who first saw them in their native state in Kansu, China, above the Blackwater Valley and later high up near the border of Tibet. "The most overpoweringly superb of shrubs" he excitedly exclaimed as he beheld "on the eaves of the world" this magnificent *Paeonia suffruticosa* in all its grandeur as a wild plant.

Because tree peonies are destined to give you long delight, you will want to make selections with great care. And incidentally a good way to obtain them is as a Christmas or birthday gift. Your family and friends are bound to consider these a respectable present as they won't the item I mentioned earlier. I hope that you can choose your plants while they are still in bloom and so reserve them in the colors you see instead of the ones you are told about. It should be possible to inspect tree peonies in bloom from May 10 until about May 20. The middle of September is the best time to have your reserved plants delivered.

Three Types

Within the three general types are included varieties in every color but blue. The European tree peonies have broad foliage and large, heavy, rather shaggy, completely double blooms, which weight down the stems. The effect is full and globular. The Japanese, also the Lutea hybrids, are characterized by fine narrow leaves and large, broad-petaled, crinkle-tipped single, semidouble or "double" flowers displaying a prominent cushion of golden anthers in the less heavy varieties. Actually there are no *completely* double types in this group. The "semidoubles" have a double look with their full set of pistils and stamens in the center surrounded by rows of ruffled petals, usually ten or more in two or three rows.

"Single" Japanese peonies have up to eight or nine petals but look five-petaled. The finest, most luminous whites are in this Japanese class, and here you will do well to make your first selection. Flowers are carried well above the foliage on straight stems, and plants are less susceptible to frost damage and so more certain to bloom well than the European types.

The yellow Lutea hybrids, the third type, are the result of crosses of *suffruticosa* varieties with the species, *Paeonia lutea*. Here are the pure yellows and yellow-to-red tones on plants which are hardy but slow to propagate and therefore comparatively rare, although some growers have recently brought them down considerably in price. You must have at least one of these!

Most tree peonies—Chinese, Japanese and Lutea—are available in five-inch pots. They flower the second year after planting. Field-grown plants, ready to bloom immediately, cost just twice as much as potted specimens since they are twice as old. Getting them safely through their first years takes care. Once they are happily established, they usually stay so.

Among the European tree peonies, Reine Elizabeth, an older hybrid, which the horticulturist Dr. John C. Wister terms "the finest of all Chinese doubles," is a lovely cherry rose. Bijou de Chusan is a delicate, green-tipped white. Comtesse de Tudor and Carolina d'Italie are both excellent pinks. Jeanne d'Arc is a vivid, free-blooming salmon. Two varieties I do *not* recommend are the undistinguished pink Banksi which in comparison to other pinks is "absolute rubbish," and Athlete which is a "dirty magenta."

Highly regarded by many enthusiasts are some of the less heavily petaled Japanese tree peonies like Kogane-Zome (Golden Dye), a semidouble, white with maroon flares at the center, or Shuchiuka (Flower in Wine), a semidouble, fragrant white, stained rose, also the fragrant, quite double Renkaku, meaning Flight of Cranes. Hodai (Reign of Chinese Emperor) is a handsome, double rose-red, one of the very best, and Rimpo, a stunning royal purple. Beside my terrace I have planted the double, crinkled, glistening white Gessekai, or Kingdom of the Moon. Generally speaking, all of these flower more freely than the Chinese and require no staking.

Among the Lutea hybrids developed by Saunders, Argosy is first class, a single and fragrant. It is not so heavy headed and short stemmed as most of the old Lutea hybrids, whose flowers hang down into the foliage. Canary, Hesperus and Silver Sails (all included in the chart at the end of the chapter) do not have this failing. L'Esperance, my choice here for a terrace plant, is one of the old Lemoine hybrids, primrose yellow, semidouble, fragrant—and expensive, definitely not a simple purchase, but an investment! Actually any tree peony is an investment so I do hope you will make your selection from a named collection in bloom. Not only are these plants costly but greatly to be respected. To the Chinese, the tree peony was sacred. Only one plant might be set out and when this bloomed, the owner and his friends would sit before it by the hour in order to appreciate it fully.

Planting of Tree Peonies

As with herbaceous peonies, the tree peonies are set out in mid-September, or seven to ten days earlier in those regions where first frosts are likely to occur before mid-October. Browning of foliage is a good indication of ripeness for moving and a month in the new place before frost is the aim. Full sun used to be considered essential to free flowering, but Dr. Wister finds his plants in partial shade doing even

better than those in the open. An evergreen planting or similar shield behind tree peonies protects them from the full
sweep of the wind and forms a barrier to the late touch of
frost.

Since such peonies are permanent assets, beds or individual
planting holes are deeply dug, as they are for herbaceous
peonies, and the soil similarly improved. If it is on the stiff,
rather heavy side so much the better. Don't, of course, cut
back the tough top growth. Indeed, the development of a
tall, free-branching frame is your object. On the strength of
this depends the abundance of the crop. If a plant grows out
of bounds, as it might at seven to eight feet, it can be pruned
back without harm.

One of the pleasantest attributes of tree peonies is their
earliness of bloom. Before mid-May the pageant commences,
with *Paeonia suffruticosa (moutan)*, the species, holding the
lead. Long before Decoration Day, while most of the herbaceous peonies are only just making up their minds, the
tree peonies adorn their woody branches with the choicest
blooms the garden ever produces. A single plant, accenting
an important point in a shrubbery boundary planting, is arresting. Two as sentinels at the garden gate are attractive.
Four in the corners of a formal garden are elegantly important, while a whole row edging drive or walk will make every
visitor exclaim at the beauty of a plant which supersedes even
the grandeur of the finest herbaceous peonies and appears
weeks ahead of them, at that.

Home Propagation

But a *row* of tree peonies! Well, that idea makes us budget-
conscious gardeners gasp—until we try our hands at propagation. Then we can count on one or two purchased plants

developing, in the course of time, into twelve or eighteen. A ten-year-old plant, for example, may be lifted and divided. Sometimes a clump readily falls apart. In other cases it is necessary to cut through the roots with a saw.

But there is another way to propagate. After your bought plant has reached four- to five-year-old flowering size, start propagating in September. For this business turn first to your herbaceous peonies, since these provide the first root system on which pieces of tree peony tops will establish themselves. Any varieties of herbaceous peonies will do but avoid species plants since these are only determined about propagating themselves.

Begin by lifting with a spading fork a clump of a herbaceous peony. Let it lie in the sun for twenty-four hours. This limbers up the fleshy roots. Next cut these into six-inch lengths. (You can then return the herbaceous peony to its former dwelling place where it will take up its old habits, little the worse for its experience in the open.)

Now cut three-inch lengths of tree-peony wood from the tops of the specimen you bought. Allow at least two leaf buds to each piece. With a sharp knife slice away one inch of bark from the *lower* end of each of these tree peony cuttings. Slice away also one inch from the *upper* part of one side of the herbaceous root cuttings. Lay the tree peony and the herbaceous peony roots so that the cut parts are side by side, cambium tissue next to cambium. Then tie these sections firmly together with raffia and cover with melted candle or grafting wax.

In a garden bed where drainage is absolutely assured, plant the grafted pieces in a row. Space them twelve inches apart and insert deeply enough to cover completely each of their tops. Now nothing will be visible of the new tree peony planting until the following spring when green shoots will appear and develop. Finally let two full years pass before transplanting the young tree peonies from this nursery row to their permanent locations. One hundred percent success will, of course, not be probable, but if you manage the average forty percent you will still be getting a big increase.

During these two years the young tree peonies will develop single stems some twelve inches long. A mass of lead-pencil roots of their own nature will also be developing above and around the herbaceous roots which nourished the grafted twigs at the start. After the second year, lift this nursery stock, and cut away the herbaceous roots entirely. Then replant your personally developed stock in its permanent location, setting the plants some two or three inches deeper than they grew before. Such deeper planting encourages the further development of roots.

Obviously such propagation is not recommended except for really patient and energetic gardeners to whom the propagating of plants is as great a joy as the sight of the finished flowering product. The moderately patient must, of course, dig into their pockets and buy all their plants, while the truly impatient are strongly advised to eschew tree peonies entirely, and stick to daylilies, iris and other plants of immediate result.

Impatient gardeners will thus miss a lot, although they probably won't guess how much, unless they happen to come upon your row of dazzling pink Reine Elizabeth or royal purple Bird of Rimpo plants some bright May morning, when these are putting on what might be described, horticulturally speaking, as the greatest show on earth.

JAPANESE TREE PEONIES (*Paeonia suffruticosa*)

(Flowering May 10–30)

Name	Translation	Color	Remarks
PINKS			
Hana-Kisoi	Floral Rivalry	Cherry-pink	Tall, double, large, prolific
Higurashi	Twilight	Coral-pink	Semidouble, brilliant, vigorous
Jitsugetsu-Nishiki	Finest Brocade	Rose, pale pink edges	Large semidouble flowers, 3-foot plant
Kintajio	Castle of Kinuta	Pale pink	Double, cupped, free-flowering
Tama-Fuyo	Jeweled Lotus	Pale peach-blush	Early, double
Terute Nishiki	Terute Brocade	Pure pink	Semidouble, fragrant
REDS AND PURPLES			
Hatsu-Hinode	Rising Sun of the New Year	Flame-rose	Semidouble, eye-catching
Hodai	Reign of Chinese Emperor	Rose-red	Double; very large; one of the best
Nissho	Sunbeam	Glistening scarlet	Double, very fine, enormous
Rimpo	Bird of Rimpo	Yellow-centered purple	Semidouble
WHITES			
Gessekai	Kingdom of the Moon	Glistening white	Over 12″, considered best by many, strong plant
Kogane-Zome	Golden Dye	White, maroon flares at center	Semidouble, shapely, with small leaves, 5′
Renkaku	Flight of Cranes	Yellow-centered, pure white	Tall, to 6′, double
Shuchiuka	Flower in Wine	White, stained rose	Semidouble, ruffled, fragrant, prolific
Yaso-Okina	Venerable Man	Pure White	Double, ruffled, cupped, showy center

LUTEA HYBRIDS

(Flowering May 20–30); all are Saunders hybrids except
L'Esperance from Lemoine; unless otherwise indicated, as single,
flowers are 4 to 8 inches across with about ten petals.)

Name	Color	Remarks
Argosy	Sulphur yellow, plum spots	Single
Canary	Pure yellow	Single, favorite, held well above foliage
Golden Hind	Cream yellow, flared dark	Thickly semidouble, large
Hesperus	Pale yellow, overlaid rose	Very lovely
L'Esperance	Carmine-marked light yellow	Semidouble, some fragrance, old variety, but blooms held well above foliage
Roman Gold	Bright yellow, red flares	Light fragrance, flowers appear *on* foliage
Savage Splendor	Cream, marked maroon	Handsome
Silver Sails	Yellow, flushed pink around orange stamens	Ruffled, unique

12. Oriental Poppies Sparkle

As spring slips into summer, the oriental poppies open crinkled silken cups of glowing pink, blazing red or shining white. As brilliant from late May through June as phlox is later, these poppies make a garden sing with color. They need a careful setting, however, or the song goes out of tune, with flaming orange protesting the propinquity of rose or a patch of cerise defending itself against yellow.

Do not on this account omit poppies unless your border or garden is so small that you cannot afford to reserve space for this plant of three weeks' bloom and six weeks' disappearance. A well-grown poppy does require room, almost as much, in fact, as a peony clump.

Keeping Company

Furthermore, in border settings you must place before or beside each poppy plant some plants of more constant quality to cover its long summer retreat. I have liked for this purpose Chinese delphinium, shasta daisies, Giant Imperial annual larkspurs or tall annual snapdragons. I secure these from the florist as blooming-size plants in order to have them ready early enough for this cover-up role. These make a charming

sequence. Another possibility is an interplanting of speciosum lilies.

In ten-foot or wider borders, the problem of covering up
for dormant poppies can be readily solved. Of course, you
can plan for a separate bed of oriental poppies. This may be
edged with August lilies if a lightly shaded location is selected.
Among the poppies that hold their colors better out of the
sun are the lilac-rose Enchantress and old-rose-toned Henri
Cayeux Improved. Or a phlox variety may be interplanted
with the poppies. This is a good plan since many a brilliant
summer phlox looks better gleaming by itself than in the
intimate harmonies of a thick-set border. Hardy asters also
make good companions for poppies since their bulky foliage
shows up even later than that of phlox. Nor do the new
crowns produced by the poppies in late summer seem to be
harmed by the temporary shading.

In the border you will probably prefer the paler poppies
like White Splendor, Barr's White or various light pinks such
as Seashell or Echo. The coral-pink Watteau, often the first
to bloom, is charming with white iris Spanish Peaks. Use
forget-me-not anchusa in the foreground and then, if you
can, place your entire masterpiece before such a climbing
rose as Coral Dawn. Helen Elizabeth is an enchanting midseason pink poppy to plant with Madonna lilies as well as
early delphinium or other June blues such as the tall Drop-
more anchusa, which is a less usual but delightful poppy
companion.

Mrs. Perry is the first of the pinks grown by most of us.
Early in June it is utterly lovely in company with pale and
deeper blue iris or those like Misty Gold which picks up the
yellow subtleties of its salmon shadings. Or for brilliant effect,
plant a lustrous scarlet poppy like Oriental with the creamy

peony Primevere and the Siberian iris Royal Herald. In time
you will, of course, work out perfect oriental poppy pictures
of your own. In planning, consider that late May and June
are poppy weeks. Since the bold peony comes at the same
time, you will probably do well to grow one or the other in
your borders, but not both. Check the catalogue descriptions
for flower sizes, which vary from six inches, which is "medium-sized" on Betty Anne, to twelve inches, which is "large"
on Lavender Glory. Eight inches is about average. Some varieties like John III produce flowers on twenty-inch stems;
Master Richard grows to five feet. Foxgloves, canterbury
bells, garden heliotrope, early delphinium and iris bloom at
the same time, and are strong enough to hold their own with
poppies.

The tall spectrum red Cowigan or dark red Tanager, the
cerise Watermelon and the double orange Salmon Glow, you
may prefer by themselves although they look well, too, combined with Barr's White or the soft contrasting grays of artemisia Silver King or babysbreath, *Gypsophila paniculata*.
Perhaps you will set Sungold in its own stark beauty before
a backdrop of yew, or Indian Chief or Tanager in front of
such white June shrubs as mockorange, weigela or snowball.
Deutzias also are excellent with poppies. In fact, these perennials are so visually forceful that delicate plants may "disappear" among them. The white, small-flowered shrubs so
prevalent at poppy time look more in scale.

Of Easy Culture

But no matter what varieties of oriental poppy you select,
you will discover that they are winter hardy, thrifty and undemanding. In fact, if your garden were all poppies you
wouldn't need spray or dust gun, hose, or even fertilizers,

which only induce rank growth. Planted two to three inches deep in a sunny or lightly shaded garden bed, in a well-drained soil originally well prepared with leaf mold and bone meal, poppies can be trusted to carry on beautifully by themselves for many years.

That doesn't mean, however, that you can't change your mind about their location and switch them around occasionally. It is just an old wives' tale that oriental poppies can't be transplanted. Take with them the same safeguarding ball of earth you do with other large, deep-rooted perennials and you will discover that your big poppies do not object to transition. Also, the former locality of the poppies is quite likely to produce a sizable crop of offspring, for poppies are great breeders. Wherever a bit of root remains, there a poppy plant springs up. Therefore, if you have a favorite variety, you can count on bounteous propagation by the simple method of root cuttings explained earlier (in Chapter 8).

Mid-July to late September is the time for drastic poppy dealings. After their spring exuberance, these perennials drop off to sleep like tired kittens. Keep their locations well marked; don't let other perennials or annuals crowd in on them through July and early August because toward the end of August each poppy plant will wake from its deep sleep and produce a crisp, fresh crown of leaves. When this is well in evidence, you can divide or transplant or take root cuttings. Of course, don't disturb happily located, flourishing plants unless you have a reason. Like many other perennials, poppies prefer untraveled intervals of three to five years.

If you are setting out new poppies in spring, obtain pot-grown plants. But in late summer and fall, field-grown clumps transplant well. In addition to the two- to three-inch depth allow a generous two- to three-foot space between plants. A mulch is required the first winter. A thin layer of straw, oak leaves or peat moss will do. Pull the material under, never over, the persisting foliage. In spring watch out for heaving. Their second year, no winter covering is needed.

Poppies to Pick

As cut flowers, poppies are excellent for bouquets and even a few plants provide an abundance. The pink variety Betty Anne, is particularly good because it flowers so freely and seems to last longer when cut than many other varieties. Curtis Salmon-Pink is worth a mass planting also just for cutting. Where a great shock of color looks well indoors, as on the grand piano or at the shuttered landing window, no arrangement will give you greater pleasure than one of oriental poppies. These are not, however, flowers for casual cutting. You must gather them just as the buds show color and before the bees get to them either in the evening or early morning. Sear the cut ends of stems as promptly as possible over a gas flame until the lower inch or so is charred.

Or follow my plan of taking a lighted candle and a pail of water to the garden for poppy cutting at dusk. I sear each stem as I cut and immediately plunge it up to the neck of the flower in warm water. The pail is placed on the porch or next to the house wall where no early eastern sun will touch the poppy buds. Indoors then in the morning the bouquet is made. The buds open their glowing chalices quickly and the flowers stay fresh four days or more.

Six- to twelve-inch blossoms, two- to five-foot plants, color that makes of the rainbow a pallid arc and a month's succession of cut flowers—all this, with less than usual routine care, makes the oriental poppy a perennial prized by every knowing gardener whose space permits its brilliant habitation.

PARADE OF BRILLIANT SINGLE POPPIES

Variety	Color	Height in Inches
Barr's White	Pure white with dark spots	30
Betty Anne	Pure pink, no spots	36
Cowigan	Spectrum red	42
Echo	Silvery pink, few maroon spots	30
Enchantress	Lilac rose	34
Helen Elizabeth	La France pink, no spots	24
Henri Cayeux Improved	Old rose	30
Indian Chief	Mahogany red	36
John III	Coral-red	20
Master Richard	Coral-pink	60
Mrs. Perry	Salmon	29
Salome	Rose-pink	36
Snowflame	White, flame border	30
Springtime	White, pink border	30
Tanager	Dark red	42
Watermelon	Cerise	30
Watteau	Coral-pink	24

13. Phlox, Song of Summer

The flowering of phlox is a symbol of summer. When in my garden the white Miss Lingard perfects its scented blooms, I know that warm days are near at hand and that with them comes one of the most glorious and lavish of perennial displays.

Phlox is no modest, shrinking subject, to be sought out and appreciated in a shady nook. Flamboyant, friendly and sun-loving, it flaunts its brilliant midseason colors in any well-tended garden. Even in deserted coutry dooryards it may be seen in every shade of rose, purple and white, neglected yet beautiful, with the gray weather-beaten walls of some forsaken homestead for background. Obviously self-reliant and persistent, such descendants of hardy phlox set out years before do not readily succumb to the blows of fate.

Wise, indeed, is the gardener who reserves space for lavish dealings with phlox, especially if summers are spent at home. But when plants are made to use this perennial either in a mixed border or in an area of its own, certain facts about it are to be kept in mind. The tall early *Phlox suffruticosa* Miss Lingard, with shining leaf and fragrant flower, gives a June effect ahead of the more diversified *P. paniculata*, and will keep flowering right through early summer. "The best pe-

rennial of all perennials," one plantsman justly described it.
You will find Miss Lingard effective with delphinium blues
and salmon sweet william, also with Reine du Jour, another
early phlox, white with a red eye. This makes a very good
companion for Miss Lingard and brings out its very light pink
tints.

Following the bloom of *P. suffruticosa*, a dwarf phlox like
the white Mia Ruys or the violet Little Lovely looks well in
a foreground position. Pleasing companions for the long-
blooming summer phlox can be chosen from delphinium,
achillea, shasta daisies, stokesia, platycodon, veronicas, gypsophila and statice and, for late phlox varieties, the hardy
asters.

SELECTING VARIETIES

The July and August-flowering *P. paniculata* (*decussata*) varieties range in height from the fifteen-inch dwarfs to the
unbelievably tall, five-foot Rose Spier. The paniculata season
extends from the end of June to the second or third week
in October, depending on frost. Many colors are so brilliant
and clashing in this group that varieties must be selected with
caution and grouped with care. There can be no artless beauty
achieved by the careless flinging about of phlox unless it is
to be viewed from a distance. To make certain of pleasing
effects, I first grow unfamiliar varieties, which I have not seen
in bloom, in a separate row-by-row bed. Here I check up on
colors and find out which goes with what, according to my
taste, before introducing them to the on-view garden.

In my test plot I also note quality of plant. I found that
Columbia was the prettiest true pink imaginable and also of
very excellent quality. I discovered that the brilliant violet

colors like Blue Boy were better alone or with white phlox and gray-leaved perennials. I noted that Sir John Falstaff was a salmon shade of real glory, Charles Curtis the reddest of all and that the cherry Augusta used sparingly among rose pinks gave them a real lift. I found that the whites with a rose eye like Reine de Jour and Prime Minister were something special, although no catalogue description had ever moved me in their favor.

It took just one visit to a nursery display for me to develop a tremendous enthusiasm for the newer English varieties of the Symons-Jeune strain. I saw plants in full bloom on a day in August following a hard rainstorm. Despite the weather, they stood proudly erect—a magnificent sight. The Symons-Jeune phlox has marked fragrance and fine strong colors in both tall and dwarf varieties. In fact, the selection of dwarf varieties (eighteen to twenty-eight inches) such as Endurance, Jean, Little Lovely and Powder Puff, is considerable. Then there are giants like Exquisite or Shenstone, to four feet. These are excellent for the rear line of the summer border. I marked as my favorites two pinks, Fairyland and Fairy's Petticoat (with a darker eye); among violets the tall Lilac Time and low Toits de Paris; two dark-eyed white varieties, counting as blush at a distance, Monta Rosa and Mt. Everest; the tall salmon Queen of Tonga and dwarf Gaiety, also Shenstone, a crimson-eyed cherry red. The selection of brilliant violets and strong rose hues was extensive, but I am hardly the one to make such recommendation here because in summer I like very little strong color in the garden. Some pleasant combinations are Lilac Time with World Peace, the lavender-pink Fairy's Petticoat with the lavender-blue Cool of the Evening, and Lady Violet in front of the brilliant rose Olive Symons-Jeune.

Agreeable Associations

As you examine phlox colors, you will see that there are
no true reds nor true blues. The so-called blues all have a
rose cast which makes them count as lavender or purple. The
pinks are of two kinds, rose with a tinge of blue and salmon
with a hint of yellow. If you keep in mind these supplementary color values, you can select phlox companions far more
effectively.

Thus the tall early, yellow-red Leo Schlageter looks well
with such a daylily as the pale yellow Hyperion or the
meadowrue *Thalictrum glaucum. Gaillardia* Sun Gold, and
the Yellow Supreme marigold will be pleasing companions
to such a later phlox variety as Salmon Beauty. The soft rose-
pink Olive Wells Durrant will be right with hardy aster Eventide, or with lavender hostas. With Harvest Fire, one of the
most brilliant of all phlox varieties, plant white regal lilies
and misty clouds of babysbreath. With the brilliant salmon-
pink Sir John Falstaff, plant purple platycodon and petunias,
dwarf Fire Chief and taller Tango, both singles, which match
this phlox exactly—a stunning combination. The very dark
Blue Boy is handsome with a white variety like Mary Louise,
and the pale pink Pinkette with the deeper Columbia and
delicate Rosy Blue. And for peacemaking admist the rival
brilliance of purple, rose or salmon phlox, it is not necessary
always to resort to blush or white varieties. You may select
one of the placating gray-foliaged perennials like *Artemisia*
Silver King, or *Gypsophila paniculata.*

If part of the phlox border is to be under the light or
dappled shade of open-branched trees, so much the better.
There set the lavenders and purples and rose pinks too, all
of which, if planted in brilliant sunshine, will go magenta as

they fade. But do not use for an edging in the shade the dwarf *Phlox subulata*, which requires the sun for ample growth and flowering.

Idea for a Phlox Garden

Even in a modest suburban place phlox can be planted to create a superb effect. I think of one garden where it has been used predominantly in a border along the entire 125-foot length of the lawn. Here a Virginia fence affords interesting background contrast to the vertical phlox plants, which occupy almost exclusively the eight-foot-deep border. A minimum of supplementary material gives other seasonal values. Since the scheme of this display is easy to duplicate I shall outline it here.

Phlox subulata White Delight makes a charming white

MIDSUMMER COLOR

April edging for the border. Behind it there are alternating colonies of narcissus Aerolite (yellow) and Monique (white and yellow), and tulips Clara Butt (pink) and Georges Grappe (lavender) with a small planting of the lavender dwarf spring *P. divaricata* separating each bulb group. Before the bulbs die down, small plants of white lantana from the florist are inserted among them. After this spring picture come the drifting masses of summer *P. paniculata*.

Commencing with lavender and purple shades, a progression of color has been worked out from the terrace, the spot from which the border is usually enjoyed. The lavender Rosy Blue is grouped with the deeper violet Lilac Time, the strongest color there. Next comes a long wave of the pale variety Prime Minister, which really is a white with a crimson eye but counts as blush a short distance from the terrace.

These blend into a mass of light rose pink varieties, Columbia, Lillian and Pinkette. Three fine whites, the midseason White Admiral and the taller, later Mary Louise compose the next group with the early Mia Ruys to the fore. These are for blending since the border is terminated beyond them by the salmon pinks in varieties brilliant as a desert sunset. The medium high Salmon Beauty here blends into the taller and deeper Leo Schlageter, the nearest to red.

This garden of *paniculata* phlox carries on all through the summer and far into fall, flowering repeatedly from new growth, as the first and finest blooms are consistently removed at the base of the fading flower head. In autumn, the garden is again supplemented with hardy asters. In this particular border the lavender variety Gay Border Blue is set behind the white and blush phlox and the white Mt. Everest behind the lavender, rose and salmon-pink varieties. Thus this wide border holds color from April almost to frost.

In my garden three white varieties—Miss Lingard, Mrs. Jenkins and Mary Louise—have given me particular pleasure. On moonlit evenings, these shine out luminous and lovely, together dispensing a sweet fragrance. Coolly beautiful, the sight of them is refreshing on the most humid night. In fact, among white flowers, white phlox is pre-eminent. You can select for a long season and in various heights. White phlox could be a beautiful summer emphasis in an all-white garden.

I also find phlox a charming landscape plant. One memorable colony was effectively set in a small green and white plot which was primarily a bird sanctuary. For background, there was a graceful hemlock tree and a clump of hybrid rhododendrons. To the fore stood strong clumps of Miss Lingard with an underplanting of lily-of-the-valley. In the midst stood a bird bath. From June on, it was the white phlox which made intermittently lovely this quiet spot at the end of the vista from a study window.

To outline shrubbery or bring color along a boundary at some distance from the house, a border of phlox is excellent. Phlox has carrying power, and I am not sure that it is not really better seen with perspective. Some plants, like bleedinghearts or Christmas roses or lilies, should be close at hand so that we can dwell on every perfect detail. Not so phlox. It serves best in a mass planting, where the individual is lost in a colorful symphony. But if you plant it so, be sure the prevailing breeze will bring its sweet scent toward you.

About Culture

Culturally speaking, phlox does best in full sun or in quite *open* shade. Out of the glare, colors are truer, especially in the dark violet varieties. Plants keep both health and looks in either situation if the soil is rich, deeply prepared and well drained, and *the plants are uncrowded*. Deep watering in times of drought is essential but overhead sprinkling is to be avoided. "Wet feet but dry clothing" is the rule.

It is also most important that each plant be allowed a full two- to three-foot area depending on variety, with a free circulation of air about it. A house wall or solid stone boundary wall, which dispenses dampness, is not a good location for phlox. The ills this plant is heir to are kept at a minimum under proper growing conditions. Often they do not put in an appearance at all. There are two principal ailments. Foliage sometimes appears rusty with leaves curling under. This indicates red spider mites. A strong hose spray directed from below the plant frequently suffices to break the tough spider webs and wash away the minute offenders. If not, a natural garden fungicide may be regularly applied. It will likely contain sulphur, which has a double value if humid days bring the second ailment, mildew, which disfigures the plants although it does little harm. The sulphur is, of course, kept as much as possible away from flower heads because it ruins color, especially reds, and it should not be applied on a very hot day.

Phlox does not, as is commonly supposed, revert in color. When lovely blues or pinks seem to change to magenta, it is because faded blooms have been permitted to go to seed and the lusty seedlings, which do not come true to the parent, have crowded out the parent plant. "Reversion" is prevented by prompt removal of blooms past their prime.

Phlox thrive on adequate feeding and by frequent enough division to keep the centers of the plant in a healthy growing condition. This means about every third year.

September is an excellent time for separating phlox. Center parts are then discarded and strong outside sections cut apart with a knife rather than a spade, into three to five budded divisions. These are then reset at the same height they grew before but in well-forked and much-enriched soil and at proper distances. If this task is completed three to four weeks before the first frost, new roots will firmly anchor the fresh division and next year's display will be lavish despite the disturbance.

Since hybrid phlox does not come true from seeds, plantings are increased either by division (as above) or by cuttings. It is indeed, a simple matter to get a fine large crop of some favorite variety if you will take tip cuttings in July or August. I have had them form good roots in three weeks.

If size of bloom is an objective, remove at the stem line from each strong phlox clump all but about five main shoots. These will then produce big heads of bloom. For general garden effect, however, this hardly seems worth while. And, of course, phlox is not the perennial for cutting. The flowers fall too readily.

The colors and values of phlox are exciting. The culture is easy. The heat endurance is remarkable. This, I think, is the pleasant combination of attributes which makes certain perennials important.

GUIDES THROUGH THE PHLOX MAZE

(S–J, Symons–Jeune Strain from England)

Variety	Height in Inches	Remarks
WHITE		
Mary Louise	36	Excellent, long-season, chalk white
Mia Ruys	15	Dwarf, fairly early, pure white
Miss Lingard	24	Early white *suffruticosa*, June on, slight pink glow, but scentless
White Admiral	30	Long-blooming, of medium height
World Peace	36–40	Late, August and September

Variety	Height in Inches	Remarks
EYED WHITE		
Mt. Everest S–J	30–36	Faint rose eye, fine for blending
Prime Minister	30	Crimson-eyed for summer flowering
Reine du Jour	15	Red eye, excellent early dwarf *suffruticosa*
PALE TO ROSE-PINKS		
Columbia	36	Light pink, pale blue shading
Fairyland S–J	30–36	Lovely shell pink, delicate
Fairy's Petticoat S–J	30–36	Dark-eyed pink, lavender cast
Lillian	24–30	Pure satiny pink, lower plant
Olive Wells Durrant S–J	36	Light rose-pink with carmine eye
Pinkette	30	Blush pink, palest in this group
LIGHT TO DARK SALMON-PINKS		
Gaiety S–J	28	Early, semi-dwarf, pure salmon
Queen of Tonga S–J	30–36	Late-flowering, vivid, crimson-eyed
Salmon Beauty	30	White-eyed bright salmon
Sir John Falstaff	30–36	Bold, strong, brilliant effect
LIGHT AND DARK RED SHADES		
Charles Curtis	30–36	Unfading light scarlet, nearest to red
Jean S–J	24	Scarlet effect, crimson eye, semi-dwarf
Leo Schlageter	36	Deep scarlet, orange glow
Shenstone S–J	36–42	Strong cherry-red, deeper eye
LAVENDER TO DEEP VIOLET		
Lilac Time S–J	42–48	My favorite of deep violets
Little Lovely S–J	18	Violet with white eye, dwarf
Progress	30	Shaded violet effect, light with darker eye
Rosy Blue	30	Valuable light lavender
Toits de Paris S–J	24–28	Fine deep shade on semi-dwarf plant

14. Delphinium, Most
Beauteous of Spires

The blue spires of delphinium, like the steeples of churches in country towns, bring even to simple gardens a charming distinction. Whether the blue wands rise in effective isolation from a green base or present the perfect foil to pale yellow daylilies or white masses of phlox, they are always important. In June and July, lilies are handsome companions for delphiniums, as the plan on page 126 illustrates. I think of lacquer-red *Lilium pumilum* or *L. concolor*, with star-shaped scarlet flowers. Various Mid-Century lily varieties—the coppery Flame or Enchantment, lemon-yellow Prosperity or apricot Valencia—are also utterly beautiful with delphinium blues. Indeed, the delphinium with its "spirited emotional appeal" has no rival for blues in the flower garden. And for bouquets it is equally handsome.

But since in our busy lives the behavior of a plant is quite as important as its beauty, we must inquire into the disposition of the delphinium. Is it exacting or is it amiable? Perhaps a charitable dictum would be—it is improving. The Pacific Hybrids, in particular, have been bred to disease resistance. However, we must realize that the delphinium is basically a native of high altitude and cool climate and there are limits to its powers of adjustment.

Mock Orange
Avalanche

3 Delphinium belladonna

3 Lilium Prosperity, yellow

3 Lilium Valencia apricot

3 Delphinium chinense

1 Hemerocallis Mission Bells

Nepeta mussini

K.B

DELPHINIUM WITH LILIES

Three Easy Delphiniums

Therefore if you live on the Pacific coast, along the Great Lakes or near the Atlantic in upper New England where the humidity is high and the heat of summer days is mitigated by cool evenings, you can expect to bring to perfection the giant hybrid beauties. If, however, your garden is near Philadelphia, or in some sections of the Midwest or around New York City, where the summers are sudden, droughty and blisteringly hot, you can enjoy the handsomest hybrids only if you will be satisfied to have them behave as biennials or even annuals. The sturdy Chinese or Siberian delphinium, *Delphinium grandiflorum chinense* (*sinense*), and the less spectacular but still very lovely hybrids of the garland larkspur, *D. cheilanthum formosum* variety *belladonna* (and *bellamosum*), will, however, usually prove perennial, and they too bring to the garden much-valued shades of blue.

The feathery, twenty-four to thirty-inch, blue or white Chinese delphiniums are nice to mass for constant summer bloom. These are the most dependable of all. Easily grown from late April sowings, they blossom their first year early in September when other true blues are scarce, and they require no staking. Cambridge Blue and Blue Mirror are light and dark varieties; *D. grandiflorum album* is white.

The three- to five-foot, light blue belladonna hybrids flower abundantly in June, and sometimes through the summer too, and again in September. Cliveden Beauty is a good variety. It is enchanting in the familiar combination with white Madonna or *candidum* lilies and with some such climbing rose as the white City of York or the deeper Coral Dawn for background, a carpeting of salmon sweet william at its feet. A more unusual picture results when, against a backdrop of evergreens, *Delphinium belladonna* is accompanied by white fox-gloves and shasta daisies. The variety *D. bellamosa* is a deeper blue. Both take five months from seed. Midsummer sowings produce first crops the next summer between the blooming time of the older established plantings. These two, and the Chinese type, are better than giant hybrids for narrow borders and also for the lower houses of contemporary design.

Handsome Giants

Whether you live in a favored delphinium section or not, the true blues of the Bishop's Hybrids and the lavenders and mauves of the Blackmore & Langdon Hybrids, both English, or our own Giant Pacific Hybrids will some day entice you. Truly lovely are the light blue Summer Skies series, the dark blue and purple King Arthurs and those handsome glistening whites of the Galahad group. Pink delphiniums are today a further invitation but still not so tempting as the translucent blues.

Challenge of Seeds

If you live in one of the difficult delphinium sections, it may be only sensible for you to forego the tedious process of seeding. There is no disgrace, indeed, in considering delphinium as a worthwhile yearly garden luxury and each spring purchasing one- and two-year old plants from a specialist. Half of these plants will pull through to the second year, and usually a few will survive into the third or even fourth year. Of course, some may succumb by fall of the first year, especialy if summer heat is continuous and intense, or plants are infected by one of the crown rot organisms, the most common cause of a short life span. Even so, these purchased plants will produce at least two and often three glorious periods of bloom. Then if they depart, you can still bless your delphiniums as annuals of extraordinary loveliness.

You may, of course, enjoy the challenge of seeds and the generous crop a successful sowing produces. If so, much advice both simple and intricate confronts you at this point. I have had best results, however, from taking the long way round with delphinium seeds and so follow the method specialists have worked out for us who live in adverse localities.

Obtain fresh seed, they urge, in July or August. Then prepare a florist's flat, the deep kind, with a sifted mixture of two parts good top soil and one part sand. Level the soil off smoothly and firm it well.

Next shake up several pinches of clean, sharp sand in each seed packet. This deters damping off. Sow the seed thickly in rows and directly on the surface of the soil. Press it down firmly with brick or block and cover with a very thin layer of sand.

Now plunge the planted flat part way into water in the kitchen sink or bathtub. Let it stay until the soil surface feels moist. Then remove the flat to some cool, sheltered place which is light but not sunny and where there is good air circulation. If you have a cool garage or shed this is a better place than on the porch or under the grape arbor.

During the next ten to fourteen days, until germination occurs, water carefully and as frequently as is necessary to keep the soil barely moist. A house plant bulb syringe sprays a finer mist than you can get from the sprinkling can. When the seed leaves are followed by the true leaves, transfer your seedlings to the cold frame.

Here set them four inches apart in a mixture of top soil, sand and leaf mold or commercial humus or compost. Place a lath screen as a shade and prop up or remove the glass top. After the first hard freeze apply a light mulch and place an old window screen over the frame to keep out mice or other unwanteds.

Early in the spring, investigate. When you see growth, remove the mulch and cultivate the bed. As soon as the

weather is fairly settled, plant your crop where you want it.
Until the plants have bloomed, apply no fertilizer.

Ideal Location and Culture

An unshaded northern site is ideal for mature delphinium
plants. Here they will be likely to live far longer than in the
full heat of southern or western exposures. However, if your
border faces south, as it is likely to, place your plants where
they will give you the most pleasure. And if they grow in the
mixed border, trim back through the summer any rampant
perennials or lusty annuals which crowd around them and so
invite disease by preventing a free circulation of air. However, I have always obtained the best flowers for cutting from
plants grown in a garden row by themselves.

If success with delphiniums means a lot to you, you might
prepare the soil an ideal three feet deep. But this involves a
terrific amount of digging, much more than the average back
can bear or the average pocketbook afford to hire. Feel,
therefore, that you have done right by your delphiniums
when in a well-drained spot you improve the soil with leaf
mold or compost and bone meal to a full fifteen-inch depth.
Provide an extra six-inch drainage area if the site requires it.
Waterlogged delphiniums, of course, rarely survive. Rich,
limey, not sour, soil, perfect drainage and plenty of moisture
at flowering time are the three essentials of successful culture.
Wood ashes, so rich in lime and potash, are fine for delphinium. If your fireplace does not supply enough for your other
garden plants, skimp on them, but not on the delphiniums.
They will appreciate the wood ashes most.

Two weeks after young plants have bloomed for the first
time, work in and water in a light top dressing of fertilizer
around each clump. Once in early spring, feed your estab-

lished delphiniums. These incidentally are better off without winter protection, except where the climate is extremely cold. As the first bloom fade, cut the flower stalks down, but leave some of the old *leaf* stalks to protect the upspringing new growth. When this is twelve inches high, cut back the old stalks to six inches.

Encourage the Comeback

After the plants have had a fortnight's rest, sprinkle fertilizer a second time under the outer leaf spread of each one. Cultivate the soil lightly then and water deeply. As new shoots develop, select two or three and pinch back the others. When this second flower crop fades, cut back as before, but do not attempt to force a third period of bloom with further feeding. It may appear anyway.

Meanwhile delphiniums cannot be left unsupported. Before the fatalities of wind or rain occur, firmly insert in the soil a number of wire or bamboo stakes long enough to support the *ultimate* height of each spire. Fasten these with Twistems or raffia to the highest current point of growth.

In summer, mulch to keep the root runs cool and so reduce heat and dryness, ever the bane of delphinium. Disease and pest controls are, of course, necessary. A mite sometimes distorts tip growth, particularly if the plants are not too environmentally content. Mildew often appears during humid July days. Certain soil-borne diseases may attack the crowns. Regular dusting or spraying with one of the all-purpose natural mixtures concocted for roses is almost essential for the big hybrids; or a natural garden fungicide containing dusting sulphur or baking soda alone may suffice. In winter, after the first hard freeze, in very cold climates, cover plants with a sifting of coarse sand plus a little dusting sulphur to deter fungus troubles, then spread evergreen boughs. (If coal ashes are by any chance available to you, cover with these instead.) In fall, set out some slug bait (put it under a piece of broken pot to keep it dry).

After this account of the depressing aspects of delphinium culture, let's think again of the great beauty which makes such attention worth while. And, of course, if it does not seem worth while, just skip delphiniums. I realize that the longer I garden the less I coddle. In most cases if plants cannot thrive under the average conditions I offer, we simply part. So it has happened in recent years with hybrid delphiniums at Stony Brook.

Lovely Companions

However, my notebooks record much previous pleasure. My first delphinium delight occurred in June when the glorious Pacific Hybrids dominated my borders. Their companions then were the tall pale-yellow meadowrue, *Thalictrum glaucum*, and the white Miss Lingard phlox with a haze of babysbreath between. White regal lilies, the easiest of all lilies to grow, supported this blue delphinium beauty while in the foreground were two annuals, yellow snapdragons and white and purple petunias, both florist-started. Another pleasing group consisted of the white delphinium Galahad, pink, long-spurred columbines and the yellow evening primrose, *Oenothera missouriensis*. The familiar combination of those two lime-loving plants, delphinium and Madonna lilies, is still delightful and culturally sound. Pinks and sweet violets could be added since these also require a sweet soil.

When after a rest the delphinium spires, not so tall this time, made a second appearance in summer their principal companion was the fragrant white-flowering tobacco, *Nico-*

tiana affinis. This readily self sows. Therefore, I think of these two as close perennial friends, their blue and white loveliness an appealing summer picture.

But one year a pink nicotiana seedling sprang up beside a rose-centered blue delphinium in a place where blush Gruss an Aachen polyantha roses made an edging. This was an enchanting trio well worth your planning for some year. Delphiniums, however, seem to look well with all other flowers. The mockorange Avalanche, for example, is a beautiful background for belladonna hybrids and pink canterbury bells and in some seasons the luscious mauve of oriental iris appears in time to create a soft harmony of color.

But why should I go on with tantalizing descriptions of this loveliness? There isn't one of you, I know, who doesn't appreciate the beauty of delphiniums. What I wish I could recommend is some certain method for making this cool, independent transient, a really heat-tolerant perennial. When this is discovered, I shall indeed have delphinium news.

15. Daisies Are a Generous Clan

"As common as a daisy" is today a completely outmoded expression. For such distinguished modern Composites as the gerbera, *frikarti* aster and new gaillardias, to name a few, now far surpass the oxeye daisies of the field and black-eyed susan of the meadow, and proclaim with the opening of each elegant blossom the plant-hunter's courage or the hybridizer's art. Furthermore, these most uncommon daisies are easily grown and may be depended on for long periods of handsome bloom in your borders as well as good keeping qualities for bouquets.

If your garden is small, one or two varieties selected for each season assure progressive color. If it has both good length and depth, many Composites can be used for massive effects of unrivaled brilliance. While singularly free of pests and diseases, daisies require more frequent division than many other perennials and more constant picking than the usual run of annuals.

Doronicum, Pyrethrum and Anthemis

There are three noteworthy perennial daisies for spring and early summer effect—leopardbane or doronicum, anthemis and the painted daisy, pyrethrum.

In my Apple-Tree Garden it is *Doronicum caucasicum*, a golden yellow daisy, which, with lavender mertensia, pink bleedinghearts, hardy white candytuft and deep blue forget-me-not anchusa, makes a delightful spring picture. This doronicum, also an ideal tulip companion, grows some two feet high, and provides that lift of yellow so essential to all plantings in all seasons. Unlike most daisies, it grows well in heavy soil, either in sun or partial shade, and sometimes produces a second crop if first flowers are promptly removed. The earliest of the perennial daisies, these doronicums are well worth investigating for they seem to be rarely grown except for the flower shows. Mark the crowns well so that you do not overlook them and cultivate them away in summer.

Anthemis, the thirty-inch pale yellow or white marguerite, is another charming rather early daisy. And such a long season of bloom, June to October! The variety Moonlight is light lemon-yellow, E.C. Buxton is a sparkling, yellow-eyed white. Anthemis needs full sun, good but not damp soil.

Pyrethrums are fine for companion groups in the border or for cutting. I like the singles best and have found plants of Robinson's Rose pleasant to face down delphinium. Robinson's Crimson and Giant White are other good possibilities. These two-foot painted daisies thrive in full sun and rich soil freely mixed with well-rotted manure. They want deep watering in times of drought.

Gaillardias and Coreopsis

The season is continued by modern gaillardias (blanket flowers) which are infinitely superior to the grandiflora blanket flowers of an earlier day. Gaillardia Sun Gold is a notable two-foot variety which adds a pleasing, all-season deep yellow to the garden. I find it curing stems also add interest to many arrangements. Flowering steadily through June and July, it is unbelievably drought-resistant and reliable provided it is planted in rich, light soil. In heavy clayey loam it proves an unsatisfactory bloomer and rarely survives the winter. Burgundy is a glowing, coppery scarlet, a little taller and longer blooming, even into October. Both these modern gaillardias are self colors with no detracting flecks or streaks. I prefer them to the familiar, almost weedy tickseed or coreopsis which seems entirely undistinguished although it does deserve recognition for utter durability and incessant production of yellow composite flowers.

Shasta Daisies and Stokesia

When I think of shasta daisies, three of them seem almost indispensable. I prefer singles and semidoubles, though all are fine, showy, long-blooming garden plants. The twenty-four-inch Alaska, a single, flowers heavily in June and July. Mark Riegel, a newer variety, may grow to three feet and the flowers have a pronounced orange center and a double row of petals, though the effect is still single. These two are particularly effective with yellow daylilies which then emphasize the yellow in the daisies. Daylilies are, of course, good with shastas since they offer contrast in both plant form and flower.

The fully double, crested-center Mt. Shasta has a longer blooming season, late June to frost, and if you like double flowers, this "probably the best white-flowering herbaceous perennial to date" is the one for you. The glistening of Mt. Shasta is well set off by the strong salmon or red tones of phlox. Indeed, all the shastas look well with phlox and delphinium, especially the dark blues. In the cutting garden, I have found a fifteen-foot row of shastas (*Chrysanthemum max-*

imum) one of the most productive sections there. With roses in a rose satin-glass bowl, they are enchanting.

To the fore of the border Stokesia Blue Moon, with charming five-inch lavender discs, appears consistently attractive through summer and autumn; its neat foliage is always in good order. A relatively unfamiliar Composite, the Stokes' aster or cornflower aster is one of the more worthwhile fifteen-inch growers, and delightful with the later shastas. If annual asters do not reciprocate your affection, stokesia is a good substitute. Avoid planting it in soggy sites.

Helenium, Helianthus and Heliopsis

Where space is plentiful and thus strong, robust, flashing flowers are suitable, there are three transition daisies which carry summer brilliance into autumn glory. Helenium, helianthus and heliopsis are no toy plants to be tucked in an inconspicuous spot; they are deep, glowing perennials for mass plantings among shrubs, for backgrounds in very wide borders, for screens along garages or, as I have used them, shields for the compost pits. Since any of the three will atain some two-foot clumps of green growth early, they are well fitted to this cover-up use.

Helenium, or Helen's flower, comes in fine named varieties; all are grand to cut. I particularly like the gilt-edged dark mahogany *Helenium autumnale* variety Peregrina, three feet high and a mass of color in July and August; the three-foot Riverton Gem, opening old gold and turning to red; the lemon yellow, four-foot Riverton Beauty and the copper-and-gold Clippersfield Orange. These last two flower in August and September. Division for all of them is necessary in alternate years at least, and preferably each spring.

Of the perennial sunflowers, *Helianthus decapetalus flore-*

pleno, a clear yellow, double, four-foot variety, blooms through July and August, and gives the effect of a small dahlia. It is a useful plant but a rampant runner and can be a pest.

As American as an Iroquois Indian is heliopsis, the "false" sunflower, which produces a molten glow of wiry-stemmed, daisy blooms from late June into early autumn. *Heliopsis scabra incomparabilis*, a three-foot rather double variety, winner of an Award of Merit in England, has now gained appreciation in this native land of the heliopsis. Gold-Greenheart—looking rather like a tall zinnia—is a variety I have admired in England. It grows three to four feet tall and makes a magnificent display in the garden or for cutting from August on. Other named varieties offer varying degrees of doubleness of the one American species, *H. scabra*. Conveniently, heliopsis stays put, though it may seed, but it does not run like helianthus.

All three of these summer-into-autumn growers need room so that it is wise to make their acquaintance with some diffidence. Start with a few plants of heleniums. You'll love bountiful summer baskets of them, for the porch or for deep window ledges in the sunroom.

Rudbeckias and Aster frikarti

Better known perhaps for late summer are the rudbeckias or coneflowers, especially such fine varieties as The King, with stiff-stemmed rose-colored flowers, and White Lustre, a dignified plant, bearing white-petaled blossoms with a metallic lustre to their prominent cones; the flowers of the latter last on the plants for months.

The rudbeckias are all somewhat coarse-growing plants but most reliably hardy and tolerant of dryness and heat. They are just the perennials, in fact, for some sun-baked corner where the best of conditions do not prevail yet where space exists for increasing your cut flower supply.

Actually, though the trade does not always make the distinction, the rose, crimson and white varieties are in the genus *Echinacea*. Thus The King and others belong botanically to *E. purpurea*. Most of the yellows are true rudbeckias, perennial forms of the handsome, old biennial black-eyed susan, *Rudbeckia hirta*, and the other species. The variety Gold Queen looks to me simply like a dwarf form of the ubiquitous Golden Glow (a form of *R. laciniata*). Gold Drop, growing under thirty inches, bears big very double flowers. Goldsturm is a large single for July to Early October, and the plant is taller.

Of distinguished hardy aster varieties there has long been a magnificent procession. Yet preeminent even among the most noteworthy kinds is *Aster frikarti* Wonder of Stafa (a hybrid derived from *A. thomsoni*), which blooms from June until November. An enchanting lavender, this aster does well in light shade but in full sun it produces not just a fair showing of bloom but a rich unfailing, long-season display of two and one-half inch flowers; they are superb for cutting. The plant averages thirty inches high; it needs a loose soil with sand and peat added where there is heavy clay. It has no crown but dies down completely and in severe areas does require some winter protection like salt hay if it is to survive. (See Chapter 18 for a thorough coverage of the many familiar and meritorious asters.)

Transvaal Daisies

Finally—since such varied members of the Composite family have been included among the autumn flowers—I pass on now to the Transvaal daisy or gerbera. This tender perennial is hardy south of Virginia and a northern florists' darling. Thus for home gardeners in the North the gerbera is absolutely dependent here on cold-frame wintering or greenhouse culture. But so elegant is its form and so enchanting its muted pastel tones, that more and more of us are finding this South African daisy essential for the summer cutting garden.

From seed the gerbera is difficult. Germination is uncertain and it takes six to nine months of careful growing to obtain first flowers. But spring-purchase plants of the Jamesoni Giant Hybrids will flower freely through the summer. If they are potted up in early September and moved indoors, they may continue as winter window-garden subjects. I have not tried this but even if you discard them, as I do, at frost time I feel sure you will consider them worth your investment just for the narrow-petaled coral, gold, primrose and cream blossoms they so constantly produce.

Every time I begin thinking over all the daisies I have grown, I get excited. Each one I've had I want to urge you to plant too. But what I really should suggest is that you find your way cautiously through the maze of Composite varieties, since the majority of them grow rapidly, produce abundantly and practically never die.

16. Daylilies for
Long Delight

Daylily is the pretty common name given to *Hemerocallis* which in the past ten years has become one of the most popular of all garden flowers. And rightly so. Although each flower does last but a day, and hence the name, the great stalks of bloom bear so many blossoms that the flowering of a single, well-grown plant is spectacular, prolonged (sometimes thirty to forty days), and sometimes repeated. Furthermore, the daylily requires a minimum of attention from the gardener.

Today there is a marvellous range of size and color in daylilies. There are dwarfs like Little Cherub, scarcely more than a foot high, and giants like Midwest Majesty well over four feet. I think I still like the pale yellows best, but there are also handsome gold, deep red, peach, rose-pink, brown, lavender and orange shades, as well as bicolor, banded and polydrome types. In fact, you can get pretty confused thinking about daylilies since I am told there are already more than 8000 varieties, and about 500 more are added each year in early, midseason and late classifications.

There are day-bloomers and evening-bloomers, and some that seem to be almost both. The "evergreen" group is *mainly* adapted to the South, the "dormant" (deciduous) or hardy daylilies to the North, although many of the best in each group thrive in climates where you don't expect them to, and the "semi-evergreen" types are quite unparticular. Catalogues of hemerocallis are a great delight—among the most informative in any plant group—so if you are a daylily enthusiast, and who is not, you will want several to peruse. (Some growers are listed in the Sources of Plants on page 295.)

Where to Plant

Daylilies seem to me to be but one more evidence of the wind being tempered to the shorn lamb, for today plants of low upkeep are absolutely essential. Knowing this, hybridizers have made every effort to provide us with daylilies so easy to grow, and so inexpensive, except in the case of new and scarce varieties, that we can use them as freely as we wish, even as ground covers (they are wonderful to hold a slope). I covered a whole bank in a new section of the Fern Garden with divisions from two great plants of Hyperion from the Apple-Tree Garden.

Take a look round your property. I know you will find many places inconvenient to mow or trim. Consider—can you plant out the nuisance areas to good foliage and pleasant flower color with daylilies? Here at Stony Brook I have found so many just-right spots for these undemanding perennials— Hyperion, Midwest Majesty, Felicity and Vesters in the Apple-Tree Garden; *Hemerocallis flava* and *H. flavina* in the foreground of the Look-Into Garden; Thistledown by the terrace, Crimson Pirate, Golden Moth and Hesperus in a corner with cinnamon ferns. On one bank of the brook, Pink Dream holds court in utter loveliness, and this is but the beginning of the brook plantings, while the Fern Garden will soon be a Fern and Daylily Garden. Cool Waters and various other pale yellows already appear almost too beautiful among the royal ferns, and I plan to add many other yellows there. Ferns and daylilies are indeed a lovely combination for an area of high open shade.

Perhaps in a sunny border, you will want your daylilies set as accent and contrast plants in the midst of a long line of iris or along the rear with tall phlox and hardy asters. Or you may plant daylillies to face down shrubs or foundation evergreens, which can have an awful sameness. Daylilies are equally lovely when grown in occasional individual clumps with a stone wall for background or perhaps a short flight of garden steps or in a dooryard or doorstep garden. You might think, too, of developing a wide, glowing late-May-into-September bed along a driveway or hedge. And if you have a brown split-cedar fence, establish before it a large planting of a tall variety of yellow daylilies like Midwest Majesty. This will make a handsome picture indeed. If there is any water on your property, by all means cluster daylilies beside it.

I think one of the most attractive plantings of hemerocallis I ever saw was in a friend's garden. Planted near a little stream were divisions from my Hyperion clumps. There in the open shade they grew to great stature, producing in July an abundance of flaring yellow blooms of fine texture, strength and quantity. The low-growing Cradle Song, Kindly Light or Little Cherub would also add distinction to the line of a small pool. In fact, this plant of recurving foliage crowned with delicate lily-form flowers belongs near any sort of water—pond, brook or pool, large or small.

In deciding on daylily associations, you may feel, as I do, that the pale yellows set off all other colors, doubtless because there is so much yellow in the throat of most varieties. For instance, I think Crimson Pirate is more beautiful with Vespers or Golden Moth, and most of the pinks like Coral Mist, Evelyn Claar and Salmon Sheen are lovelier for the contrast of a pale yellow like Atlas, Fond Caress or Colonel Joe. And yellows are essential to set off dark brown and mahogany varieties. Tall varieties look best with a house wall or fence behind them or with a background of evergreens. But these are matters to investigate for yourself. The Chart of thirty-six excellent varieties at the end of the chapter will start you off.

Easy to Grow

Culture is simple. Daylilies require at least two feet of space between all but the dwarf varieties, better three if you hope to leave plants unattended but uncrowded for three or four years. And the space between is fine for groupings of early narcissus. You can plant daylilies at any time, even in bloom, but early September in the North is most propitious because it gives plants time to establish before cold weather checks growth. And in the North, you will be selecting mainly "dormant" types; if you choose "evergreen" ones also, wait until spring to plant and the next winter give these a mulch. The dormant varieties aren't likely to need this, unless the area is one of considerable thaw and freeze. I know I have never mulched daylilies. In the South, July and August are a period of summer dormancy in many areas, so midsummer is the best time to plant there. Also, in the South many plants rebloom, offering a dividend of color in the cool of September.

Daylilies will live and, to a degree, bloom under almost any conditions, but they perform handsomely if granted at least four hours of sun a day and if they are grown in well-drained, fertile soil. Prepare the soil as you do for your other perennials with plenty of compost and, in this case, perhaps add peat moss to retain moisture. Then in spring apply a fertilizer for flowering plants with the accent on phosphate and potash rather than on nitrogen. Spread out the roots in the planting hole and set the union of roots and stalk just an inch to an inch and a half below the surface of the soil, but no deeper.

Plenty of water is important when plants are producing buds and bloom. If you have varieties with possibilities of rebloom, fertilize and continue to water them after the first flowering, particularly during a summer drought. Staking even for the very tall background varieties is seldom necessary; only in some wet seasons will the tallest growers need support. However, this is not the usual thing. Of course, where it comes to demands for spraying or dusting, the self-reliant, pest- and disease-resistant daylily is mercifully silent. I am told that thrips and leaf spotting are possible problems to be controlled by insecticidal soap sprays and a natural garden fungicide, but I have had no experience along this line.

Time of Bloom

The blooming season of hemerocallis is long, extending from the little *Hemerocallis minor*, which opens about May first, to the late August-into-fall varieties like Autumn Prince, Farewell and Sonata. Some varieties like Dawning Light give a very long display, while others like Hyperion are most beautiful but in flower for less than three weeks. A number of fine varieties like Colonial Dame, Salmon Sheen, Golden Moth and Vespers, in favorable seasons or as the result of plenty of food and water, repeat after the first blooming.

I believe we get the most pleasure from the daylilies that

stay open in the evening and that a longer term of beauty for each bloom is most appreciated by most of us than enormous flowers. Flower size is always of great interest to the hybridizer and, of course, to many hobbyists. Some of the finest pinks and reds are, alas, as one gardener describes them, "rags when I walk around the garden in the cool of the evening, and the larger the flower the larger the rag. I certainly don't want my flowers to look the way I feel after a blazing summer day!"

If your garden means most to you late in the day and evening, choose from among the extended diurnals, or long day-blooming varieties like Fond Caress, Dawning Light, Midwest Majesty and White Caress. These stay open well into the evening. Or select from the nocturnals, or true evening bloomers. These are usually pale yellow, fragrant, and do well in light shade. They are the ones to plant beside porch or terrace to enjoy at night. Cradle Song, Cool Waters, Golden Moth and Vespers are sure to please you in the evening, and they will be lovely with your moonflower vines (calonyction), flowering tobacco and white phlox for as late as you want to stay up to enjoy them.

Daylilies are charming for indoors too, but for bouquets rather than "arrangements," since the limited life of each blossom results in continuous shifting in the points of interest and rhythm in each flower cluster in accordance with the sequence of bloom. However, this does not preclude using daylilies in flower-show work since a long day-blooming variety will give at least eighteen hours of beauty.

Many daylilies—Hyperion, Fond Caress, Lemon Lustre, Dawning Light—also offer fragrance, but not the outpouring kind, rather a sweetness to the searching nose. Indoors, the scent is more noticeable. And here a word of caution—when you are searching for scented daylilies and bending down to smell the flowers, don't get pollen on your white hat. It stays there!

When You Select

Here then is a short list of daylilies from which you can plan a long succession. Peonies as companions for the early daylilies are delightful. For the long midseason sweep of hemerocallis, you have a wide selection of perennials—shasta daisies, delphinium, phlox and many others. The hardy asters and early chrysanthemums will look lovely with the late varieties.

Necessarily my list reflects my own taste. The emphasis is on light colors, fragrance, and extended day or evening bloom. You won't find some classifications here since they are no favorites of mine. For instance, I simply can't bear the bicolors like Howdy or Caballero, and I'm not very fond, either, of banded varieties, except Colonial Dame where the contrast is not strong, or of polychromes. A flower that involves "cinnamon brown and yellow, flushed red, with a coral throat," is just not for me. But you should look at a large planting of hemerocallis for yourself; maybe you won't agree with me. Anyway the Chart includes many I feel sure you will find irresistible, though perhaps not the very late ones. Most of them aren't as big and handsome as the midseason varieties, but they do extend the season in case you haven't had enough of daylilies by late August and want a *full* season, even to frost.

HEMEROCALLIS IN BRIGHT SUCCESSION

(D, dormant—E, evergreen—SE, semi-evergreen; ext, extended day-bloomers—noc, evening bloomers. Dates (*i.e.*, May 15–June 1) indicate the usual range of time in which a given variety *starts* to flower in the Philadelphia-New York areas.)

Variety	Color	Height of Stem in Inches	Type	Remarks
			EARLY: *Beginning May 15–June 1*	
Flava	Lemon	30	D. ext	Ancient "lemon lily," fragrant; color still rare at this season
Flavina	Lemon	24	D. ext	Miniature *H. Flava*, slightly fragrant; bit earlier to bloom
Judge Orr	Golden yellow	30	D. ext	Good with tall yellow or henna iris; very fragrant
Little Cherub	Yellow	18–24	E. ext	Low, full-flowered; nice shrub edging
Tangerine	Orange	20–24	D	Best of early oranges: floriferous
			EARLY MIDSEASON: *Beginning June 15–21*	
Colonel Joe	Light lemon	40	D. ext	Very large and fine
Colonial Dame	Apricot-buff, rosy halo	36	SE. ext	Large ruffled; repeats
Cradle Song	Golden yellow	24	E. noc	Prolific; low because stems bend; useful in high positions
Evelyn Claar	Salmon-rose	24–30	D	Prolific; orchid tone develops after few hours
Fond Caress	Pale cream-yellow	30–34	E. ext	Broad-petaled; very fragrant

148

| Lady Bountiful | Soft yellow | 40–48 | D. ext | Well-branched; profuse |
| Salmon Sheen | Salmon-pink | 33–36 | E. ext | Broad-petaled; prolific; reblooms |

MIDSEASON: Beginning July 1–July 10

Cool Waters	Pale sulphur	42	D. noc	Smooth; tailored; fragrant
Coral Mist	Light coral	24	D.	Useful-sized plant; refreshing color
Crimson Pirate	Carmine	30	D. ext	Handsome; bright; well-branched
Golden Moth	Pale yellow	30–36	E. noc	Unusual form; quite fragrant; vigorous; prolific; may repeat
Hyperion	Pale lemon	40	D. ext	Old favorite; very fragrant; needs some shade
Kindly Light	Sulphur yellow	30	D. ext	Very large; petals narrow; curled; ruffled; "spider" type
Lark Song	Medium yellow	38	D. ext	Wide-petaled; bright; fragrant
Midwest Majesty	Golden yellow	44–50	D. ext	Large; stately; very fragrant
Pink Dream	Good pink	36	D. ext	Small but lovely; one of very few pinks good in evening
Rajah	Burnt orange	40	D. ext	Prolific; handsome replacement for *H. fulva*, with yellow hollyhocks, blue hydrangeas
Ringlets	Golden yellow	30–34	SE. ext	Small but perfect; many open at once
The Doctor	Scarlet	36	D. ext	Wide-petaled; brilliant; one of few reds open at night
Vespers	Pale yellow	36	D. noc	Classic form; quite fragrant; repeats when established
White Orchid	Almost white	24	D. ext	Broad-petaled; excellent in foreground

HEMEROCALLIS IN BRIGHT SUCCESSION (Continued)

(D, dormant—E, evergreen; SE, semi-evergreen; ext, extended day-bloomers—noc, evening bloomers. Dates (*i.e*, May 15–June 1) indicate the usual range of time in which a given variety *starts* to flower in the Philadelphia–New York areas.)

Variety	Color	Height of Stem in Inches	Type	Remarks
				LATE-MIDSEASON: *Beginning July 25–August 5*
Aten	Orange	36	D. ext	Large; wide-petaled; intense color; vigorous; well-branched
Dawning Light	Canary	40–46	SE. ext	Smooth; tall; fragrant; long season
Lemon Lustre	Lemon	40	D. ext	Child of Hyperion; wide-petaled; fragrant; handsome
Shooting Star	Light cream	38	D. ext	Wide-petaled; well-branched; an improved North Star
				LATE and VERY LATE: *From August 15 on*
August Pink	Rose-pink	34	D	Small; multiflora-branched; lovely with hardy asters
Autumn King	Yellow	48–60	D. ext	Very free-flowering; until October
Farewell	Buff-yellow	30	D. ext	Widely branched; handsome with orange-berried shrubs
Harvest Sunshine	Yellow	36	D	Large; broad-petaled; as good as most mid-season varieties; fragrant
Reginald Steed	Orange-red	38	D	Very large; with recurving petals
Sonata	Pale sulphur	36	D. noc	Unusual color at this season; lovely with vivid chrysanthemums

150

17. The Handsome Hostas

Perhaps it is because they are so utterly undemanding that my great favorites, the hostas or funkias, have been until recently so completely unsung. Certainly their lack of acclaim has not been my fault since I have wearied my fellow gardeners with hosta praises. But so completely charming is the white and fragrant August or Corfu lily and the small, pale *Hosta minor alba* in my garden that I cannot bear to see them neglected. And for the house, especially in clear green glass, hostas are the coolest-looking hot weather flower I know. Indeed, every arranger should have five or six different ones in the garden or somewhere on the place.

Is there a plant which combines so many attractive attributes with a practically self-supporting nature? No, emphatically no—and here's why: Prepare the soil to begin with, give a little early spring fertilizer, and *assure moisture* by occasional deep summer soakings or by locating near a stream, and what do you get? First a plant of handsome heart- or lance-shaped foliage, pleasing from the time the early green spears push up in May until growth is checked in late October by frost. Then a strong-stemmed flower of white or lavender, sometimes scented, and for most species pretty enough, indeed, to have right beside the porch all summer long. Even a place in the sun is not required since the hostas prefer light shade. They will even grow in quite dense shade. And finally no pest or disease will appear and not a stake be required.

For many years I enjoyed a panel planting of the August lily along the south side of a wisteria-hung veranda. The young leaves first appeared with a foreground setting of purple and yellow pansies and a backdrop of tall yellow tulips. As the hosta foliage developed the heat-ridden pansies were discarded and the hostas readily covered their retreat. Meanwhile self-sowing nicotiana seedlings from the border were placed among the tulips. Thus in summer nicotiana and hosta flowered in fragrant unison and where the house formed the fourth side of a garden, this three-foot bed was consistently colorful. You too may prefer by your porch such a flower bed rather than a typical all green "foundation planting." Furthermore, I commend to you a summer evening scented by Corfu lily and nicotiana.

Hosta subcordata grandiflora is still my favorite hosta, and I find thirty-nine species and varieties offered by at least one firm; general nurseries usually include six to eight. (Of course, you will want the fun of perusing a specialist's catalogue; see the Sources of Plants on page 295.) And they don't by any means give the same botanical names to the same hostas, although plaintain lily is the accepted common name. Also, there's no relation, I assure you, to the lawn weed also called plaintain (plantago). As a gardener, rather than a botanist, the confused nomenclature need not disturb you. Under the listings for hosta (or funkia), read the facts about flower, leaf, plant size and blooming time before you order and then don't worry about what your choice is called. *Hosta plantaginea* and *H. subcordata grandiflora* are apparently the same old-fashioned fragrant August lily, and *H. seiboldiana* and *H. glauca* make the same or very similar dramatic mounds of large silvery, puckered leaves.

Like their relatives, the hemerocallis, hostas have also been called daylilies because the flowers of most of them last but twenty-four hours, opening in the daytime and closing at night, a few at a time on the stalk. However, *H. plantaginea* opens one evening and remains open until the next, while its hybrid Honeybells opens one morning and does not close until the next. And these are the only two fragrant ones.

Flower and Foliage

You will find that there are hostas to bloom from late June until October with flowers from up to six inches for the fragrant plantain lily to two inches for most of the others, and mainly white or in shades of lavender. *Hosta caerulea* is the deepest "blue" and has the next largest flowers to *H. plantaginea*. Although their flowers are pleasant and mainly effective, it is as enduring foliage plants that the hostas are important. Give them room and a couple of years to establish and they will need no division for five to ten years when giant types could make a clump to cover more than four square feet.

The foliage is frequently very colorful, ranging from bright to dull to bluish or silvery green, sometimes, as on the Siebold plaintain lily, with a "bloom" you can actually rub off. Some hostas have splashings, stripes, or bandings of white or yellow or another shade of green. I particularly like the greenrim plaintain lily (*H. fortunei viridis marginata*) which early in the season has deep green edges on a yellowish green leaf. This becomes all green in summer. Using this range of leaf coloring to advantage, you could with hostas alone develop a very interesting "green" garden which would look cool as the proverbial cucumber through all the steaming summer days.

Height and Use

As you choose varieties, keep in mind the plant heights and the fact that the flower scapes may rise far above them. The dwarf plaintain lily makes a mound only ten inches high while the flowers go to twenty-six. The plant of *H. fortunei marginata alba* is but twenty inches, while the flower sprays rise to forty-two. But with the handsome-leaved *H. sieboldiana* the flowers barely escape the two-foot leaves and so count for little.

In general, if you want ten- to twelve-inch plants, consider *H. minor alba*, *H. lancifolia tardiflora*, *H. undulata* or *H. decorata*. If you need something taller, say to fifteen to twenty inches with a spread of two to three feet, there is *H. fortunei marginato alba* and *viridis margenata*, *H. lancifolia* and var. *fortis* and var. *albo marginata*, *H. undulata* var. *univittata* and var. *erromena*. The really big ones are *H. sieboldiana*, *H. fortunei* var. *gigantea*, *H. caerulea*, *H. plantaginea* and Honeybells. Count on these for foliage from twenty-four to thirty-six inches high.

Once you have eyes to see hostas, you will find many places on your property for which they are the perfect answer, keeping a mind always that they are heavy not airy plants. If you have lightly shaded areas which have proved difficult, if you need plants for naturalizing so as to reduce upkeep, if you have struggled over an angle by the cellar door or the kitchen steps or a narrow northern walk which presents one long plea for weeding, try one or more of the hardy hostas.

To face down shrubbery borders or accent a pool, they are also effective.

Attractive Associates

Hostas associate beautifully with ferns and daylilies, or they can be used as specimen plants like small handsome shrubs. At Stony Brook, the August lily is again beside the terrace steps, on one side with mountain laurel and royal ferns, on the other with azaleas. But one place I never plant hostas is in the border or with groupings of perennials. Except with hemerocallis—and I really like only the broad, heart-shaped types, not the lance-leaved ones with daylilies—I find hostas too dominant for mixed plantings. Shrubs, of course, can hold their own above them.

Today with low upkeep such a necessary aspect of our planning, hostas have become interesting to hybridizers, and we are seeing more and more worthwhile introductions. New varieties like the rich purple Betsy King and dainty white Tinker Bell are still expensive but prices always come down as supply increases. I really can't urge you strongly enough to find out more about these plants. I know you will bless every hosta you plant for its beauty as well as for its marvelous, long-lasing self-sufficiency.

18. Asters Herald the Season in the Sun

As summer wanes, the garden reaches a final peak of beauty. With hazy drifts of color in the sun, the Michaelmas daisies achieve a rich fruition. Now with the heat of the season almost past, a new freshness begins to come both to the garden and to us, as we linger among our flowers through the last delectable summer days and enjoy these autumn daisies, which make a lovely transition from the late phlox to the first chrysanthemums. The hardy asters, or Michaelmas daisies as they are so delightfully called, come in soft, light and dark shades of lavender, purple, rose, pink and white. Even the wild untended New England asters of my meadow are handsome plants. The cultivated ones vary in height from nine-inch cushions like Niobe to four- to five-foot sentinels like Harrington's Pink. This variation makes it possible to use the hardy asters in a number of ways in the border or garden, with shrubs, or beside a path. If stems on the tall ones are pinched back several times in June or July, growth is more compact and there is less staking to do.

Dwarf Types

The very low dwarfs make good edging plants if you prefer late bloom at your border's rim instead of spring concentration there. Since aster foliage is good, you can achieve a pleasant sequence by alternating one-color groupings of asters with plantings of May pinks or, if you like autumn emphasis alone, you can achieve unusual September color with a completely fresh outline for your garden. The white Niobe and shell-pink Constance with Lilac Time would make a very pretty sequence.

The dwarf and semi-dwarf Oregon asters are also useful as edging plants or as substitutes for the taller asters in small gardens. Extremely hardy and entirely insect-free like most asters (only the New England varieties seem to be subject to aphids), the Oregon strain offers charming possibilities in under-one-foot plants like Bonny Blue, Pacific Amaranth, Snowball and Violet Carpet. Combined, these would make a telling, richly colored edging for a shrub border whose color came all in spring, as it usually does. The fifteen-inch or higher ones like Persian Rose, a marvelous shade, and Twilight, a deep purple—and nice together—might be planted in the bays of the foundation evergreens to bring color there from mid-August into October. (Most doorway plantings are *so* drab!)

For the center of the border, or any place where twenty-four- to thirty-inch plants would look well in colorful array for late summer into autumn, there is an almost too rich selection. You could have a pretty complete color representation with the white Alaska, pale lavender Aquilla, light orchid Erma, silvery mauve Mother of Pearl and purple Archbishop.

Mid-border asters prove more tractable if only three stems are allowed to develop on each plant. These are staked with inconspicuous bamboo. Fine cloudy growth then results without too much space consumption for each plant. If these mid-border asters are planted next to oriental poppies, however, one extra side stem is allowed each plant, and these side sprouts are pinched back a few inches early in July so that a shorter, bushier spray is available to fill in during the time when the poppy no longer has height.

Taller Asters

For the rear of the garden or in luxurious masses among shrubs, nothing is handsomer than the taller four- to five-foot asters. Harrington's Pink and the late-flowering carmine Picture will reach this height and the soft blue, late autumn species *Aster tataricus* will exceed it. Many of the finest varieties grow only to three feet, like the white Charity, deep, deep violet Eventide, the crimson-pink Ernest Ballard, crimson Brocade (such a lovely one), Radar (nearest to red) and the brilliant salmon Ambrosia.

Any of the three- to five-foot varieties can also be set to the rear of a border, as the plan on the next page demonstrates. There I value them particularly as early green backgrounds for beds which have to be free standing and so lack an important backdrop of evergreen or flowering shrub. Their flowering then is but an additional blessing. Let this type have four stems to a plant. These, though stiff, must still be staked. Pinching off six inches of growth in July results in more grace but in less height, of course, so in shaping your plants be guided by purpose.

FOR LATE SUMMER INTO FALL

Pleasant Partners

Good companions for Michaelmas daisies in September are the early chrysanthemums. The white aster Clarity is charming with a single pink chrysanthemum like Astrid or a double pink like Sparkling. Since chrysanthemums lack blues, however, you may prefer these tones, especially a deep rich aster like Royal Velvet or Violetta, to go among them. The orchid variety Erma is also pleasing with such a lingering salmon-pink phlox as Duchess of Gloucester. And when you grow easy-from-seed dahlias of the Coltness hybrid strain, plant these with hardy asters for background. You will like the strong contrast of bold, shiny-foliaged dahlias with pale misty clouds of aster bloom. I like, too, the combination of marigold Yellow Supreme with any of the blue varieties.

Perhaps outside the border where space is no object, you have growing on a trellis the brilliant fall-fruiting firethorn shrub, *Pyracantha*. If so, set the rampant mauve species, *Aster tataricus*, which grows almost to six feet, before it with plants of chrysanthemum Bronze Queen near by. Then in sections where November first concludes the garden year, these three will wave a gay flamboyant farewell.

Cultural Clues

Hardy asters have four cultural requirements—full sun, plenty of room (crowding promotes mildew), adequate summer moisture (mulch plants by all means) and frequent division (in spring). Your average garden soil, spring-enriched along with the other perennials, will be just fine. You may need to divide some varieties yearly or in the second year (Harrington's Pink doesn't need it so often), rather than the third which is usual practice. If the growth gets too thick and centers get woody, plants decline and eventually disappear, so keep an eye out for this. When you do pull the clumps apart, throw away the woody centers and put three of the outside rooted shoots in one hole to form a clump. Improve the soil, of course, with humus and bone meal or other fertilizer while you are at it. Do avoid crowding. Like phlox, these asters are fresh-air fiends. If mildew shows, get out the captan or sulphur, but don't use the latter in very hot weather.

In vases too you will enjoy these easily arranged Michaelmas daisies. For the mantel, I fill urns of them in blending colors. They keep fresh for a week if only I remember to add extra water daily. If you are on the flower committee of your church, depend on these luxuriant late summer and autumn perennials for your Sundays. You will find that they are large and important enough to be effective, instead of overwhelmed, when they are used for altar adornment. Late daylilies and dahlias go well with them. Buy your first aster plants. A few will go far for you by the second year. Only the species like *A. tataricus* will come true from seeds.

19. Aconites and Anemones for the Shadows

In light shade the cooler nights of late summer and early autumn perfect the blue flames of aconites and the delicate pastel tints of the Japanese windflower, *Anemone japonica*. These are plants to round out our lovely gardening year and to give special pleasure because they are somewhat less familiar than the iris and peony of almost every garden.

ACONITES

The monkshood, so called for the shape of its blossom, adorns its long spikes with a multiple blue array. Plant it, however, only in areas of light shade since aconite fails in full sun. Its other preferences are for a protected location, a great deal of moisture and a soil rich in leaf mold or old manure.

The Sparks variety of *Aconitum napellus* is the best late summer aconite. It has deep blue turrets, five feet tall. These are charming contrasts to masses of salmon and white phlox and lavender mistflower, *Eupatorium coelestinum*, all of which are shade tolerant. The Croftway Pink beebalm (monarda) is another attractive Sparks companion.

The first year don't be surprised, however, if all you enjoy from aconites is finely wrought foliage. Color will appear the next year when the plants feel more at home.

Aconitum fischeri, a dark blue monkshood, blooms in September and October. One of the hardiest, it grows but two to three feet tall and appears at a time when spike flowers of deepest blue are valuable. Latest and tallest is *A. fischeri wilsoni*, the violet monkshood, a six- to seven-foot mauve variety which gleams through the October mists. Try either of these monkshoods with white *Anemone alba* against a yew hedge and you will achieve an autumn memory which will last the winter through.

Unfortunately aconites are not the easiest of perennials to raise. Too many gardeners, indeed, report they "used to have aconites but they seem to have disappeared." Drought for one thing affects them most adversely, often causing leaves to blacken and curl and stalk by stalk to turn brown and collapse. Then, of course, no flowers appear. If this happens to *Aconitum wilsoni* which you have awaited clear into October, it is a far from happy circumstance. Drought thus makes aconites appear diseased. Before you lift and burn and renew the soil of plants so affected—as you must do if it is verticillium wilt which has attacked your aconites—consider the season and the possibility that dryness alone has caused the trouble. Usually the diseased plant reveals a progressive dying upward of leaves while the drought-afflicted plant browns all over. Crown rot, mildew and poisonous roots, which must be handled carefully, are other aconite debits.

Considering all this, I still urge upon you the acquaintance of the aconites. If you soak them well in dry spells, mayhap no ailments will develop. Certainly aconites are desirable if healthy, well-grown plants are at all possible.

ANEMONES

The Japanese anemones, growing two to three feet high, bring
to the rich season of autumn the delicate tints of spring. From
September until killing frosts, they offer their white and rose
sequence of waxen blooms, lovely for garden or house. *Anemone alba* is the single, yellow-centered white, now superseded
by Marie Manchard. September Charm is a silvery pink. Alice
has lilac tones in its pink and the newer Profusion, growing
only to two feet, is a rose-pink, valuable for both low growth
and an early season—late August to late September.

Be patient with anemones in their early days and they will
reward you with a bright future. When they arrive late in
spring, plant them in sun or light shade and in a spot where
there is protection from wind but still a good circulation of
air. It is fine if a wall or shrubbery border can protect them
from the north while the plants themselves face south. The
site must also be well drained and the soil richly and deeply
prepared.

Anemones are, indeed, no casual sojourners in your garden. Therefore place them judiciously and let them become
well established until each plant has the root power to bear
a great mass of flowers. In summer, cool the root runs with
a mulch and be indefatigable about watering. In winter, cover
the plants well with leaves.

Time will suggest many charming companions for these fall
perennials which come into flower while many annuals are
still at their height and the hardy asters and chrysanthemums
are also staging their show. Aster Eventide, anemone Profusion and yellow zinnias are a lovely trio, or against an evergreen background you may prefer aster Crimson Brocade,
Aconitum fischeri and *Anemone alba*. The mistflower is a good

companion for anemones, too, and also the tall daisy-decked
Boltonia asteroides.

If, however, you share the opinion that for sheer loveliness
of blossom no other flower equals the fall anemones, you
may prefer to plant them by themselves. Perhaps along a gray
ivy-covered wall you will colonize alba or dwell upon September Charm as it justifies its name before the feathery
green of hemlock. Alone or with companions, they inevitably
become your autumn delight.

20. Chrysanthemums Dare the Garden to Die

Long after the anemone and aconite have said farewell, long after we have put away summer's chintz and started the heater fires, chrysanthemums challenge winter with late and lavish blooms. Indeed, in some favorable seasons these perennials, which come into final flower at a time when nature seems most hostile to the garden, carry on even into December and in the very teeth of frost present fresh, crisp and beauteous blossoms.

These last beauties terminte a procession which begins in August and reaches its height in October. Through these months chrysanthemums appear in many forms and a multitude of colors. You may select them from some seven major classifications. Soon there may be further diversity since development among these perennials is still going forward rapidly. Especially are there signs of increased earliness of bloom. This does not interest me, however, since my concern is not with varieties which appear when asters and dahlias are still at their height. At that time chrysanthemums have garden rivals. I prefer them and appreciate them most when they stand alone.

Cushions and Rubellums

Consider first the dwarf cushion mums growing one foot high and two feet or more wide. Such kinds as Bowl o'Gold, Corsage Cushion and Yellow Cushion, Bronze Queen and Lipstick flower freely from September, or even late August, for many weeks into fall. These cushions are a good landscape type to use as edging for a *wide* perennial bed, as outline for a shrubbery border or along driveway or walk. If your garden space is tiny, plant instead the small English lilliputs, like Happy and Redbreast. They grow but eight to twelve inches high and ten to eighteen across, depending, of course, on variety.

The *rubellum* hybrids, of which Clara Curtis is the famous one, are, as in this case, low and bushy—twelve to eighteen inches high and up to two feet across. More often the rubellums are not such compact growers as the cushions and seem to me more attractive. With their airier manner of growth, the rubellums look like hugh bouquets of colored daisies in August and early September. They are truly hardy and can be counted on to be perennial, as all chrysanthemums cannot. The salmon-pink Anna Hay and the velvety red Royal Command are kinds you will be sure to like.

Koreans and Articum Daisies

The single and semidouble Koreans are tall, rather loosely formed plants with handsome, mainly October flowers. Plants of these—and the rubellums as well as various doubles—are readily raised from seed, flowering five months after sowing. However, to my knowledge, seeds come only in mixture, but you can select and discard to get the colors you want after the first fall. Or you can buy plants, sometimes simply listed as singles. You will like the bronze Apollo and pale yellow Ceres, which make a lovely planting together; also the old-rose Daphne, purple Dubonnet and the most excellent red Fred Stone. This last, a semidouble with fine four-inch blooms in sprays, is well worth disbudding.

Somewhat later the buds of the daisylike *arcticum* hybrids or Northland daisies open. These are iron-hardy and fully disease resistant. I have always loved Astrid, which has three-inch shell-pink blooms with bright yellow centers and light green foliage. Good Morning is the yellow form. For easy gardening these Northland daisies and the Koreans are an excellent choice but, of course, they do not have the distinction of many of the other chrysanthemums.

Spoons and Spiders

The spoons are another type of single with petals formed like narrow teaspoons. These are choice in lovely shades of white, ivory, coral, yellow, orchid and garnet. They are not reliably hardy, however, and in general, need some coddling, which I for one have always considered worth while.

Also exacting are the spiders or Fuji chrysanthemums so dear to flower arrangers, but not blooming until late October. These can well be disbudded. Consider when you choose Fujis that those large, exquisite, thread-like blooms in melting colors are not to be yours just for the wishing. Plants need good culture throughout the season and in most places wintering in a cold frame.

Important Garden Doubles

Double chrysanthemums are mainly of two types. The pompons, including the buttons, have a tight inflorescence, one to two inches across, and are represented by Canary and White Wonder, Crystal, Jubilee, Lavender Button and Pepita. The pompons last almost eternally as cut flowers. Some catalogues do not list pompons separately from the other doubles.

The larger, loose-flowered decorative or garden types of chrysanthemums are the ones most of us want in quantity. According to your preference, select them in an early-to-late sequence to make your garden glow and your home lovely with bouquets from late September until frost—or even beyond.

To begin with consider this group of twelve which I think of as a good All-Season, All-Color Dozen—baker's! It includes favorites of mine which for one reason or another have received many good marks in my chrysanthemum notebook. Later, your own experience and taste will indicate the perfect dozen for you, or very likely more. But for a start you will enjoy Avalanche and Quicksilver, both excellent whites; in shades of salmon, pink and lavender, Betty, Sparkling and Old Lavender; in yellow and bronze tones, Yellow Avalanche, Bronze Giant, Lee Powell, Eugene A. Wander and Admiration (peach); with the deeper Red Velvet, Mardi Gras, a bronze-copper cactus type and an All-American Chrysanthemum Selection for 1960, and Dark Knight added for contrast. First flowers, beginning probably with Mardi Gras, will appear in mid-September, and the show will continue far into October.

Like the spiders, the big double football chrysanthemums are really for the hobbyist who doesn't mind giving some extra attention to feeding and disbudding. A few plants of this kind are really fun. For instance, I have grown the old

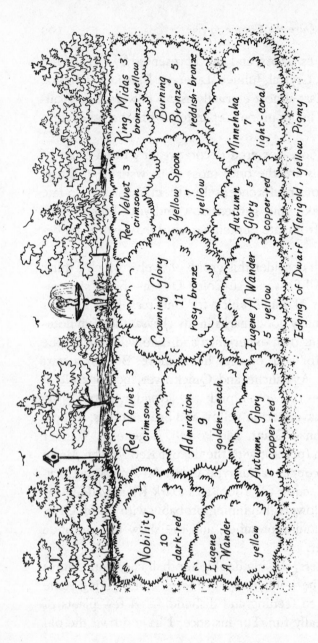

Nobility
10
dark-red

Eugene A. Wander
5

Autumn Glory
5
copper-red

Red Velvet 3
crimson

Admiration
9
golden-peach

Crowning Glory
11
rosy-bronze

Eugene A. Wander
5
yellow

Autumn Glory
5
copper-red

Red Velvet 3
crimson

Yellow Spoon
7
yellow

Autumn Glory
5
copper-red

King Midas 3'
bronz-yellow

Burning Bronze
5
reddish-bronze

Minnehaha
3
light-coral

Edging of Dwarf Marigold, Yellow Pigmy

BORDER UNIT OF CHRYSANTHEMUMS IN
RICH AUTUMN SHADES

Numbers in sections - number of plants required

0   1   2   3   4   5   6 feet

170

light-yellow variety, Mrs. H. E. Kidder, with great success—
and without special protection—outdoors in Philadelphia.
The pink Fascination, cactus Bronze Giant and yellow-centered White Swan are other temptations in this class.

I prefer to grow chrysanthemums either in cutting rows
among the vegetables or in separate beds featuring either
whites and pastels or else rich deep yellows, bronze reds and
a few pale blends like the coral Minnehaha. A friend of mine
who has the handsomest chrysanthemum border I know, over
a period of four years has selected and associated plants which
on a bright October day always lead me to ask, "Is there a
sunset missing?" Her border with its background of shrubs
grows on a little slope to the south of the house, and is
particularly beautiful looked down on from the dining-room
window. (The plan on page 170 emphasizes the rich colors.)

I have richly tinted chrysanthemums running along my
hawthorne hedge since I do not include them in my mixed
hardy border. Unless a bed is wider than my eight-foot al-
lowance, it seems to me chrysanthemums take up too much
spring and summer space there without offering color. Furthermore, when in October my favorites do flower, there is
a very tired end-of-season look to the borders and few desirable companions for these late perennials. Therefore, I
prefer to feature chrysanthemums separately as in the plan
on page 172, "Pastel Chrysanthemums for Late September
Into October."

But it's easy enough to grow them through the summer in
a place of their own and then to move them, on a cloudy
September day when they are in bud, to the border. There
space is easily made by pulling out some of the weariest
annuals. If roots are well soaked before and after moving,

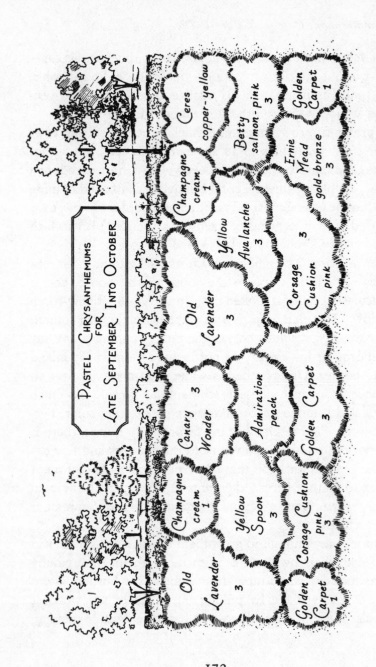

PASTEL CHRYSANTHEMUMS FOR
LATE SEPTEMBER INTO OCTOBER

Ceres
copper-yellow

Betty
salmon-pink
3

Golden
Carpet
1

Champagne
cream
1

Ernie
Mead
gold-bronze
3

Yellow
Avalanche
3

Old
Lavender
3

Corsage
Cushion
pink
3

Admiration
peach

Canary
Wonder   3

Golden
Carpet
3

Champagne
cream
1

Corsage Cushion
pink
3

Yellow
Spoon
3

Old
Lavender   3

Golden
Carpet
1

0 1 2 3 4   5 feet

the chrysanthemums bloom on without missing a beat. For all the early varieties this is particularly good procedure.

If you want chrysanthemums for late fall cutting and cherish hopes of early December bouquets, set out, in as protected a spot as you have, such varieties as the white Grace Bradshaw, bronze Carnival, dark red Nobility, coral Trevania and bronze Ernie Mead. In the Philadelphia area, any chrysanthemums dated late just may continue to flower until the first week of the last month in the year. If autumn has its droughty spells, be sure to water them to keep up their spirits for this much-appreciated late season role. The spiders do not bloom until far into October, but unless these are given some special protection, such as a canvas screen at night, they are best grown only in areas of late frost.

Where to Plant

Location is an important factor, of course, for all plantings. It should be protected where winds will not rock the plants about or a hot early morning sun destroy tissues sometimes frozen the night before. I notice that if flowers can recover slowly, not suddenly, from severe cold, their endurance is remarkable. Undoubtedly a southwestern exposure is best with house wall, fence or shrubbery behind the planting for a windbreak.

Good drainage is essential, particularly in its relation to winter hardiness. Plants which are alternately ice-locked and thawed rarely survive an average open winter. Plants on a little slope covered, after the first crusty freeze, with salt hay or oak leaves held in place by boards or the more slightly evergreen boughs, pass safest through outdoor winters.

If even under such conditions your chrysanthemums have

proved poor survivors, either treat them as indispensable annuals to be purchased every spring or take up a plant of each variety you cherish and afford it safe wintering in the cold frame. This is the method: After plants have flowered and well before a hard freeze, cut back the tall tops to crown growth. Soak the roots well and transfer the plants to the cold frame. Water again after planting and each week thereafter until a hard freeze occurs. The idea is to encourage as much rooting as possible in the new location. Then cover lightly with oak or other hardwood leaves or salt hay and fasten down the glass of the frame. To avoid overheating by the sun, cover the glass. If you have a lath screen used for summer shading, lay this on top.

From January on as warm middays occur, prop the glass up for short periods of ventilation. When in March examination reveals green growth, remove the leaf covering and the cold frame shade. By the first of April you can usually let the glass stay up all day and, as weather permits, at night too. This hardens plants so they can face open conditions again. Separate and transfer your chrysanthemums back to the garden when new growth is a few inches high. This is a fairly arduous business but the only sure way I have found to hold over certain exquisite but often tender ones like the spoons and other favorites.

Soil Preparation

Chrysanthemum beds need be prepared but twelve inches deep unless natural drainage is poor. Then an extra six inches is dug and a layer of cinders or broken bricks laid in the bottom. This leads off water which otherwise would linger dangerously around the roots and be a real hazard to safe wintering.

If new beds are prepared in autumn, there is plenty of time for settling before spring planting. This is in May for new plants from the grower's but mid-April for home wintered stock, which is at that time regularly separated (except for the cushions which are divided every second year) into as many small rooted divisions as the outside of each crown will supply. Discard the hard woody centers. Then set the divisions out twelve to eighteen inches apart depending upon the nature of their mature size. A lilliput, for instance, needs but a square foot to a plant while Red Velvet and Old Lavender take much more. *Plenty of room and a free circulation of air are essential for both looks and health.*

Average cultivated garden soil grows very nice chrysanthemums but the bed made fertile with manure, humus or compost and later enriched with additional plant food, produces very fine flowers indeed. For extra feedings I use a dried manure product or some balanced plant food. Either is scattered in a ring under the outermost leaf spread of the established plant about the middle of June and again the first and middle of July. It is *immediately* watered in.

To Keep Them Low

When after the spring resetting, your plants have six leaves, pinch the tops out to induce side branching and a type of growth to minimize staking. As each new branch develops six leaves, pinch these too. Discontinue this practice by mid-July for early varieties like Avalanche, Yellow Avalanche, Eugene A. Wander, Prairie Moon and Vulcan. Continue until August for later flowering ones. Let growth go on then or flower formation may be fatally delayed. Be guided also by the time of first frost in your locality. In periods of prolonged drought, usually about three times a season, water chrysanthemums deeply with a soil soaker or by placing a slow-running hose on a board for at least an hour in each area of the bed.

Health Measures

As a routine matter, and before pests appear, spray plants with insecticidal soap on a weekly basis until buds begin to open. If there is a complaint against chrysanthemums—and I hesitate to admit one since these are my most cherished perennials and this my favorite chapter—it is that in some seasons and for some varieties an unattractive browning of the lower foliage occurs. This may be due to the effect on plant tissues of drought followed by wet spells; it may be caused by poor air circulation in overcowded plantings, or it may be the result of a nematode attack. Attention to deep watering through rainless weeks, adequate spacing, and application of a deterrent dust will minimize or even eradicate this foliage trouble. Avoid overhead watering, use a mulch and if you have reason to suspect nematodes, propagate by tip cuttings rather than crown division.

Staking for the taller Koreans seems inevitable.

Bamboo or wire stakes fastened separately to each main stem by a twistem or plant tie look well, or you may set three stakes around each plant and encircle it with a piece of green twine or raffia. I have seen in certain of our public gardens, and in many English gardens, a quite adequate supporting job done by thrusting strong, much-branched pieces of brush among the plants, just as we have long done here in the vegetable garden for peas, usually with privet clippings. Cushions and rubellums, of course, need no such attention. If you have special tripod supports for your peonies, these are also fine for chrysanthemums.

As for the practice of disbudding, single varieties are more charming in great undisbudded sprays, though large-flowering types like Girl Friend or Stylish will produce even finer blooms if you remove some of the side buds from each cluster. Large-flowering doubles like Mrs. Pierre S. du Pont, III, Old Lavender and Mardi Gras could be disbudded to advantage. But in the garden where mass loveliness rather than greenhouse individuality is desirable, few of us enthusiasts find disbudding worth while.

What to Select

It is a good plan with chrysanthemums to select only the earlies if you live where the growing season is brief and frost comes soon, but choose late September and October varieties if your garden grows where so long a pagent is in most years possible. If you want chrysanthemums for cutting, choose colors that suit the decoration of your house through the autumn months, and be sure to include a few of the gerbera-like spoons. If you prefer the garden effect, I recommend these as charming color groupings:

For early September:
    Mardi Gras, Vulcan (red) and yellow Lilliput Happy (foreground)

For late September:
    Avalanche (white), Abundance (bronze-yellow), Chippa-Red and golden Eugene A. Wander (foreground)

For very early October:
   Pink Bett, White Gardenia, Old Lavender, ivory-pink
      Corsage Cushion (foreground)

For early October:
   Canary Wonder, Admiration (peach), Yellow Spoon,
      bronze Ernie Mead (foreground)

For mid-October:
   White Grace Bradshaw, pale yellow Ruby Breithaupt,
      coral Trevania, copper-yellow Ceres and dark-eyed,
      lilac Masquerade (foreground)

Finally here is a chart of my own favorites to use until your preference and experience dictate a more valuable one for your own garden.

CHRYSANTHEMUMS YOU MUST NOT MISS!

Singles

WHITE	PINK	LAVENDER TO PURPLE
North Star	Daphne	Garnet Spoon
Radiant	Jimmy Spoon	Orchid Spoon

BRONZE TO COPPER	RED	YELLOW
Apollo	Fire Engine	Gold Daisy
Ceres	Fred Stone	Yellow Spoon
Clarke Coral Spoon	(semidouble)	Moonlight Spoon (dwarf)

Doubles

WHITE	PINK	LAVENDER TO PURPLE
Avalanche (early)	Betty	Lady Fair (orchid)
Gardenia	Sparkling	Old Lavender
Quicksilver (early)		Purple Heart

BRONZE TO COPPER	RED	YELLOW
Abundance (early)	Cinnabar	Eugene A. Wander (early)
Admiration	Fred Stone	King's Ransom
Burning Bronze	(semidouble)	Lee Powell
Headliner	Royalist	Newton
John Furst (late)	(pompon)	
Mardi Gras		Tonka (early)
		Tranquillity (low)
		Yellow Avalanche (early)

21. Christmas and Lenten Roses Bloom in the Snow

When the firm hand of winter is laid upon our gardens, it seems impossible that a fresh crop of flowers should start blooming there. Yet where the Christmas rose is planted, blossoms appear in December, since this hellebore scorns the sun and ease of summer and waits for the cold to flaunt unrivaled its white drifts of waxen bloom and bud. According to legend this is the rose which bloomed on the first Christmas Eve. Now when temperatures are not far above zero, its flowering seems as miraculous today as it did centuries ago.

Yet this is a miracle which readily occurs since these perennials are culturally simple to deal with and, once established, richly productive. Clumps of Christmas roses are filled with fat and numerous buds long before the late chrysanthemums are spent, while their close relatives, the Lenten roses, are in fine flower before the spring crocuses show a trace of color.

Varieties for the Collector

If you are an enthusiast with a desire to make a hobby collection of these hellebores, you can with determination and time locate a number of them. One of the loveliest, *Helleborus niger*, the Christmas rose species, as well as the usual mixed varieties of *H. orientalis*, the Lenten rose, are readily available from many growers. *H. niger* grows eight to ten inches high with deply serrated evergreen leaves and, in time, twenty to thirty flowers to a plant. These blossoms on sturdy stems, frequently in pairs, resemble the single-flowered tuberous-rooted begonias or some of the anemones. As the months go by from October to March, the flowers pass from white through many beautiful rose-pink shadings, and finally turn a pleasant enduring green.

When I cut them for bouquets, I select both white and pink blooms and, in order not to sacrifice their important evergreen foliage, I use instead sprays of yew, or pieces of English ivy or pachysandra. For a special centerpiece, Christmas roses with hemlock are unusual and exquisite, and the flowers stay fresh for three to four weeks, although the hemlock does not. *Helleborus niger altifolius* is the largest-flowering of the niger strains. It grows twelve to sixteen inches high and produces flowers three to five inches across, often several on the same stem. Consider, too, February Star, with four-inch flowers in midwinter, and Chalice, also with large blooms, but these appear toward spring.

In the beginning it takes patience with these hellebores. Usually they do not flower either the first or even the second year after planting since they must, before setting buds, not only attain an unusual degree of maturity but also have made themselves completely at home. It is therefore important at the outset to select permanent quarters for them.

Where to Plant

I have planted hellebores in various places, mostly close to the house where I can see the flowers from a window when very cold weather makes garden strolls less inviting. I have a few plants of *niger* under the dining-room windows among ferns and mountain laurel, but the planting I enjoy most, becuse I dwell on it at breakfast time all through the year, is in the Kitchen Look-Into Garden (see page 28). Here the Christmas roses grow with the Christmas ferns, but more about this when I tell you about the Fern Garden in Chapter 22. The Lenten roses I have planted away from the house at the end of the Fern Walk as a pleasant objective late in February when an unexpected warm day makes it fun to poke about and see what's doing. Sometimes flowers do appear that early on the Lenten rose.

One happily located group of fifteen *niger* plants, which my friend Isabel Fasel developed from one plant set out some thirteen years ago, opens each year, well before Christmas, some sixty flowers in a lively white-to-rose profusion. They make a surprising winter picture with an ancient oak tree spreading above them and the protecting wall of an old spring house for background.

In some years this planting, which is in West Chester, Pennsylvania, begins flowering by October tenth with new buds still opening at the New Year. Until late in March the blossoms, by that time green, linger on the plants. As a rule, however, bloom on *H. niger* is not to be expected there before November.

Near the *niger* plants grow also several varieties of *orientalis*, a species originally found in Asia Minor. The palmate foliage reaches twelve inches while the Lenten roses, so called becuse they always are present at Easter time, although they start blooming earlier, rise on twenty-inch stems. More than a hundred blossoms may appear on a well-established plant. *Orientalis* has exceedingly beautiful foliage which inclines to die down once very cold weather arrives in January. The color range of the flowers is from pale green through white, rose, claret and purple to light brown and a deep chocolate-red. Some varieties are maroon spotted.

The very handsome flowers suggest certain cypripediums and are as charming as orchids for corsages. You can readily obtain *H. o. astrorubens* and *deicatissima* and the varieties Mons. Prosper Perthuis, Albert Dugourd, Marco Polo, Ariadne and Mirande.

Bearsfoot Hellebore

Choice and lovely is *Helleborus foetidus*, a species from Western Europe called bearsfoot hellebore. It produces a thick two-foot stem of slimly segmented leaves in the center of which develops a loose pale green globe of inflorescence. The flowers start slowly to open before Christmas, are perfected late in January and continue to look well for three to four months longer. Several stems spring from each crown in four- or five-year old plants, thus producing the effect of a small shrub, which is reminiscent somehow of leucothoe and just as attractive for the foreground of a shrubbery planting.

For an indoor arrangement *H. foetidus* is also a treasure. Late one January, I placed a single tall spray of it in a dull gold jar with a black Chinese base. The deep green of the foliage and the pale green of the flowers blended beautifully with the yellow and looked particularly well with my eighteenth-century furnishings. And incidentally for an unusual flower showpiece nothing could be more interesting that *H. foetidus* since it immediately commands attention and as a keeper is unexcelled. When after two weeks mine wilted, I revived it for another charming ten days by recutting the stem and steeping it for five minutes in a cup of boiling water and then plunging the spray again into its tall vase filled with ice water.

Flowers on *H. foetidus* usually do not appear until early in December, but in some particularly fortuitous seasons first color is seen a month ahead of schedule, in November. This species readily self-sows but seedlings do not bloom until the third year.

St. Patrick's Rose and Others

Helleborus viridis (St. Patrick's rose) can also be obtained. It bears smaller, greenish veined flowers of special interest to those who are collecting hellebores. It sometimes starts budding as early as December but the flowers do not open until March and appear before leaves, since this hellebore is deciduous. I have liked it for miniature arrangements. It too keeps fresh for weeks. The holly-leaved hellebore, *H. corsicus*, and *H. cyclophyllus*, with a delicate sweet fragrance, are rare and interesting varieties in this most interesting plant group.

Ease of Hellebores

Elegant and unusual as these hellebores are, there is no great skill required in raising them. In your average garden soil, they will do well enough but because of the permanency of their residence, it seems worth while to prepare an ideal plot of loam well mixed with leaf mold and sand until it feels coarse and light and is reliably moisture-retentive. A top dressing of leaf mold and rotted manure with slight yearly additions is always recommended for hellebores, but you will find that an inch layer of composted material is an entirely satisfactory substitute. Mrs. Fasel's large planting has been grown without either manure or mulching, but it is in leafy soil to which she has added bone meal each November.

Most important of all is location. A cool, moist, lightly shaded situation with protection fron north and west winds which tend to burn foilage, seems best. The closer plants are to a protecting wall the earlier they will bloom. Their taste for shade makes these hellebores a special boon if you crave flowers but are frustrated by the deep shadows of trees. Beneath these in a fern bed or at the edge of shrubbery plantings, hellebores will do beautifully. (An idea for a planting is offered in the plan "Winter Color Beside the House," page 186.)

Set plants out at any time from spring to October. August, however, will prove to be a particularly propitious time.

Let the roots stretch down, not out, in each sixteen-inch hole with the crown just under the surface of the soil. E. W. Luedy, the well-known hellebore specialist, advises bone meal or a little superphosphate at planting time and liquid manure or a commercial fertilizer in solution in spring, but with rather less attention my plants have been satisfactory. Good drainage is, of course, the great essential; standing water will not be tolerated by the fleshy roots.

New leaves appear in spring and when a plant has reached the six- or seven-leaf stage, it may be time to divide it. Sometimes the buds on niger, for example, come up so thickly they can hardly find space in which to open. Even in the first year of flowering there are six or seven blooms to a plant. In the course of a decade one *niger* specimen will be capable of sufficient division to provide some thirty plants. However, hellebores are generally slow-growing perennials and are better off if divided only for good reason.

Niger does not produce seed in some localities, possibly because most of the flowers are fertilized just before extremely cold weather sets in and the seeds do not have a

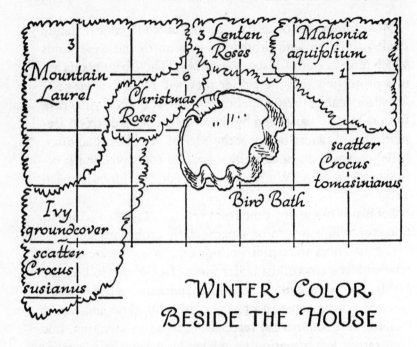

3 — Mountain Laurel

3 Lenten Roses

Mahonia aquifolium 1

— 6 Christmas Roses

scatter Crocus tomasinianus

Bird Bath

Ivy groundcover

scatter Crocus susianus

WINTER COLOR BESIDE THE HOUSE

chance to develop. In the same place both *orientalis* and *foetidus* may seed freely. *Foetidus* will produce quantities of seed which ripen in June from flowers fertilized in February and March. All hellebore seed grows best when it is planted immediately after ripening. Seeds need cold weather, however, before germination is likely to take place. And signs of growth may not occur for two years! Then perhaps three more years may elapse before flowers appear. Obviously, I cannot recommend seed-grown hellebores to the impatient.

In Summer

Through the summer your hellebores will change little. They seem simply to wait for autumn. Occasionally in times of prolonged drought the foliage wilts a little. Soak the soil around the plants deeply if this occurs. Otherwise even extra watering does not seem necessary for these most easy-to-grow perennials which rest in summer and work in winter.

In fact, more trouble is often taken with the hellebores than is necessary. I see recommended the practice of lifting and forcing plants. Since despite cold and snow the hellebores bloom outdoors anyway, I can't see the point of forcing.

It is indeed part of the pleasure of growing hellebores that they afford us the special delights of inconsistency. Gathering fresh flowers in the garden in December, with one hand to reach for galoshes as snow protection and with the other holding the picking basket and shears, is for most of us a rare experience. Midsummer blooms grown in the open on mid-winter plants—therein lies the charm of the hellebores.

22. Ferns Are Valuable
Garden Perennials

Ferns are among our most valuable perennials. Beautiful and varied, almost unattended, they come up year after year. I have only recently thinned out the Fern Garden which I first planted seven years ago, soon after I came to Stony Brook Cottage. It was then that I really discovered ferns, and every year since I have appreciated them more. In fact, I shall always think of 1960 as the "Year of the Fern" because that year I made the acquaintance of a number of new ones, and I extended their use here in so many ways.

It seems to me that ferns belong in every garden. If you are busy and want an effect easily and quickly, ferns are for you; if you are pressed with garden chores and get little outside help, ferns will prove your ally. If you appreciate plants with through-the season good looks, you can certainly rely on ferns.

In early spring, ferns are utterly delightful as the fiddle-heads thrust upward and then unfurl, quite slowly over a matter of weeks, into exquisite and varying types of fronds. Indeed, there is no monotony among the plants called ferns. In their own haunts, they vary from a few inches to five feet (without considering the tropical giants), and the fronds can resemble green lace veiling, as in the maidenhair, or sharply-cut dark green leather, as in the Christmas fern. Some fronds are pale and feathery like those of the northern lady, New York or the hay-scented ferns; some put up fruiting sprays like "flowers," as the royal and cinnamon ferns. All are fascinating, and in all seasons. Perhaps they mean most to us on hot summer days when their green composure looks so cool.

You can properly set out ferns early in spring or late in fall, though I admit I move them any time that suits my convenience, last year late in June. Transplanted in full leaf, they suffer some, but sprayed lightly with the hose every evening for a week or so afterwards, they will survive. Anyway, I didn't lose a plant, although I shifted about a multitude of them.

Ferns with Bulbs

Ferns have so many possibilities and vary so in size and effect that you should really start by deciding *what you want them to do for you.* Perhaps you have a piece of woodland on your place and would like to have a garden there predominantly of ferns. If so, choose the shade- and acid-lovers and arrange these in both related and contrasting foliage groups on each side of a wide (at least four- to five-foot) grass path. Such a path can be mowed along with the rest of the grass and will serve as important transition from lawn to woods (But don't put in stepping stones that require clipping; I took mine out.)

Where lawn meets woodland, you might plant, as I have, a ground cover area of Christmas ferns interspersed with clumps of narcissus. Ferns with spring bulbs, wild flowers or other early perennials make a wonderfully carefree association. As the bulbs retreat and their foliage matures, or as the earliest flowering plants grow shabby, up come those sturdy fern crooks, unfurling their fronds at just the most appropriate time. The brittle, evergreen wood, New York and lady ferns all make attractive companions for bulbs.

With this fern-and-bulb association, you aren't harassed into cutting down bulb foliage before it has really ripened for its more unsightly weeks are quite unseen. I grow my Christmas ferns with White Lady narcissus and both through the years seem extremely pleased. Plants of flowering tobacco are introduced late in June, when at long last the bulb foliage can be easily pulled away.

Besides its evergreen nature, a great asset, the Christmas fern has the virtue of staying put. The clumps spread very slowly, as do many of the "crown growers," but they do eventually send out short stocky runners to form another clump or so which can be cut off. And that's important because the more ferns you have the more you find you can use.

My Fern Garden

Along the grass path then, as you pass into the Fern Garden, is en edging of blue and white wood hyacinths (*Scilla campanulata*) and pink-lavender wild geranium, which self-sows luxuriously. Then behind this edging are more Christmas ferns, here some distance apart with groupings of the native purple *Iris versicolor* between, its lance leaves an excellent contrast in form to the ferns beside and behind it.

The Fern Garden slopes down to the brook on one side, but on both the high and the low side of the path are similar large groupings of big ferns from the osmunda group—cinnamon, royal and interrupted, all of them beauties. And how they thrive! Yellow evening primroses and great bulbous orange lilies (*Lilium superbum*), to seven feet, are interplanted with the ferns. This makes a garden of primarily just four kinds of ferns, but this has sufficient interest for royal and Christmas are in strong contrast to the somewhat similar cinnamon and interrupted.

At the end of the Fern Garden there is a featured area dominated by a huge elm with practically the whole trunk kept clear and visible from the house terrace above. (I don't like to see the base of trees hidden as when they rise from shrubbery clumps; on that account, I cleared away the natural growth around the tree before I made this woods a garden.) So, at the base of the tree there are a few scattered Christmas ferns again for unity, interplanted with narcissus, and with two kinds of woodferns introduced, the evergreen marginal or leather, and the semi-evergreen toothed or common woodfern. (Some sensitive fern has recently volunteered here too but its residence will depend on behavior: usually it is too aggressive to be tolerated in garden quarters, but it offers pleasant foliage contrast.)

The flowering feature of this terminating area is Japanese iris in lavender, pink, but mainly white varieties. Wet in spring, well-drained in summer, with adequate sun and very rich, acid soil, this is a lovely place for Japanese iris, and also for the white astilbe which itself has such ferny foliage. You will like both of these as companions for your ferns. (The plan on page 192) shows the planting of this area.)

Ferns as Specimens or Colonies

The large ferns also make fine speciments in the manner of small shrubs. Because these big growers will tolerate so much shade, they are fine for odd places where you don't want to go groping in after weeds. I use the interrupted fern

DRAWING BY KATHLEEN BOURKE

thus in a corner behind the wisteria, and it adds grace there and is a background for the bare wisteria stems. I fitted a plant of cinnamon against the house behind a viburnum bush, and in a very shady spot under a maple I planted both cinnamon and interrupted as backdrop for a forward, sun-reaching planting of daylilies.

The evergreen woodfern makes a fine specimen elsewhere on the edge of the woodland below a wild cherry tree with periwinkle at its base and yellow evening primroses and mauve tradescantia as good companions. Indeed, there are a number of choices to use as specimens. Cinnamon, interrupted, royal, leather woodferns and goldie fern stand excellently alone, but not the northern lady fern which grows somewhat jumbled and can get rusty in dry weather.

Fern colonies you will find are pretty almost anywhere. I have them—royal, cinnamon, leather woodfern and, at the edge, a fine, gray-leaved, silver-marked Japanese variety—in a planting of evergreen mountain laurels, azaleas, Oregon grape—and always several of a kind together to avoid a spotty picture. Here the ferns shade and cool the soil. Then along my New England stone boundary "fences," I have areas of New York, lady and royal ferns with bulbs and periwinkle. In the bog garden, still so far from "finished," royal doesn't mind wet feet (in fact, enjoys it) and neither does the lady fern. Both colonize charmingly there. Colonies are also pretty as foundation plantings. In New England, they are often used with ancient lilacs at the corners of white houses, and I have seen the hay-scented fern planted to retain a bank and combined with cinnamon and interrupted and with pink climbing roses along a tottering wall. Bright-colored coleus or impatiens with ferns makes a charming doorstep planting, especially in shade, and at the seashore, the interrupted endures the sun.

The maidenhair, surely the most beguiling of ferns, is lovely in a bed with tuberous begonias for summer, or following spring flowers like mertensia and bleedingheart, which eventually disappear altogether. This brings me to one of the most valued uses of ferns: in association with flowering perennials. In my Apple-Tree Garden, the cinnamon fern is a perfect interspersing background plant, and goldie fern is a handsome specimen beside daylilies. Both bring fresh interest there as this predominately spring garden takes a long breather before the blooming of the summer monardas and daylilies. Smaller northern lady and New York ferns make an appearance midway in the bed where the color has gone from doronicums and trollius.

For rock gardens, there are many small treasures which naturally seek the companionship of rocks and boulders. Ebony spleenwort, polypody, lipferns (the *Cheilanthes),* woodsias and grape ferns are all possibilities to plant with your forget-me-nots, small phloxes, Jacob's ladder, primroses, violets and veronicas. Of course, the larger maidenhair, but only to twenty inches, belongs here too. Plant it in descending order and it will look like a cool green waterfall coming over the rocks.

For Ground Covers

Another marvelous value of ferns lies in their use as ground covers. When I took away the fence to the Rose Meadow—it was supposed to act as a psychological barrier to further expansion, but alas it didn't—I found myself with a rather rough area, too large and too expensive to turn completely into grass. So here in the worse places, we chopped out bittersweet and other unworthies and in light shade in well-dug soil planted some of the creeping ferns, as the hay-scented, lady and New York for ground covers.

The hay-scented is the lovely pale green feathery fern you have seen along roadsides, under trees, beside rocky out-croppings or in abandoned cellar holes. Planted directly under a fence, it makes clipping there unncessary. It looks fragile but is so strong it always reminds me of one of those delicate women who turn out to have a whim of iron. In the Rose Meadow (so-called for the collection of the old shrub roses there), it won't matter how invasive the hay-scented is for there's lots and lots of footage there which I'll be glad to have it cover.

Other possibilities for sites that need a green covering of *your* choice—Nature always fills in if you don't—are the coarse bracken and the sensitive fern (sensitive only to cold and drought that is, and most insensitive in appearance). These with the hay-scented—whose fresh fronds in full sun smell so sweet, and whose dry fronds in fall are even sweeter —should never be admitted to the garden, and if they show up there or in a small woodland, as well they may if it is a haven for other ferns, pull them out. On occasion, the ostrich fern can be too pervasive. One year it had to be weeded out by hand so intent it was on smothering an important planting of Christmas ferns. I have used the lovely New York fern as ground cover for a pine tree in the Rose Meadow, and it does an attractive and suitable job there.

The Look-Into Garden

My newest planting, the last made in my "Year of the Fern," involved an association I have come to enjoy tremendously, for it is in the Look-Into Garden—that is, look-into from the kitchen casements. I have told you before about the association here of Christmas ferns and Christmas roses when I discussed Doorstep Gardens (Chapter 3). For me, the Look-Into Garden is just another triumph for the fern. (The plan on page 28 shows the lay-out.)

The only thing against ferns is their jaw-breaking names which the botanists make worse by changing them all the time. Otherwise ferns are perfect. However, like all that lives, they need *some* care, mainly a spring clean-up of fallen leaves, and later when the new fronds are well developed, some removal of old basal fronds. After this is finished in the Fern Garden, and the bulb foliage is removed, I mulch with buckwheat hulls. That ends the weeding problem here, as elsewhere, for the year. (You can more sensibly but less neatly for a not-so-prominent planting, let all the old fronds remain and with oak leaves encourage the development of a natural mulch.) In time of drought, I see to it that my ferns get a good deep soaking about once a week. In general, they prefer a soil with leaf mold, and they don't mind a mixing in of some stones, which is lucky for me at Stony Brook. No fertilizer is ever needed.

The Fern Chart which follows is a quick reference for some twenty kinds. Before you choose, consider which ones will best suit the conditions you can *easily* offer. You will notice that there are evergreen and deciduous types, ferns for sun as well as shade, neat crown growers and spreaders from root stocks. Watch out for these creepers because some of them really do take over and will grow just about anywhere in sun or shade, wet or dry. If you have a patch of woodland, you will be sure to have some ferns there already, and fern enthusiasts can always spare you a few plants of the kinds you like. Collecting from the wild should only be done with good conservation practices in mind, but don't mind rushing in with trowel and spade if a woodland is being torn up for a new road or a development.

Most perennial nurseries carry a few ferns, while nurseries specializing in wild flowers usually offer a goodly number, as in Sources, page 295. When the environment suits them and the ground is steadily moist, all ferns will propagate themselves by spores, and in three years the new plants may grow as large as the parents. In addition, those that spread by creeping do so at various speeds, while the vase-forming ones grow steadily larger and but two or three new plants spring up beside them in the course of years. You will indeed be glad of the day you discovered ferns. For low upkeep and high pleasure, I find them unequalled—and so will you.

TWENTY EXCELLENT AND USEFUL FERNS

Name	Height in Inches	Foliage Type E—Evergreen D—Deciduous	Light Requirement	Soil Requirement	Behavior and Appearance	Remarks
1. *Adiantum Pedatum* —Maidenhair Fern	8–20	D	Woods, dense shade	Neutral, rich leafmold, drainage important	Creeping, unique, dainty circular, lacy tops—wiry dark stems	Early appearance, most lovely with spring wild flowers or perennals, with laurel, etc.
2. *Asplenium platyneuron*—Ebony Spleenwort	8–20	E	Light shade	Stony or sandy leafmold; indifferent to soil reaction	Narrow fronds in a crown	Pretty for a rock garden; nice in terrariums
3. *Athyrium angustum, A. felixfemina*— Northern Lady Fern	12–36	D	Partial shade or full sun	Dry to wet woods	Delicately green, finely cut, creeping	Adaptable and strong grower; has naturalized in my woods
4. *Athyrium goeringianum pictum*—Japanese Gray Fern	10–15	D	Open shade	Leafmold on acid side, adaptable if moist	Slow creeper, makes a clump not a whorl	Gray-green with silver markings. Fine accent plant, as beside a rock

198

5. *Cystopteris bulbifera*— Berry Bladder Fern	18–30	D	Shade	Neutral or sweet, not acid	Long narrow tapering fronds; pinkish stems, produces baby ferns in pellet form	Suited to rock garden or small areas, nice shade for clematis, daphne or other lime-lovers; naturalizes readily, amusing to children
6. *Cystopteris fragilis*— Brittle Fern	4–12	D	Shade, sensitive to drought	Rocks, ledges sometimes moist stony woods; in sweet soils runs madly about	Deeply toothed and very brittle; spreads into crevices	Early croziers uncurl before others; good cover for earliest bulbs
7. *Dennstaedtia puncti-lobula*—Hay-scented Fern	12–30	D	Shade or sun; on exposed slopes good soil holder	Good or poor soil; wild grower in acid, more circumspect in sweet	Feathery growth, creeping; spreads from root mats; rampant	Aroma of hay in sun, or when dried in fall. Turns light rust color

TWENTY EXCELLENT AND USEFUL FERNS (Continued)

Name	Height in Inches	Foliage Type E—Evergreen D—Deciduous	Light Requirement	Soil Requirement	Behavior and Appearance	Remarks
8. *Dryopteris goldiana*—Goldie Fern	24–36	D	Shade	Rich humus, neutral to slightly acid, must have steady moisture	Dark blue-green, broad oval fronds, lighter beneath	Palmlike and tropical, fine specimen type, considered by some our most beautiful native
9. *Dryopteris intermedia*—Evergreen Woodfern	16–32	E	Partial shade	Moist, rich woods	Deeply cut, prickly fronds; good deep color	Late to develop, so excellent with bulbs
10. *Dryopteris marginalis*—Leather or Marginal Woodfern	12–36	E	Shade but adaptable	Rich wood soil, rocky shelters	Blue-green fronds in vase form, very lovely, crown	Firm textured, not toothed, fruit dots underneath along edges or "margins"
11. *Dryopteris spinulosa*—Toothed or Common Woodfern	14–28	Evergreen sterile fronds; deciduous fertile ones	Among rocks and trees	Acid, moist but adaptable	Circular clumps, lighter than *D. intermedia*, very lovely, crown	Volunteered under my apple tree and along wall; lacy but less so than *D. intermedia*

Ebony Spleenwort (See #2)
Evergreen Woodfern (See #9)
Goldie Fern (See #8)
Hay-scented Fern (See #7)
Interrupted Fern (See #14)
Japanese Gray Fern (See #4)
Leather or Marginal Woodfern (See #10)
Maidenhair Fern (See #1)
New York Fern (See #20)
Northern Lady Fern (See #3)

12. *Onoclea sensibilis*—Sensitive Fern	D	12–36	Shade or in full sun	Bog or drier soil but best as bank-holder along water	Rampant creeper; coarse, showy, not for small garden	"Sensitive" to drought and first frost—good texture contrast
13. *Osmunda cinnamomea*—Cinnamon Fern	D Red-brown spore "flowers"	24–60	Rather deep shade	Must have rich acid soil	Mighty grower where conditions suit, crown looks tropical	Fine bold accent; showiest fiddleheads; lovely with Pieris Japonica or daylilies
14. *Osmunda claytoniana*—Interrupted Fern	D	30–36	Shade or sun	Deep rich woods soil	Somewht coarse fronds, good specimen plant, crown	Frond "interrupted" by separate branchlets of spores; interesting growth; not so handsome as Cinnamon

TWENTY EXCELLENT AND USEFUL FERNS (*continued*)

Name	Height in Inches	Foliage Type E—Evergreen D—Deciduous	Light Requirement	Soil Requirement	Behavior and Appearance	Remarks
15. *Osmunda regalis*— Royal Fern	24–48	D	Light to dense shade, no sun	Moist, acid soil, in drier locations only with special care	Brown spore clusters like flowers, vase form, fine for contrast	Lovely and graceful for a bank planting along a path; mixes well with Cinnamon and Interrupted, or with Japanese iris and astilbe
Ostrich Fern (see #18)						
16. *Polypodium virginianum*—Polypody	3–10	E	Light shade	On rocks in moderately dry leafmold; sometimes on fallen logs	Dense spreading mats, a creeper	Darling small fern for right environment
17. *Polystichum acrostichoides*—Christmas Fern	15–30	E	Shade—of dogwoods and witchhazel	Fairly damp rich leafmold but adaptable	Refined, crown spreads slowly; fine ground cover	Edge of my woodland, next lawn; interplanted

18. *Pteretis nodulosa*—Ostrich Fern	24–48	D but fertile July fronds stay through winter, brown though, not green	Shade to full sun if near water	Deep, rich soil, moist to wet	Plumy vase form but creeps by ropelike stolons, even under paving, turns brown early	Not for refined locations; hard to eliminate but attractive where plenty of room; looks like an ostrich plume with narcissus, followed by flowering tobacco
19. *Pteridium latiusculum*—Eastern Bracken	8–36	D	Part shade or full sun, open hillsides, pastures, banks	Anywhere acid or alkaline even in sterile areas	Triangular frond, creeper, great violence, coarse grower	Much too invasive for home garden but has uses elsewhere
Royal Fern (See #15)						
Sensitive Fern (See #12)						
20. *Dryopteris (Thelypteris) noveboracensis*—New York Fern	8–24	D	Partial shade	Adaptable, late in coming up, about mid-May	Shallow creeper, delicate light green, harmless among stronger plants	Excellent ground cover; fronds taper *both* ends; lovely contrast to deeper greens
Toothed Woodfern (See #11)						

23. Secondary Spires

In the long border, especially if it can be seen from a distance, several spires other than delphinium are also rhythmically effective. Repetition of the same flower form gives continuity to the whole as if the same chord were struck over and over again in a prelude. And this primary rhythm should be syncopated with a secondary theme of lower spire flowers. For example, if the yellow thermopsis dominates June, blue lupines become perfect secondary steeples with white Miss Lingard phlox the repeated chord.

Large groups of spires, however, are not placed together or the valuable pyramidal form of the individual is lost. Usually sufficient is a single developed plant of any of these flowers considered spire-like. A well-grown chimney bellflower, for instance, will send up from a single crown several purple or white rockets while others of the steepled clan are often even more prolific.

The background of the spire should be unassuming. A flowering shrub or brilliantly berried bush may vie with the turrets of garden flowers and so rob them of their restful beauty. A plain wall of hemlock darkness, the quiet green of euonymus, the soft rose red of a brick wall, the gleam of a white picket fence, or the peaceful blue of sky or sea are ideal backgrounds.

In selecting our primary spire flowers for the various seasons we must require definite qualities. Obviously the predominant characteristic must be height, not usually less than five feet. The blossom must be of steepled form, preferably with the leaves growing in a low crown so that a long line of stem is visible. Plants must be moderately sturdy too, never even artistically loose in the manner of the carefree hardy aster. Their night value for the garden, sought at twilight, is also worth considering.

Spires of Spring

The spires of spring are slow to appear for it takes a long stretch of growing weather to perfect a five-foot flower spike. Perhaps for the sake of an early show, and that not until June, it is wise to lower the standard and admit for this season the two- to three-foot beauty, *Digitalis ambigua*, a pale moonlit yellow. This is an excellent foxglove, with yellowish flowers marked with brown, and fine for our purpose because of its definite, sturdy form. Also unlike most foxgloves, *D. ambigua* is usually perennial.

Foxgloves give strength and dignity to any border planting and "consort well with nearly every other flower, and certainly with every other color." The biennial Giant Shirley Hybrids, reaching a three- to four-foot height, are particularly fine in their wide range of color from white and shell pink to deep rose. For the yellowish *ambigua* a foreground planting of yellow columbines is attractive with masses of lavender *Nepeta mussini* in front of these.

And for late spring the beautiful *Thermopsis carolinianum*

is also not to be overlooked. How rarely I see this in gardens,
although it is easily grown in the sun and choice for cutting.
Indeed, where delphiniums are too difficult, this five-foot
yellow thermopsis is a charming steepled substitute, and it is
readily developed from seed too, if this is sown in early spring
while the soil is still cool. Age increases its stature, the third-
year thermopsis being mature while the second-year plants
are only twenty-four-inch infants.

Lupine and Baptisia

There are two choice secondary spires for this season—of
similar form and both blue—lupine and baptisia or wild indigo. I do not include the strain of Russell lupines. These,
of course, grow taller and produce a wide color range but
since they do not care for my garden or thrive in any of my
friends' plots either, I am not well acquainted with them.
Evidently even the selected American seed is still dependent
on the cool humidity its English ancestors enjoyed. Of these
the remark seems true, "the weather that grows corn, kills
the lupine."

The more reliable *Lupinus polyphyllus* and its pink and
white relatives develop two- to three-foot spikes of enchanting blooms in June. These rise from finely-cut, soft gray-
green leaves. White lupines are particularly lovely grown with
the pink oriental poppy Helen Elizabeth, and blue masses of
Chinese delphinium which help to hide the lupines' usual
summer retreat. After lupines fade, cut the stalks low and let
the plants rest for several weeks. Then water them deeply
and feed them to encourage a September crop. If they disappear for a time, keep the space for them open and marked.
Do not interplant.

Since our hot, dry summers are not at all to the lovely

lupines' liking, it is essential for their survival that the conditions we can control be ideal. A well-drained site in full sun but with protection from wind is good. There prepare a light, moisture-retentive rich soil. I always add plenty of sand to the lupine bed too and in the spring work a dried cow manure product among the plants. During their growing season and after their midsummer rest, an abundance of moisture is essential. Transplantings are best managed in autumn.

Baptisia australis is a pet of mine. It is three feet high, deep blue and lupine-like but easier to grow, and with a large generous plant form reliably handsome the entire growing season. This makes it fine for important placement in a sizable border even though its blooming season lasts but a few May or June weeks. If you are not acquainted with baptisia, do seek it out. It is a lovely thing especially for busy gardeners who want continuously attractive borders on a minimum attention schedule. Buy a few plants to start with. Then increase your stock, as you will certainly want to, by sowing your own freshly gathered seed in a cold frame in midsummer. There it will germinate, though probably not until the next spring.

SUMMER VERTICALS

Summer spires are more numerous that those of spring. In June and July the lovely astilbe Peach Blossom reaches its peak of perfection. The distinctive yucca, too long disgraced by unskillful planting, shakes out its bells in June. The chimney bellflowers appear in July when "flaunts the flaring hollyhock" as well.

When the background is a white fence or brick wall, hollyhocks are the inevitable choice. They are most effective, as Gertrude Jekyll has pointed out, if the wall is not too high and the spires shoot up "telling well against the distant tree masses above the wall." They are particularly effective too if the garden slopes down a hill and their varying heights outline the declivity. I saw them thus, both singles and doubles, in all the pink shades with Dorothy Perkins roses strewn over the wire fence behind them and larkspur and ragged robins complementing their hues. A mulberry tree in the background emphasized the cheerful uprightness of the holly-hocks.

Useful Yucca

Yucca has long had the unhappy fate of growing singly and centrally in front yards of unhappy visage. Used with some relation to its surroundings it displays an unusual and individual beauty, its "tall columns like shafts of marble against the hedge trees. In the daytime the yucca's blossoms hang in scentless, greenish white bells, but at night these bells lift up their heads and expand with great stars of light and odor—a glorious plant. Around their spires of luminous bells circle pale night moths lured by the rich fragrance." Yucca can be counted on to emphasize the framework of a design. It is unexpectedly fine too as an individual accent plant in each corner of a small formal garden.

For midsummer, *Cimicifuga racemosa*, snakeroot or bugbane, is a lovely spire suited to a shady place. Each spike is covered with feathery white blossoms. Let the tall fragrant white *Clematis recta*, the lower white veronica Icicle and blue *Clematis integrifolia caerulea* stand near *Cimicifuga racemosa*.

Campanula pyramidalis is one of my favorite steeples for strong summer effect. It is either purple or white with star-shaped blossoms. This chimney bellflower, although often perennial, is not reliably hardy in some sections and is often, like most of the foxgloves, therefore best renewed every year. Purple and white hostas and the tall heat-loving betony contrast pleasantly with this bellflower. Where a border is free standing and lacks shrub or wall background, this bellflower and the taller delphinium interplanted maintain a fairly constant rear guard.

Astilbe, Dictamnus and Veronica

For secondary points in summer, selection can be made from the Japanese astilbes. These are the feathery branching flowers the florist forces at Easter time. Gift plants can be set out permanently in the border. With my passion for fine plant form, I am keen on astilbes of all kinds. In a shaded section of one border, I had a colony of astilbe Peach Blossom, a pale pink variety which earned a special blessing every June. Deliciously fragrant, we all enjoyed it on the table, while a plant which in five years has required absolutely nothing of me beyond yearly fertilizing and a few summer soakings is one to elicit paeons of praise.

Some time when you are weary of the vagaries of columbine or the infections of delphinium, plant a lot of astilbes and enjoy a few seasons of utter peace. Varieties to consider for foreground are the white Deutschland, pink Peach Blossom, garnet Fanal and salmon Granat. Usually the pastel pinks are fairly tepid, a fact I don't mind, however. I now have a big planting of the paler astilbes with Japanese iris in the Fern Garden. I think astilbes are plants that have everything, and I do most strongly recommend them.

The gas plant, *Dictamnus fraxinella*, is another undemanding gem. With an eye to permanence, select for it a sunny location in deep, rich loam. When it thus has its way, it lives and thrives in the same spot for generations. Slow to establish, it eventually grows to thirty inches. From the midst of fine, ash-like foliage appears a rose or white turret of exquisite form and color. This is a foreground spire of undeniable worth to all who wish to garden for the future as well as the present. Here is plant quality of the finest kind. Space dictamnus at five- or eight-foot intervals just behind the edging of a border and let its companions be iris and blue flax. You will then have added a note of real distinction to the planting.

I enjoy, too, the lemon odor of the foliage and the fun of seeing the flowers flash when touched with a lighted match. Because of the volatile oil emitted as a vapor from these, the dictamnus is commonly called gas plant or burning bush. It is grown from seed sown an inch deep in the open as soon as it is ripe. The next spring sprouts show but not until the third year are flowers likely to begin appearing. For an unusual arrangement, dictamnus also have fine possibilities.

Likewise good to cut and of long-season border value are the veronicas or speedwells. These produce find stalwart foreground spires of purple, rose or white for July, August and into September. They are easily propagated by seed or division and a constant joy because of good foliage and easy culture.

It is important, however, to select veronicas with care and under no circumstances to take in gift plants whose habits are not known to you. *Veronica longifolia* is a weedy grower you will be likely to wish you had never met, but *V. l. subsessilis* is one of the best, two feet tall, with continuously good foliage and showy deep purple spikes through midsummer. The eighteen-inch pink Pavane is a worthwhile improved *spicata* for late June through August, and noteworthy for heat- and drought-resistance.

AUTUMN TURRETS

For early fall, I like the well-named gayfeathers. *Liatris sca-riosa* September Glory lifts a fine strong purple cone some five feet tall. White Spire is a beauty too, and a better choice if red, orange or purple abounds in the border, since September Glory clashes with most rich warm shades.

Finally for late autumn there are the shade-loving aconites, marvelous when they thrive, which could be more often. Plant them in that section of the border which passes under a tree. There they will rise like dark blue torches.

These spire flowers are a fascinating group but not all of them, of course, would be right in any one garden. Their value both outdoors and in bouquets lies essentially in the contrasts they afford. Plant them therefore near loose, massive material and in arrangements note how interesting they are when combined with the globes of daisies or the mists of gypsophila. Purple veronica with white shastas, for example, make a charming, clean-cut appearance while blue baptisia contrasts effectively with yellow gaillardia Sun Gold. And in the shrubbery border too, especially when it is in an all-green summer stage, the ivory spires of yucca are a splendid sight.

24. Grace Notes for
the Garden

Variety is the spice of gardens too. When borders are exclusively planted with masses of lance-leaved iris, grassy daylilies and globular phlox, they inevitably lack grace. It takes the lilting sprays of columbine, flax and coralbell, or the gossamer clouds of gypsophila and sea lavender skillfully interplanted with these heavier subjects to produce that air of delicacy and charm which makes a garden an enchanted spot.

Yet who would seek a reason beyond their own attractiveness to plant columbines? Captivating in their own right, those poised butterfly blossoms are a delight for garden or vase. In May and June they flower just on the heels of the early tulips and since their heights—according to the species or variety—vary from low to medium, their place is in the foreground of the border just behind the edging plants.

If you are are not acquainted with the columbine (aquilegia), you can obtain a good survey picture by purchasing in fall or very early spring a plant each of such species as *Aquilegia chrysantha*, a thirty-inch yellow which is likely to go on flowering up to July; *A. caerulea*, the twenty-inch pale blue Rocky Mountain columbine; and the ten-inch white fan columbine, *A. flabellata nana alba*, with the best foliage of

them all. Then obtain three plants of the eighteen-inch
McKana Hybrids and at least one of that choice variety, Crimson Star. Personally I would not lack a single one of these.
You will find, however, that they are usually not very long-
lived perennials though some may last into the third year. If
this happens, you can increase your stock by dividing the
crowns in September.

Crop of Columbines

It is more likely, however, that you must keep your crop
of columbines in hand by sowing seeds about every other
June. The seeds will germinate slowly so keep the bed
watered until actual green appears and don't stop a week
short of success because you think your crop has failed. Allow
the separated seedlings then to remain in the cold frame until
spring, transplanting them as early as weather permits to their
flowering positions in the border.

A packet of Wayside Giant Pinks or Giant Blues produces
something pretty special, I assure you. For effective border
contrast, try a colony of these in front of a blue iris like Blue
Rhythm with the pale yellow meadowrue, *Thalictrum
glaucum*, behind the iris. Use columbine freely between the
Darwin tulip stretches and if your garden is tiny and every
plant there must count for succession, precede the columbines with a dozen early tulips, among which you can scatter
annual larkspur seed in September. Follow the columbines,
then, with your favorite perennial phlox and a few chrysanthemum plants. Never a dull week will be the result of even
such a limited procedure.

Species columbine seem to prefer a rather heavy, clay soil
but for your hybrids you must prepare a sandy, humusy home.

Both thrive either in full sun or light shade but are not drought resistant and so need extra summer watering. In the Apple Garden I enjoy bleedinghearts with the fan and *chrysantha* columbines which have been reliably perennial there. I hope your plants will be spared leaf miner attack. Mine recovered from the labyrinthian tunnelings of these pests when I was constant about cutting off attacked foliage and dusted plants several times with rotenone. If you are using an insecticidal soap elsewhere for aphids, this will discourage the leaf miner too.

Linum and Heuchera

The feathery, true-blue linum or flax, also blooming in May or June, is another means of grace. Although there are also white and yellow varieties, they do not compare with the enchantment of the blue *Linum perenne*. Charming with white or yellow tulips, with iris and with white phlox Miss Lingard, this fifteen-inch plant is most pleasing for a foreground planting.

Select a sunny spot and supply a well-enriched sandy soil or you will find, as I once did, that its sojourn with you is much too brief. Its azure shower of fine petals is as pretty on the plant as on the ground which it literally "blued" around it every June morning in one of my gardens. By removing at the earth line the shoots which have flowered you can induce thicker growth and longer flowering. I couldn't say of *Linum perenne* that it is as indispensable as is peony or iris, only that you'll love it and treasure it for color and pleasant individuality.

The coralbells, or heucheras, enter the picture a few weeks later than linum, though for a time their pink and blue blooms can be delightfully concurrent. The heucheras produce twelve- to fifteen-inch airy racemes of rosy or white blooms from late May to July with some sporadic flowering even into autumn. The coral-red variety Pluie de Feu and the pink Rosamundi are choice. Indeed, I know no prettier small plant. The crowns of finely edged heart-shaped leaves with reddish tints never fail in beauty from spring till fall so that you can use heucheras prominently, even as edging, knowing they will always look well. Their delicate panicles are a particularly attractive contrast to intermediate iris or late tulips, and for bouquets are an adorable filler.

I once had a long line of Pluie de Feu beside a flagstone walk. Divisions every third year from the original six purchased plants produced these undeniable treasures but you can readily get a stand from seeds as well. I am told heucheras want sun but they have done well for me in light shade too. The soil, however, must be rich and, of course, well drained. A spring top dressing of well-decayed or dried manure seems to delight them and increase their flowering.

Gypsophila and Limonium

For tall early summer and lower late effect there is the gossamer babysbreath. Only a few plants of this are needed since in time each one covers almost a three-foot area. In each of my thirty-foot units beside the blue delphiniums I had two specimens of the double, choice white variety, *Gypsophila* Bristol Fairy. This is a lovely sight in June. It reaches three feet or more then but continues into fall to bloom on new growth which never attains more than eighteen inches. Consider this change in height when you plant *G*. Bristol Fairy.

If you have room for but one variety, let this be it but try to deal in small sizes since gypsophilas form strong, thick tap roots which prefer not to be transplanted. In fact, I always try to obtain potted plants of gypsophila because they move better. Full sun and usually some extra lime in the soil are advisable with removal of faded shoots so new clouds of growth will develop. This cutting of shoots, however, usually occurs before fading since I never have enough babysbreath for bouquets.

Gypsophila repens Rosy Veil is also lovely, flowering two weeks ahead of Bristol Fairy and for just as long but not growing so tall, only to two feet. For the small garden Rosy Veil, a form of *G. repens*, is good because in every way it is a more limited plant. You can increase your stock of either of these gypsophilas from tip or root cuttings but not from seeds with Rosy Veil since the hybrid does not come true. A pleasing white for the smaller plot is *G. repens bodgiri*.

Not until late July or early August does my last grace note open in the border. This is the great sea lavender, *Limonium latifolium*, which is erroneously but quite commonly known as *Statice latifolia*. It produces from a shining crown of stalwart basal leaves a fine twenty-four-inch lavender cloud of branched panicles which seem never to fade. Even after five weeks or so the flowers will be fresh and full of color.

The sea lavender, not to be confused, of course, with the fragrant true lavender *(Lavandula)* always poses a problem. Shall I cut it for a bouquet where in water it will stay fresh for some two weeks, or leave it for longer loveliness in the garden? Usually the garden wins out, since what happens outdoors in summer is always more important to me than any bouquet effects inside. (Both statice and the gypsophila variety *paniculata* can also be dried for winter bouquets though I am not very intrigued by such uses for these two.)

Limonium (Statice) latifolium, given sun and a sandy soil, seems to be completely happy. It never needs extra water or spraying or anything else beyond average, routine care and it looks so pretty next to my yellow snapdragons. A nice child, well behaved and unexacting, I think, as I note its contented condition in the border.

25. Quality Edgings Make the Border

"A garden is only as fine as its edges" is one of those pleasant, homely adages which the experienced gardener likes to trot out for the benefit of the novice. Actually no piece of gardening advice I can give is sounder than this adage which urges the careful selection of first-rate edging plants. For it is certainly true that the general good looks of a planting depend tremendously on the way the front lines of beds and borders are terminated. Indeed, during out-of-bloom periods a well-chosen edging will do as much for your garden as a new satin binding on a shabby blanket or a piece of fresh, even fringe sewn along the ends of a worn carpet.

Too often edging plants are afterthoughts whereas they should be important primary considerations. In fact, when I am making a new garden with definite budgeting in mind, I always allocate at the outset what might seem a disproportionate amount to the purchase of high-quality edging plants and save by filling in behind them with annuals. This produces a finished appearance even during the first season.

And the possibilities for the purpose are practically endless even though many of the so-called edging plants are not included on my own preferred list. For I feel strongly on the subject of omissions and do not consider worthy any plants which are not, first, either evergreen or of good foliage tendency from spring through fall and, second, of attractive and fairly prolonged blooming habit. In the back of my mind there is always a third criterion which I think of as style.

EVERGREEN "BINDINGS"

For the formal garden, distinguished by straight lines or by definite curves and circles and by a certain balanced plan of planting, the evergreen edging plant of permanently neat and distinguished appearance is ideal. Think of varieties for this purpose as "binding" rather than "fringe" plants. They should appear as smooth and straight along the fronts of the beds as lengths of strong green ribbon firmly stretched there.

First choice obviously falls on the slow-growing English boxwood, *Buxus sempervirens suffruticosa.* This box forms the great object lesson of the Williamsburg gardens which during certain off-season periods have little to commend them but their important edges. These alone make them lovely. Despite its beauty this box, however, has certain drawbacks. If where you live, for example, an unsightly burlap screen over the planting in winter is going to be essential to its life, omit box by all means. It is expensive too. Where temperatures are not too low, however, and this is the wanted plant, you can develop young specimens from cuttings which, if first dipped in one of the root-encouraging hormone substances, will in six weeks develop a root system the size of an egg. Then the young plants are set out, and tended for a year in what is termed a "nursery row," that is, a place in the cutting or vegetable garden where care can be easy and constant.

However, because of its capriciousness many of you will not care to be bothered with boxwood. For you there are

various beautiful substitutes, some but recently developed
and charming enough to rival the older favorite. *Pachistima
canbyi*, for example, is a choice dwarf evergreen shrub which
does not grow above eight inches tall or eighteen wide. It
may be trimmed as a binding plant or left natural as a graceful,
feathery fringe. Tolerant of twenty degrees below zero with
no tendency to burn or discolor and of equal beauty in sun
or light shade, it is first rate wherever an evergreen edging
is desired.

Another possibility, if not too tall for the bed to be edged,
is the blue-leaved willow, *Salix purpurea nana*, hailing from
the Arctic Circle. It can bear those wet or heavy soils which
spell demise to most plants and may likewise be enjoyed in
a formal or natural state. It is quite possible by judicious
pruning to keep the height to twelve inches and the width
will be about the same.

The old-fashioned germander, *Teucrium chamaedrys*, a pic-
turesque, aromatic plant reminiscent of knot-garden days,
grows twelve to fifteen inches high. Its glossy green foliage
is often mistaken for that of boxwood but the plant is far
hardier. This is a delightful substitute.

Ivies and Periwinkle

Then there is English ivy, *Hedera helix*, a gem of a plant
for locations out of full sun. Where the perennial border or
the shrubbery line is somewhat shaded, this shining-leaved
vine makes a charming binding. It must, of course, be sternly
trimmed to check its gadding proclivities. And English ivy
has, of course, the great advantage of being very easily and
quickly developed from cuttings. The Baltic type has smaller
leaves and withstands lower temperatures and a greater degree of sunshine, but it is a coarse undistinguished plant,

super-hardiness being its only real value. Other attractive small-leaved ivies include shamrock, Green Feather, pin oak and sweetheart.

Then there is the blue- or, more rarely, white-flowered hardy periwinkle or myrtle, *Vinca minor.* This is a gem for sun or shade. It will bloom unless the shade is dense, and it will grow well even in quite heavy shade. Runners are shorter than those of English ivy and you don't have to clip very often to keep an edging of periwinkle in shape, once or maybe twice a season at most. More fringe than binder, I think, this is a plant to which I am really devoted and I use it in various ways. As an edging, it grows along a flagstone walk bordering the northwest foundation of mountain laurel and ferns—an extension of the doorstep garden. Here periwinkle has proved to be a lot less trouble than grass and a pretty planting in its own right, too.

As a ground cover, periwinkle is also marvelous. If you have a tree under which grass simply won't grow, mark out the irregular shadow it casts, work up the soil, improve it as best you can, and fill in the area with periwinkle. Such a planting under a maple tree, with narcissus clumps set among the green vines, has turned a constant irritation into an attractive garden spot for me. To keep the narcissus blooming in this set-up I find it needs a heavy spring feeding, but *V. minor* is undemanding. There are other places at Stony Brook adorned with this excellent evergreen plant, sometimes with ferns, sometimes alone on a bad slope. (You know, of course, that this periwinkle is different from the one used in window boxes. That variegated green-and-white vine is the tender *V. major.*)

But to return to edging plants, there is then really a wide choice of evergreen types. English boxwood, pachistima, the

Arctic willow, germander, English ivies and periwinkle in
their natural or sheared state, comprise a most distinguished
selection of edging material for formal or, in some cases,
informal plantings. It will depend on how energetic you are
about clipping.

"FRINGE" PLANTS

For the informal border of the garden laid out in balanced
beds informally planted, a number of good-foliaged, flowering subjects immediately suggest themselves. Foremost
among these is the hardy evergreen candytuft, *Iberis sempervirens*. It has for years, during which I have tried many other
kinds of plants, remained my favorite and this despite the
fact that July weather occasionally brings on attacks of red
spider if the plants are not dusted (or sprayed if you prefer)
once or twice that month with a natural miticide insecticidal
soap. I cling to the old-fashioned type, *Iberis sempervirens*.
Something of a sprawler, it produced a most soft and lovely
fringe for my four oblong flower beds in Philadelphia which
were in full view at all times from porch and study, and now
I love it as the edging of my Look-Into Garden where it
blooms with pink hyacinths and early yellow daylilies.

During the growing season this sturdy sub-shrub has no
shabby moments, while its six weeks of snowy spring bloom
appears, with the yellow and cream narcissus, as the first sweet
enchantment of the gardening year. Directly the flowers fade,
I sternly shear the plants to keep in line the fresh new growth
as it develops. Little Gem and Purity are more compact iberis
varieties while Snowflake bears larger individual blooms. I
like any of these compact growers for rather narrow borders.

A number of other flowering plants measure up to my

standard of fine foliage and prolonged bloom. Unless the border is over thirty feet long, however, I feel that a stronger effect is achieved by planting but one or maybe two types or blending colors of one kind. For example, attractive and so easy to get abundantly from seed is a mixed edging of the old-fashioned, May-blooming, spicily fragrant clove pink, *Dianthus plumarius.*

For lengthier borders I prefer a rhythm of the plumarius garden pinks in a repeated series of such low-growing, fine-foliaged varieties as the fringed pink Essex Witch, crimson Little Joe and the double white Her Majesty, all notably fragrant. The series looks best if composed of uneven numbers, that is, three or five different varieties, of five or more plants of each variety to a stretch, and the series repeated at least three times. Only for an over thirty-foot bed, however, is this likely to look well. And with such long lines to fill in, the gardener who is fond of variety may quite rightly select a repeated series of different kinds of plants, such as the double white rockcress, *Arabis alpina florepleno*, the pale yellow perennial alyssum, *Alyssum saxatile citrinum*, not *compactum*, and the lilac rainbow rockcress, *Aubretia eyri.*

E Pluribus Unum

My own preference except for very extensive plantings is for a one-color, one-variety line-up. For those who, like me, find such a planting restful and not mechanical I suggest, next in quality to the hardy candytuft, the almost evergreen coralbells, *Heuchera.* Its shapely geranium leaves and slender clouds of pink or white bloom have long been a delight in my garden where foliage is top quality throughout the season and plants show considerable shade tolerance. (Groups of this heuchera alternated with arabis now make a nice informal edging for my Apple-Tree Garden, with an April and a June succession of bloom.)

Attractive for a long edging by itself is *Nepeta mussini*, or catmint. It makes a lovely billowy border, aromatically fragrant, its gray-green silvery foliage and spikes of lavender flowers a long delight. Each plant may spread to eighteen inches and in bloom be twelve to fifteen inches high. You can count on six to eight weeks of early summer flowers and then, if you cut them off, intermittent bloom until frost. If you have visited English gardens, you know how this plant is treasured there but it is a quality edging for us too. Nepeta thrives in hot, dry, sunny places where the soil is sandy or only medium good. It doesn't take well to continued dampness. Along a flagstone walk, it is particularly effective.

For shade, however, nothing is prettier than clear yellow primroses of the true English type, *Primula vulgaris*. One small suburban garden I know is thus completely edged, along evergreen and shrub borders as well as flower beds. Behind the primroses are clumps of narcissus in many cream and white varieties. When other gardens are just waking up in April, this one appears in full glory. And through division a few English primrose plants soon go a long way. I like, too, to strengthen the picture with the lavender-blue Jacob's ladder, *Polemonium reptans*, placed in bold clusters among the narcissus. In fact, this polemonium with its fine ferny foliage can well qualify for an informal edging.

Not in Favor

Certain other low-growing plants often suggested for edging I cannot for various reasons recommend. These include the Persian stonecress and Geneva bugle, the forget-me-not anchusa, *Anchusa myosotidiflora*—which I think belongs behind the edging strip or else as a strong interruption to it— the fringed bleedingheart, *Dicentra eximia*, the wild blue phlox, *Phlox divaricata*, *Iris cristata*, which does not line up well, and the violas, except perhaps Jersey Gem. If future viola varieties prove sufficiently heat-resistant, however, I am all for placing these long-flowering plants on the preferred list.

And don't overlook strawberries. These make an edging which is unusual, dependable and enchanting. Those tiny kinds of the *fraise du bois* type we used to eat in France, with heaps of thick, almost sour cream are finds of the first order. One summer I saw a whole garden edged with them, variety Baron Solemacher, and the owner reported constant flower and fruits from May on to frost. (The variety Charles V is also pretty for this purpose.)

In selecting anything so important as edging plants, how-ever, it is not wise to depend entirely on anyone's advice. Decide for yourself whether you prefer a "binding" or a "fringe" and consider which seems most suitable for your own garden planting. Then, whether you plan to proceed via seed, cutting, or plant, try to see for yourself just what your preferred plants look like in the nurseryman's row. After all there's no better criterion for such an important selection than your very own eyesight.

SOME EXCELLENT EDGING PLANTS

Name	Deciduous or Evergreen	Height-Width in Inches	Flowers	Season	Remarks
Arctic Willow (*Salix purpurea nana*)	E	12 by 12			Sun; must be clipped to keep low; endures wet, heavy soil
Boxwood (*Buxus sempervirens suffruticosa*)	E	Indefinite			Not reliably hardy in North; needs clipping; sun or light shade
Candytuft (*Iberis sempervirens*)	E	12 by 15	White	Spring	Sun or light shade; 6 weeks trim after flowering
Coralbells (*Heuchera sanguinea*)	Almost E	12 by 15	Pink	Early summer	Sun or light shade
English and other Ivies (*Hedera helix*)	E	6			Light shade; clip runners
Germander (*Teucrium chamaedrys*)	E	12 by 12			Sun; clipped to resemble box; very hardy

Plant		Size	Color	Season	Conditions
Jacob's Ladder (*Polemonium reptans*)	D	12 by 12	Lavender	Spring	Sun or light shade; open, ferny
Nepeta (*N. mussini*)	D	12 by 18	Lavender	Spring	Sun; trim back after bloom
Pachistima (*P. canbyi*)	E	8 by 18			Sun or light shade; very hardy; naturally dwarf
Periwinkle (*Vinca minor*)	E	12 by 18	Blue or white	Spring	Sun or shade (light or heavy) occasional clipping
Pinks: Clove (*D. plumarius*)	E	6 by 18	Red, pink, white	Spring and intermittent	Sun; lime-loving; fragrant
Primroses, English (*Primula vulgaris*)	D	8 by 12	Yellow	Spring	Light shade; disappears briefly in July
Strawberry (*Fraise du Bois* type)	E	8 by 12	White	Spring and intermittent	Sun; summer fruits

26. Biennially Yours

Biennials are the puzzlers in our gardens. Sometimes they seem to behave more like annuals because many of them produce an early, if sparse, fall crop of flowers from prompt spring sowings. Often they tend to be perennial, living on from year to year or else appearing to, because they propagate themselves by self-sowing. Indeed, when we want a lot of hollyhocks, foxgloves, Chinese pinks or canterbury bells, the definition of a biennial as a plant which "sown one year, flowers and dies the next" is only moderately helpful. It is individual behavior we must know about and with these particular plants, this varies with the location of our gardens.

My approach, therefore, for a long time has been to treat as biennial those plants which *give the best results* when they are sown one year and harvested the next. The point is, I am afraid, that I like everything on my place to be "in the pink." I have no time to coddle the weary or make strong the faint. So when in my garden the foxglove, so important for early June height, rings out its last sweet steeled bell or the pansy edgings get that exhausted look, I whisk them out with complete finality and fill the precious space again with autumn chrysanthemums or midget marigolds. Meanwhile the double white hollyhocks for me carry on as perennials, producing their charming crêpe paper rosettes year after year in the original lovely form. So they remain undisturbed.

Generally speaking, biennials are more trouble than either annuals or perennials. They take two years of handling to produce what annuals do the same season and their seasonal flower display is then only about as long as that of the average perennial. These are their disadvantages. (And they can be most easily overcome by buying your biennials as well-started plants.)

In their favor we must admit that biennials include unusually lovely plants which seem to flower just when we need them most. Foxgloves, for example, bring early height in June while the delphiniums are only making up their minds. Sweet william is colorful when the rest of the garden is recovering from its first spring spurt and has not yet gathered strength for summer. Nothing surpasses the canterbury bells for June drama, while the alpine forget-me-not produces a blue cloud which the perennial type never equals.

CULTURE OF BIENNIALS

Where winters are not particularly severe, biennial culture can be simplified to summer sowing in an open seed bed, early autumn transplanting to a reserve bed, and spring setting-out in the border. Where winter temperatures drop to twenty degrees Fahrenheit or lower, a cold frame is required to insure safe dealings with biennials.

I like to concentrate on one or at most two varieties of biennials each year. Then I grow a thumping big crop of the chosen kind. This results in a strong seasonal effect in the garden and reduces sowing and transplanting to a two-day scheme—the days separated by a number of weeks, of course.

I make my plantings as late in the season as the type of biennial allows. This permits sowing when the spring rush of work is past and also reduces care by a couple of months. When possible, I sow after a rain on a cool summer day rather than during a stretch of torrid summer heat which is not conducive to good germination.

Once the seedlings attain their second crop of leaves, which are noticeably different from the first, they are set out at about three-inch intervals in rows in the vegetable garden or else replanted in the cold frame where they were first sown. The soil is now enriched for them with a little balanced plant food and made somewhat heavier too by the addition of more garden loam. This transplanting which occurs before mid-September has a strengthening effect on root systems. In winter if the plants are not to be in a cold frame, they are protected with a covering of crisp oak leaves which do not mat or with an inch or so of finely pulverized peat moss. Varieties with green tops having the covering pulled around them and *under* their crowns, not above them. If left in the cold frame they are lightly covered in November but the glass (or plastic) cover is not fastened down until after the first hard freeze. After the New Year the cover is raised during warm sunny afternoons for fifteen minutes or so at a stretch.

These are the biennials which I have found worth while: Chinese pinks, canterbury bells, forget-me-nots, foxgloves, hollyhocks, honesty, Iceland poppies, Siberian wallflowers, sweet williams and violas. For English daisies and pansies raised at home I have only a maybe-so feeling.

Chinese Pinks and Canterbury Bells

The Chinese pinks, *Dianthus chinensis* or *heddewigi*, may be sown the third week in June. Then they flower lightly by September with a much stronger display prepared for next summer. Once they are established in your garden you can count on them to flower from early spring until late fall. They are fine for bouquets (though, alas, scentless), merrily colored and excellent for bedding. Best sown where they are to grow, they are thinned out in April. Indispensable for the cutting garden, they are not to be confused with such truly perennial pinks as *D. plumarius*.

Probably the handsomest of all biennials are the canterbury bells, both the single *Campanula medium* and *C. calycantha*, the double or cup-and-saucer variety. Both came in particularly good purple shades, also in rose and white. My vote goes to the calycanthas in "dark blue" and lots of them. These are biennials to be sown before the end of July, moved before crowding to a reserve bed or slatted cold frame with afternoon shade and finally transplanted the next spring after growth has started but before buds are set, to the borders. Almost three feet high, they flower in late May and June. Some supplementary summer bloom is later produced from basal shoots but I am not inclined to keep the campanulas after the peak of their effect is past, preferring to use their space for summer-flowering nicotiana or miniature dahlias. If the handsome chimney bellflower, *C. pyramidalis*, does not stay with you, it too must be given this biennial treatment.

Forget-me-nots

Forget-me-nots are one of the choicest of the smaller flowering biennials. *Myosotis* Alpestris Blue is a sky-blue gem to

be introduced into the garden at your earliest possible convenience. Let it go to seed there each year and from April
into June you will have something special in the way of a
true-blue foil for tulip and daffodil. Plan for late July or early
August sowing. It will be worth while to prevent any tendency
to damping off by sterilizing the seed bed first. These forget-
me-nots, sown in place, readily winter in the open even where
it is very cold. You will bless the day you established this
delicate blue charmer in your garden.

Foxgloves and Hollyhocks

The most important biennials are probably the foxgloves
because they give height to the garden composition early in
the season. The Giant Shirley Hybrids of digitalis produce
in June stately three- to four-foot steeples of crimson-spotted
white to rose blooms. *Digitalis ambigua*, a thirty-inch yellow
species with brown markings, is attractive for the woodland
garden. These two *usually* behave like perennials. There are
also pure white and rose varieties as well as one called Yellow
Queen. These and the mixture of Shirley Pastel Shades are
best considered biennial. The fine seed is sown thinly before
the end of July and the young plants set out six weeks later,
ten inches apart, in row or frame. Foxgloves requires a lot
of water through the summer to avoid any possible check to
growth. They are wintered in the same manner as canterbury
bells and moved in spring with a good ball of earth. Foxgloves
do best with shade for part of the day.

The althaeas or hollyhocks are almost too rampant for the
border since they require nearly three feet for each plant but
they are perfect in a generous corner by themselves, or in
bold groups associated with shrubs. Single mixed kinds are
no trouble whatever. They grow five to seven feet high,

flower from mid-July to mid-August and, if there is good
drainage, either survive or resow very freely. If you want
choice doubles, see first if the roots prove winter hardy for
you. If not, then treat them strictly as biennials. I found that,
in the doubles, one color at a time, preferably salmon pink
or white, it was an effective plan. If several colors are grown
and self-growing permitted, the bees arrange an interesting
cross-fertilization program for you. Hollyhocks, one of the
most robust of the biennials, need not be sown until early
August.

Some Lesser Lights

The shining silver seed pods of honesty, or *Lunaria*, are
far more important than this biennial's violet and white spring
flowers. So consider lunaria for cutting in the fall when you
can do lovely arrangement things with it in pewter. Not an
important biennial, it is a nice extra for sowing in August.

Seldom listed as biennial, the Iceland poppy, *Papaver nudicaule*, gives best results for me when so treated. It is a small
darling bearing crinkle-petaled cups on twelve-inch stems all
through spring and early summer and sporadically thereafter
if seed pods are removed. These poppies look well in the
border behind the hardy candytuft and between the narcissus
colonies.

The bright orange of the Siberian wallflower, *Cheiranthus
allioni*, has a sparkling April effect on a spring border which
features *leedsi* narcissus and the subtle blues of Virginia blue-
bells, violets and *Phlox divaricata*. The plants grow twelve to
eighteen inches tall and because of a fibrous root system are
able to withstand transplanting easily. I like to sow them early
in July and transplant in September to a reserve garden row.
Then in early spring I move them to the border after the

bulbs and perennials are in evidence there. September placement is not very practical because what looks like a vacancy
then may be actually a dormant mertensia plant. The Siberian
wallflower winters healthily in the open.

The old-fashioned spotty sweet william, *Dianthus barbatus*,
is easy enough to keep in abundance either because the roots
remain or there is self-seeding. And this has pleasing flowers
too for a cutting row. For borders, where color schemes
matter a lot to me, I prefer separate sowings of Newport
Pink, Giant White or Scarlet Beauty. Sometimes plants of
these too last more than one season, more often they "revert"
or rather a seedling crop develops from the seeds of a faded
flower I didn't cut in time. As far as behavior goes, it seems
that the best sweet william turns out to be biennial rather
than perennial. And it is one of the very easiest. A grand
crop can be readily obtained from a late June sowing in an
open seed bed in almost any location.

Violas, English Daisies and Pansies

Happy the gardeners (and rare) who can depend on *Viola
cornuta* for perennial effect. It has a crop which flowers freely
the second year from April sowing but heat prostration is
likely to get the plants down the next summer. Violas, except
perhaps a very few like Jersey Gem or Catherine Sharp,
therefore prove more satisfactory when grown biennially for
April, May and June effect. If you live where summers are
very hot, permit them to make a quick and dignified exit and
don't waste time on summer mulching, clipping and feeding
and soaking. Results are not worth the effort. For spring and
early summer, however, violas are delightful for edging, while
small petunias, perhaps, are being perfected elsewhere.

Violas are supposed to do best in light not heavy shade,

but I have them also in the sun, and I find they bloom better
and longer if I thrust some twiggy supports among them to
keep them off the ground. Like pansies, violas need a lot of
picking to prevent seed formation. A favorite variety of mine,
Chantreyland, is a charming pure apricot to plant with anything clear yellow like the Dutch iris Gold Harvest. I have
these two in the Kitchen Window Garden and the violas don't
really lose their looks until well into August. (The pale yellow
Viola Vixen or Better Times is a better choice if there are
also pink flowers in spring like *Daphne cneorum*.) Awkwright
Ruby, Avalanche and Blue Perfection are other viola varieties
which have given me much pleasure, and I usually buy well-
started or in-bloom plants of one or two varieties every year.

As for English daisies, *Bellis perennis*, to be sown in early
August, they do make a charming edge if enough plants of
a variety like Snowball can be raised to outline the whole
garden. Cold frame quarters and careful attention to ventilation in early spring are, however, essential to bring them
into full flower early enough in April for them to perform
well before hot weather. For me this is a much too arduous
crop to attempt when anything as attractive and final as hardy
candytuft is mine for the one raising.

I feel the same about pansies of which I prefer to buy some
flowering plants each spring. They are not worth growing
tediously from seed unless there are enough cold frames in
which to winter them. This is not because they are not cold-
weather tolerant—actually it's our roaring summers which
prevent their permanence, not the winter's cold. But to get
the most out of pansies, they must be forced to finest flower
by early April. Grown in the open, this does not seem possible. If you go in for them, sow them in August. Big blooms
are dependent on variety rather than on special culture, so

consider Coronation Gold, Lake of Thun or Snow White. Even one frame of these provides distinguished spring accompaniment. Mixtures and small-flowering kinds have charm—all pansies do—but they are not very telling for an important edging position though always nice to cut.

Here then are a dozen possible biennials for you to consider. Do pick at least one for planting this summer. The next time something you like is marked biennial in the catalogue, don't be mystified. It's really either a long-lived annual or short-term perennial and you now know how to manage either.

27. Grown to Be Gathered

The cutting section is by rights an extremely personal, if not a prejudiced aspect of the garden. It is not meant to display. Therefore eye-searing mixtures and one-of-each plantings are conveniently in order there. A cutting garden is meant to supply its individual owner with exactly the right flowers all through the growing season for house arrangements, as well as for bouquets. I must include these since simple bunches of flowers are also a highly respectable part of interior decorating and a most comforting inclusion for those who still feel uncertain about their technique of arrangement. When, however, arrangements are taken seriously by those who frankly state, "I only plant to pick," then generous space is allotted for cutting at the expense of "display" plantings.

In your plot, plant only according to your needs. Have in mind the color schemes of the rooms your bouquets will adorn and the months when an abundance will not be wasted. If, for instance, you spend August in the mountains, let the lull in the cutting garden come in that period.

Some for Fragrance

Choose some flowers just for fragrance (see the plan on page 238). A jardiniere of the pure pink peony Therese, for

FRAGRANCE for CUTTING

instance, will be a delight if placed on a deep window sill at the landing where it will perfume the halls, upstairs and down. And keep in mind variety of form. Since globular forms predominate among perennial flowers, you should plant some spikey perennials such as aconite, lupine, thermopsis and delphinium, though the last is a "faller." And have clouds of babysbreath, sea lavender, coralbells and the gray-leaved artemisia Silver King, for blending. If in your house you have space for great telling massive bouquets, freely grow the coarse sunflowers and asters but if your rooms are small, select for cutting in-scale material, the delicately wrought bleeding-hearts, the refined oriental iris and the graceful anemones.

My Philadelphia cutting garden was most satisfactory to me when I had a conglomeration. For instance, one year I grew plants of single crimson hollyhocks for the great blue stone jar I placed on the piano in hot weather when the summer living room needed warm accents to relieve its cool muted grays and greens. There was a half row of geum Red Wings and two plants of helenium Chippersfield Orange for the same purpose. I had a whole row of assorted "fillers" and gray-leaved material and a half row of the rampant feverfew, *Chrysanthemum parthenium* (*Matricaria*). I didn't allow this species to run loose in my tidy borders but I prized it highly (as I still do) for white urn arrangements in early July. Then it is companion to yellow daylily and blue hydrangea. With a passion for white I had a whole sparkling area reserved for shastas in four varieties, a generous space for delphinium Galahad and, in the shade, a great satisfying spread of the white August lily, *Hosta plantaginea*. This arranged in a clear green glass bowl surrounded by a frill of its own waxen heart-shaped leaves appeared as cool as a lily pond in the yellow dining room. Finally I had a least fifty chrysanthemum plants, more than any well-balanced gardener would select for such a modest place, but chrysanthemums happened to be my hobby then so the cutting garden, being mine, was plotted to my individual taste.

In laying out yours, consider a most favorable location none too good, since you are expecting a heavy year-round perennial crop from this one plot. Select a southeastern location if possible, with a spot of light shade for the spring crop. Don't be afraid of size since a garden laid out in rows easily permits every necessary process of gardening—cultivating, watering, feeding and spraying—to be an easy, straightforward, up-one-row-and-down-the-next-business.

Neat Boundaries

For the sake of the over-all view, however, place some neat regular boundaries. A picket fence is pleasing if it suits the architecture of your house, or the plot may be outlined with shrubs or evergreens which also yield material for cutting. If the area is quite small, it will be unwise to surround it with tall strong material which tends to cut off air and light. I had a peony boundary on one side because it was attractive all season and gave me the kind of lavish display of peonies I wanted for a house with deep window sills where large bouquets are always in order. Boxwood then on the other three sides looked well because it fitted the cutting oblong into the general scheme of the place. Otherwise it might have appeared that I had dropped this great block of color down on one corner of the lawn just for the fun of it. A cutting garden, despite its highly useful and specialized character, needs thus to be related by proper boundaries to whatever else exists on the property.

If you have shade, plant there material for spring cutting. Plan for many small at-the-elbow bouquets of basket-of-gold, rockcress, English primrose and candytuft, and for the table, grow bleedinghearts, columbines and doronicum to go with your tulips. A clump of soft yellow Lady Bountiful hemerocallis, and a row of white Snow Flurry, Blue Sapphire, Pink Sensation and golden apricot Melody Lane iris will, when set in the sun, richly supply the hall. And, of course, at this time there can never be too many lilies-of-the-valley and sweet violets. These indispensables, however, can usually be placed elsewhere on a property. They are not row by row growers.

Seasonal Display

For late spring and early summers, select peonies, one of each color you like in early, midseason and late varieties. Six plants will yield richly. Be sure to pick the pale ones in bud so they will hold their delicate coloring indoors. Think, too, for this season of fragrant astilbe, sweet rocket and garden heliotrope, as well as pinks and the larger-sized "carnations." Veronica, gas plant, Chinese delphinium and baptisia are fine spikes and, of course, there must be oriental iris. Nepeta is feathery and soft for variety while many of the daisies like the shastas, coreopsis, pyrethrum and gaillardia Sun Gold conveniently continue to frost.

These in midsummer are supplemented by scabiosa, stokesia, helenium, coneflower and sunflower. Physostegia and hollyhocks are good short and tall spires while the various hostas provide foliage as well as flowers. Phlox you can have if you will, but, like delphinium, it requires constant cleaning up.

For autumn, hardy ageratum is a good filler. So are hardy asters with aconites for accents. For final grandeur, there are anemones and chrysanthemums in as many forms and colors as your space permits. Nor are they really final, if you have Christmas and Lenten roses in a sheltered place outdoors to carry you through to spring, or *Iris stylosa* in one cold frame for December and January and sweet violets in another for March.

In recent years I have had a flowering meadow instead of a well-laid-out cut-flower garden. The meadow is always lovely to look at and a wonderful source of wild flowers for bouquets from spring hawkweed through white fleabane, daisies, Queen Anne's lace, yarrow, black-eyed susans, blue chicory and pink clover to purple thistles, goldenrod, and fall asters. Upkeep is reduced to a late September mowing after seeds are all self sown. My flowering meadow supplements what can be spared from the perennial plantings and the wild garden, and it *is* fun to lean over the post-and-rail fence and, without even going into the meadow, to reach in and help myself to the rich untended abundance there. I found five kinds at arm's length one July day, all charming for a brown jug in my yellow kitchen. And after a full week, Queen Anne's lace, yarrow and the susans were still fresh and pretty on the breakfast table.

TO MAKE CUT FLOWERS LAST

The most lasting bouquets you will discover are composed of hellebores—three weeks one January for mine—chrysanthemum, hardy aster, columbine, scabiosa, shasta daisy, pyrethrum, stokesia and doronicum. All bouquets, however, last longer if you avoid drafty places and a hot, dry atmosphere. Certainly nearness to a radiator or register usually means a quick demise. Of course, wash the containers between uses with hot water and soap to remove any lingering bacteria.

Time of gathering is no longer considered important. However, for my own pleasure and comfort, I always gather early morning or early evening, and then steep flowers and foliage for at least two hours or overnight in hot (bath temperature, about 110 degrees F.) not cold water, as we used to. Hot water moves faster through the stems than cold and probably also clears any blocking bubbles.

Before arranging, take off a small piece of stem to insure a fresh cut, and make this on a slant so as to open up a maximum area for absorption. (And if you rearrange, make a fresh cut each time.) With tree and shrubs, crush stem-ends with a hammer and cut off some of the foliage. This is particularly helpful with lilac and mockorange.

For the steeping, place your pail of flowers in a cool basement or other low-temperature place where flowers and water will cool naturally. As an extra precaution, wrap heads loosely in paper. This reduces air movement and subsequent water loss.

In the final arrangement or bouquet, be sure to remove any foliage which would rest below the water line. If left on, it soon fouls the water and shortens life. And do use one of the commercial cut-flower foods that contain sugars and acidifiers to arrest the maturing life cycle of flowers and so retard their wilting. Two trade-named products you can buy are Bloomlife and Floralife. They were developed as the result of Professor Alex Laurie's investigations at Ohio State University. Today the florist usually supplies a packet with each order.

When flowers aren't on display keep them cold at 30 to 35 degrees. A friend of mine, who has the good fortune to have a supplementary refrigerator in the basement, keeps her cut flowers fresh for weeks and weeks by putting them there between occasions. Send her carnations at Christmas and you might see them at a dinner party later in January, and as fresh as if newly picked.

We are often advised to change the water and recut stems every day. I would never bother to do this but I do have an eye to the lowering water level in vases and bowls. Adding more water each day is little trouble, and I notice that my meadow flowers, even after steeping, seem to drink up a lot.

28. Flowers for
Church Yard and Altar

The planting of the church property and the adornment of the altar are the natural concern of all the gardening members of a congregation. Yet how often his pleasant obligation is completely overlooked by those whose own homes are never without colorful flower arrangements! In fact, I recently attended a church in a community where many of the members had unusually handsome gardens but where the entrance to their place of worship was bordered by an indifferent barberry hedge and surrounded by a most meager grass plot. In the bright month of September there was not a flower to be seen. Furthermore, whoever had filled the altar vases that Sunday had little knowledge of the keeping qualities of various materials since through the entire sermon from autumn branches of japonica one piece of fruit after another dropped in loud and awful succession.

Value of Church Gardens

In a number of communities, however, there seems to be an awakening to the value of gardens in church yards whether these be open to public view or in enclosures. Certainly members who give time to the planting and maintenance of such gardens discover they have a rich and continuous reward in the appreciation of the entire congregation. For we all experience a gracious uplifting of spirit and a quieting of mind, a kind of preparation for service, when our path to the church door lies between lines of fragrant peonies or glowing drifts of chrysanthemums. Indeed, what visitor to Stoke Poges will ever forget the sweetly burdened rose trees which from a step-by-step accompaniment to the door of that ancient little English church made famous by Gray's Elegy? It is also pleasant at any time, weekday or Sunday, to leave a busy street for a brief time of meditation in a secluded church yard garden serene with the beauty of larkspur and lily.

Bishop's Garden in Washington, D.C.

When I lived in Washington, D.C., I used frequently to spend quiet half hours in the Bishop's Garden beside the great Washington Cathedral. This most lovely garden—planned by Olmstead Brothers with the late Florence Brown Bratenahl, a gifted landscape designer and the wife of a former dean, and kept up devotedly by many members—was not only beautiful but rich in spiritual qualities. There is a moving statue of the Prodigal Son in the center of a rose planting, a herb garden at the foot of an ancient cross, with small musical fountains and streams for the birds, easy steps and many comfortable benches. The garden is on several levels and is full of interest and beauty at any season. I enjoyed it in the green of December as well as in the fragrant, colorful weeks of Easter time.

Churches in little towns can rarely plant on so large a scale but even small gardens can make a rich contribution. Here in Westport I have been watching a garden being developed at the Congregational Church which is set far back from the street but still is actually on the Post Road. Despite the impact

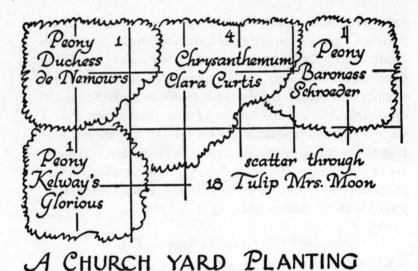

A CHURCH YARD PLANTING

or traffic, there is peace in the garden and I love to visit this one, too. A landscape-architect member of the congregation made the plan, and a plan is essential for a church garden. At first most of the money, largely memorial gifts, went properly into stone work, paths and an important evergreen hedge, which reduced the street noise. Now there are trees—four corner dogwoods—and many memorial plants, each gift recorded by a permanent plant marker. This garden, well suited to weddings and summer services, church fairs and festivals, might well serve as a model to garden enthusiasts in other congregations who want to serve their church in a particular and appropriate way.

If the making of such a garden is a new undertaking in your community, you will find it a good plan in the beginning to use perennials which are to a degree lasting and undemanding. A peony path with plantings of narcissus between the plants would be a long delight in spring and require little but routine care thereafter. If the property is small, however, this would be too space-consuming a selection. A broad border edged with hardy candytuft and filled with intermediate and taller iris and summer phlox would give a better through-the-season effect.

In one small cloistered garden I know, where a seasonal choice had to be made, spring is passed over but from June on color is constant and the deep corner plantings are bright masses of bloom. Pink hollyhocks, *belladonna* delphinium, regal and *candidum* lilies, oriental and Shirley poppies and various yellow daylilies with self-sowing Korean Hybrid chrysanthemums weave a brilliant tapestry. Paths are edged with dwarf marigolds, portulaca and ageratum. An interested Committee for the Garden maintains this lovely plot which was started with plants from the members' own gardens. None of this material is cut since its outdoor value is so deeply enjoyed.

Means to Cut Flowers

When the church property is large enough to support a cutting as well as a landscape garden, that is an ideal situation. One flower committee not finding this possible, however, worked out an uncomplicated but most satisfactory plan for supplying the altar without drawing upon its cloister plantings. A list was made of the most useful flowers for church decoration. These were apportioned to the committee members for separate growing. Then without telephoning or further consultation the person responsible for a given Sunday was privileged to go where, according to her list, the current supply was to be found and to pick what she required.

Arrangements for Churches

Experience soon indicates what flowers are effective and which colors most telling. Blues and violets which first come to mind as fitting, must frequently be omitted since these gray out completely in the dimness of a church interior. But red, pink, yellow and quantities of white are invaluable with plenty of large greens for background. Particularly if vases stand against a figured wall must there be a screen of rhododendrons or something similar in the back of the vase to set off the flowers. An unusually beautiful arrangement is possible with magnolia branches placed to silhouette Madonna or regal lilies. The green leaves are oiled a little to give them gleaming highlights.

In arranging church flowers it is wise to strive for broad masses and to avoid spotting, which is unpleasantly obvious the farther back one sits. Since so many view the flowers a long way off, the final effect must be tested from the very rear of the church. Suitable and beautiful arrangements are possible with these perennials: peonies, August lilies, chrysanthemums, oriental poppies, iris, anemones, hardy asters and most of the coarser daisies. Delicate things like columbines do not carry enough weight.

Delphinium and phlox are also better in the outdoor planting because they are poor keepers. Since the vases must usually be filled and placed on Saturday and left in a close atmosphere until morning, it is important to select flowers which last well. These may then be carefully prepared (see Chapter 27, page 237) so that they will hold up as long as possible, both in the church and later when they are taken to the sick. On Sunday morning it is a good precaution to add some fresh water. It would be better, of course, to change it completely but that usually involves disturbance of the carefully wrought arrangement.

Memorial gifts to most churches fill the vases, of course, on many Sundays. Even so, many supplementary flowers are needed and it seems a pity that these should always be bought or even that memorials should not sometimes be grown rather than purchased. The gift that is grown is somehow more lovingly offered while that church is certainly richer which is regularly adorned through the efforts of its own gardening members. Of course, in some churches, notably the Protestant Episcopal denomination, the color of the flowers for any Sunday is dictated by the church calendar.

Lists for Ready Reference

I. CULTURAL INDEX TO VALUABLE PERENNIALS

(If no information follows entry, refer to botanical-name entry—in parenthesis.)

Name Botanical and Common	Height in Feet	Color	Season of Bloom	Remarks
Achillea				
filipendulina	3	Yellow	July–September	Coarse, dry places, for border and cutting
ptarmica Snowball	2	White	July–September	Much-cut gray foliage, flat heads, self-sows
taggetea	1½	Lemon	May–October	
Aconitum				
fischeri	2–3	Purple	September and October	Shade, not drought-resistant, lovely when they thrive
sparksi	4–5	Dark blue	July and August	
wilsoni	6–7	Deepest	October and November	
Adam's Needle (*Yucca*)				
Althaea rosea	5–7	All but blue	July and August	Requires much space
Alyssum saxatile citrinum	1	Pale yellow	April and May	Fine edging plants
Anchusa				
Dropmore	4–5	Blue	June on	Valuable tall blue
myosotidiflora (*Brunnera macrophylla*)	1	Blue	May and June	Brilliant, dwarf, invaluable
Anemone japonica	2–3	Red, pink, white	September on	Among best for autumn
Aquilegia				
cerulea	1½	Lavender	April–July	Dainty, airy plants for border contrast and cutting
chrysantha	2½	Yellow	May–August	
Crimson Star	2	Red and white	May–June	
			May and June	

flabellata nama alba	2–3	White	May–July	
McKana hybrids	1½–2	Mixed		
Arabis alpina florepleno	½	White	April	Edging, early
Artemisia Silver King	3	Gray foliage		Good gray mist for "peacemaking"
Asperula odorata	1	White	May	Fragrant, shade
Aster, Hardy	½–5	All but yellow	September–October	Essential, autumn border background, lacy effect in bloom, also for edging
Astilbe	1½–4	White to red	June–August	Shade, marvelous plant
August lily (*Hosta*)				
Babysbreath (*Gypsopbila*)				
Bachelor's button (*Centaurea*)				
Balloonflower (*Platycodon*)				
Baptisia	2	Blue	June	Foliage and flower good
Betonia	2–3	Purple	June–August	For dry places, coarse
Blanket flower (*Gaillardia*)				
Bleedingheart (*Dicentra*)				
Bocconia	5–6	White	June–September	Coarse, use with shrubs
Boltonia	5–6	White	August–September	Like wild aster. Divide every spring

I. CULTURAL INDEX TO VALUABLE PERENNIALS (*Continued*)

Name Botanical and Common	Height in Feet	Color	Season of Bloom	Remarks
Campanula carpatica medium	1	Blue, white	June–October	Edging, snip faded flowers
	2½	Purple, pink, white	June	Large bells on stalks, biennial cup-and-saucer
persicifolia	2½	Purple, white	June–July	Peach-leaf type
pyramidalis	4–6	Purple, white	June–September	Important delphinium supplement, biennial
Canterbury bells (*Campanula medium*)				
Carnation (*Dianthus caryophyllus*)				
Centaurea macrocephala	3½	Yellow	July–August	Thistle-like blooms
montana	2	Blue	May–September	Sturdy
Cheiranthus allioni	1–1½	Orange	April	Easily moved among bulbs
Chrysanthemum	1–3	All but blue	September–December	Fall indispensables, list, p. 179
maximum	1½	White	June–November	Fine white cut flower
Cimicifuga racemosa	4–6	White	July–August	Shade and moisture
Columbine (*Aquilegia*)				
Convallaria majalis	1	White	May	Fragrance, shade

Coralbells (*Heuchera*)				
Coreopsis	2½	Yellow	June–September	Undistinguished, reliable
Cornflower (*Centaurea*)				
Cup and saucer (*Campanula medium*)				
Daylily (*Hemerocallis*)				
Delphinium chinense	2½–3	Blue, white	June–October	Good blue, constant bloom
hybrids	3–6	Blue, pink, lavender, white	June–November	Exceptional blue, temperamental except for medium growers
Dianthus		Red, pink, white		Lime and grit in soil
barbatus	1		June	Usually biennial
caryophyllus	1		June–September	More humus in soil, fragrant
chinensis	1–1½		May–October	Usually biennial
plumarius	1–1½		May	Fragrant grass pink, old-fashioned type
Dicentra		Rose		
eximia	1		May–October	Plumy type, sun or shade, persistent foliage
spectabilis	2		April–June	Handsome, but summer disappearance, shade
Dictamnus	2½	Pink, white	June–July	Permanent placement

I. CULTURAL INDEX TO VALUABLE PERENNIALS (*Continued*)

Name Botanical and Common	Height in Feet	Color	Season of Bloom	Remarks
Digitalis ambigua gloxinaeflora	2–3	Yellow	June–July	Wild garden, perennial
	4–6	White, rose		Usually biennial
Doronicum	1–1½	Yellow	April–May	Summer crown
Eupatorium	1½	Lavender	August–Frost	Sun or shade, cutting, rampant
Evening primrose (*Oenothera*)				
Feverfew (*Chrysanthemum parthenium; Matricaria*)	1½	White	June–October	Tiny daisy, bouquet filler
Flax (*Linum*)				
Forget-me-nots (*Myosotis*)				
Funkia (*Hosta*)				
Gaillardia	2	Red, yellow	June–November	Drought-enduring
Garden heliotrope (*Valeriana*)				
Gas plant (*Dictamnus*)				
Gayfeather (*Liatris*)				
Gerbera	1½	Yellow, pink, orange	June–September	Cold-frame wintering
Geum	2	Orange, red	May–October	Moisture, brilliant
Globeflower (*Trollius*)				

Gypsophila Bristol Fairy	3–4	White	June–October	Essential for garden misting and bouquets
repens, bodgiri	2	White		
repens, Rosy Veil	2	Pink		
Hardy ageratum (*Eupatorium*)				
Helenium	1½–4	Yellow to red	July–October	Showy, divide every spring
Helen's flower (*Helenium*)				
Helianthus	4	Yellow	August–October	Coarse plant, dahlia flower
Heliopsis	3–4	Yellow, orange	July–November	Strong, fine to cut
Helleborus	1–2	Pink, white	November–April	Shade, see pp. 180–187
Hemerocallis	1½–4½	Yellow, orange	May–October	See chart p. 148
Hesperis matronalis	3	White, lavender	June–September	Fragrant
Heuchera	1–1½	Rose, white	May–September	Edging, splendid plant
Hibiscus	3–4	Red, pink, white	July–September	Enormous, hollyhock-like
Hollyhock (*Althaea*)				
Hosta	1½–2	White, blue	July–August	Fine foliage, see pp. 151–157
Iberis	1	White	April–June	Evergreen edging
Iceland poppy (*Papaver nudicaule*)				

I. CULTURAL INDEX TO VALUABLE PERENNIALS (Continued)

Name Botanical and Common	Height in Feet	Color	Season of Bloom	Remarks
Iris				See chart p. 87
bearded	2–4½	Various	May–June	Familiar bearded type
cristata	½	Lavender	April	Shade
intermediate	1½	Various	May	Fine forerunner
kaempferi	2½–4	Various	June–July	Handsome flat blooms
Siberian	3–4	Purple, white	May–June	Foliage grassy
Japanese iris (kaempferi)				
Larkspur (Delphinium)				
Leopardbane (Doronicum)				
Liatris	4–5	Purple, white	September	Excellent spires
Linum perenne	1½	Blue	May–August	Delicate, airy growth
Lupine (Lupinus)				
Lupinus polyphyllus	3	Blue, pink, white	June	Some later blooms
Mallow (Hibiscus)				
Meadowrue (Thalictrum)				
Mertensia	1–1½	Blue to pink	April	Enchanting for shade
Michaelmas daisy (Aster)				

Name	Height	Color	Season	Notes
Milfoil (*Achillea taggetea*)				
Mistflower (*Eupatorium*)				
Monarda	2–3	Pink, white, red	June–August	Fragrant foliage, rampant
Monkshood (*Aconitum*)				
Myosotis		Blue	April–June	
alpestris dissitiflora	½			Prefer damp location
palustris semperflorens	½			May be biennial Perennial type
Nepeta mussini	1–2	Lavender	April–August	Gray foliage, soft effect
Oenothera missouriensis		Yellow	June–August	Sandy soil, evening flowers
Paeonia albiflora	2–3	Red, pink, white, yellow	May–June	Familiar, fine foliage
moutan	3–4	Same colors	May	Tree peony species
officinalis	2–2½	Red	Late May	Old-fashioned "piney"
tenuifolia	1½	Crimson	May	Finely cut leaf
Papaver nudicaule	1–1½	Yellow, scarlet, pink, white	May–October	Often biennial
orientale	2–3	Red, pink, white	May–June	See pp. 109–114

I. CULTURAL INDEX TO VALUABLE PERENNIALS (*Continued*)

Name Botanical and Common	Height in Feet	Color	Season of Bloom	Remarks
Peach-leaf bellflower (*Campanula persicifolia*)				
Penstemon	1½–3	Scarlet, pink, white, blue	June–September	Several fine named vari- eties
Phlox				See chart, p. 124
decussata (*paniculata*)	2–4	All but yellow	June–October	Hardy summer phlox
divaricata	1	Lavender	May	Indispensable for shade
subulata	½	Rose, purple, white	April–May	Creeping mat-like growth
suffruticosa	2–4	All but yellow	June–October	Early tall phlox, fine
Physostegia	1½–4	Pink, rose	July–September	Coarse, reliable for cut- ting
Pinks (*Dianthus*)				
Platycodon grandiflorum	1½	Purple, white	May–October	Fine for foreground
Plumbago larpentae	1	Deep blue	August–October	Good edger, late growth
Plume poppy (*Bocconia*)				
Polemonium reptans	1	Blue	May–June	Delicate edging plant
Poppy (*Papaver*)				
Primula vulgaris	¾	Yellow	April–May	Edging for shade

Pyramid bellflower (*Campanula*)				
Pyrethrum roseum	2	Rose, red	May–June	Fine to cut
Rockcress (*Arabis*)				Never failing
Rudbeckia	3	Crimson, purple, white, yellow	July–September	
Salvia				
azurea	3–4	Light blue	August–September	Fine for late true blue
pitcheri	3–4	Deep blue	August–September	More branching
Scabiosa caucasica	1½	Lavender	June–October	Nice to cut
Sea lavender (*Limonium; Statice*)	1½	Lavender	July–August	Good for misting, green crown
Shasta daisy (*Chrysanthemum maximum*)				
Snakeroot (*Cimicifuga*)				
Speedwell (*Veronica*)				
Spiraea (*Astilbe*)				
Statice latifolia (*Limonium latifolium*)				
Stokesia	1½	Lavender, white	July–August	Lasting cut flower
Sunflower (*Helianthus* or *Heliopsis*)				
Sweet rocket (*Hesperis*)				

I. CULTURAL INDEX TO VALUABLE PERENNIALS (*Continued*)

Name Botanical and Common	Height in Feet	Color	Season of Bloom	Remarks
Sweet william (*Dianthus barbatus*)				
Thalictrum glaucum	5	Yellow	June–July	Spring background
Thermopsis caroliniana	5	Yellow	June–July	Lupine-like
Tradescantia	2½	White to purple	May–July; September–October	Shade or sun, dies down in summer
Transvaal daisy (*Gerbera*)				
Trollius	2	Yellow, orange	May–July	Rich blooming in shade with moisture
Valeriana officinalis	4	Blush white	June–July	Heliotrope scent
Veronica	1–3	Blue, purple, pink, white	June–September	Clean, foreground plant, choose varieties
Viola cornuta	½	Yellow, white, purple, apricot	April–October	Some varieties not heat-resistant
Woodruff (*Asperula*)				
Yarrow (*Achillea*)				
Yucca filamentosa	6	White	June–July	Large coarse accent

II. COLORS BY THE DOZEN

In selecting plants listed below, consider variety descriptions carefully, both in the separate chapters in this book and in the catalogue from which you are ordering.

White

Althaea (Hollyhock)
Anemone japonica (Windflower)
Aster (Michaelmas daisy)
Chrysanthemum
Chrysanthemum maximum (Shasta daisy)
Dictamnus alba (Gas plant)
Gypsophila (Babysbreath)
Hosta plantaginea (August lily)
Iberis sempervirens (Hardy candytuft)
Iris
Paeonia (Peony)
Papaver orientale (Oriental poppy)
Phlox

True Blue

Anchusa (Alkanet)
Baptisia (False indigo)
Centaurea (Cornflower)
Delphinium
Linum (Flax)
Lupinus (Lupine)
Myosotis (Forget-me-not)
Plumbago (Leadwort)
Polemonium (Jacob's ladder)
Pulmonaria (Lungwort)
Salvia (Meadow sage)

Veronica holophylla (Speedwell)
Veronica spicata

Lavender and Purple

Aquilegia (Columbine)
Aster (Michaelmas daisy)
Aster frikarti (Wonder of Stafa)
Campanula (Bellflower)
Delphinium
Eupatorium (Hardy ageratum)
Iris
Limonium (Statice) latifolium (Sea lavender)
Mertensia (Virginia bluebell)
Phlox
Platycodon (Chinese balloonflower)
Polemonium (Jacob's ladder)
Statice (Limonium)
Stokesia (Cornflower aster)
Veronica (Speedwell)

Pink

Althaea (Hollyhock)
Aquilegia (Columbine)
Aster (Michaelmas daisy)
Campanula (Bellflower)
Chrysanthemum
Dianthus (Pinks)
Dicentra (Bleedingheart)
Dictamnus (Gas plant)
Lupinus (Lupine)
Monarda (Beebalm)
Paeonia (Peony)

Papaver orientale (Oriental poppy)
Phlox
Physostegia (False dragonhead)

Yellow

Achillea taygetea (Milfoil)
Althaea (Hollyhock)
Alyssum
Anthemis Moonlight
Chrysanthemum
Coreopsis (Tickseed)
Gaillardia (Blanket flower) Sun Gold
Helenium (Helen's flower)
Helianthus (Sunflower)
Heliopsis (False sunflower)
Hemerocallis (Daylily)
Iris
Oenothera (Evening primrose)
Primula (Primrose)
Thalictrum (Meadowrue)
Thermopsis

Orange and Rust

Chrysanthemum
Gaillardia (Blanket flower)
Gerbera (Transvaal daisy)
Geum
Helenium (Helen's flower)
Hemerocallis (Daylily)
Rudbeckia (Coneflower)
Tritoma (Red hot poker)
Trollius (Globeflower)

Cerise and Red

Althaea (Hollyhock)
Aster (Michaelmas daisy)
Chrysanthemum
Dianthus (Pinks)
Gaillardia (Blanket flower)
Lychnis (Campion)
Lythrum (Loosestrife)
Monarda (Beebalm)
Paeonia (Peony)
Papaver orientale (Oriental poppy)
Penstemon (Beard tongue)
Phlox
Pyrethrum (Painted daisy)

III. SPREADERS FOR CUTTING OR MASSING

These plants are to be introduced to the border only after due consideration of their present and future space requirements. Since they are all desirable subjects and especially useful when great masses of cut flowers are wanted, they can often be planted to advantage among shrubs or in odd corners or sections rather than in the herbaceous border where more controlled material looks better and is easier to handle.

Achillea (Yarrow) The Pearl
Althaea (Hollyhock)
Bocconia cordata (Plume poppy)
Boltonia asteroides (False camomile)
Coreopsis grandiflora (Tickseed)
Eupatorium (Hardy ageratum)
Helenium (Helen's flower)
Helianthus (Perennial sunflower)

Hibiscus (Mallow)
Monarda (Beebalm or bergamot)
Physostegia (False dragonhead)
Rudbeckia Golden Glow
Salvia (Meadow sage)
Valeriana (Garden heliotrope)

IV. SHADE-TOLERANT BEAUTIES

Try to consider shade an opportunity rather than a problem and you will discover that you can create many a charming effect not at all possible in the blaze of the sun. Under an apple tree, for example, set bleedinghearts, Virginia blue-bells, spireas and forget-me-nots with colonies of narcissus among them. Such a planting is one of the most delightful spots in my spring garden.

All the perennials listed below will bloom in the light *open* shade of fruit trees, hickory, red birch and dogwood. If you are planning a balanced garden layout—part in sun and part in shade—select plants only from the shade-endured list. These like the sun too and will thrive both ways for you.

If the whole garden is shaded, select from both shade-enduring and shade-preference lists, placing plants from the second group where shadow is strong. In areas of little light, depend upon green alone. The lady ferns and many of their kin will there delight you. Be mindful, however, of soil conditions. Especially if the shaded area is dry, must you do considerable conditioning with humus.

Shade-Endured

Anchusa
Anemone (Windflower)
Aquilegia (Columbine)

Aster (Michaelmas daisy)
Campanula (Bellflower)
Chrysanthemum
Dictamnus (Gas plant)
Digitalis (Foxglove)
Doronicum (Leopardbane)
Eupatorium (Hardy ageratum)
Hemerocallis (Daylily)
Heuchera (Coralbells)
Hibiscus (Mallow)
Iberis (Hardy candytuft)
Iris
Monarda (Beebalm)
Nepeta (Catmint)
Oenothera (Evening primrose)
Paeonia (Peony)
Phlox
Physostegia (False dragonhead)
Platycodon (Chinese balloonflower)
Polemonium (Jacob's ladder)
Thalictrum (Meadowrue)
Trollius (Globeflower)
Veronica (Speedwell)
Viola

Shade-Preferred

Aconitum (Monkshood)
Asperula (Woodruff)
Astilbe (False spirea)
Cimicifuga (Snakeroot)
Convallaria (Lily-of-the-valley)
Dicentra (Bleedingheart)

Hosta (*Funkia* or August lily)
Iris cristata
Mertensia (Virginia bluebell)
Myosotis (Forget-me-not)
Primula (Primrose)
Trillium
Viola (Violet)

V. FLOWERS FOR FRAGRANCE

Fragrance is a blessing added to beauty in many perennial species and in some varieties. When the fine qualities of two varieties are equal, if one is scented, by all means select that one. A garden is lovelier too if some plants are included just for the aromatic quality of their foliage. Especially in the night garden is fragrance desirable and for all plantings which are near the porch or beside frequently open doors or windows of the house. A breeze bearing the sweetness of garden heliotrope or the spiciness of pinks is delightful in the dining room while a bouqet of lilies-of-the-valley or of lemon lilies in the hall is pleasant to come home to. Near the porch let the white August hostas, Festiva Maxima peonies or Miss Lingard phlox perfume each hour of contemplation and rest. Gardens where only fragrant flowers are welcome have proved a deep delight.

Aquilegia chrysantha (Columbine)
Artemisia
  abrotanum (Southernwood), aromatic leaf
Asperula odorata (Sweet woodruff)
Astilbe (False spirea)
Cheiranthus (Wallflower)

    allioni
    cheiri
Convallaria majalis (Lily-of-the-valley)
Dianthus
    allwoodi
    caryophyllus (Carnations)
    plumarius (Grass pinks)
Dictamnus albus (Gas plant), aromatic leaf
Hemerocallis (Daylily)
    citrina
    dumortieri
    flava
    minor
Hemerocallis varieties
    Cool Waters
    Dawning
    Fond Caress
    Hyperion
    Lemon Lustre
    Midwest Majesty
Hosta subcordata grandiflora (White daylily or Corfu lily)
Iris (most blues)
    Great Lakes
    Missouri
    pallida dalmatica Princess Beatrice
Lavandula vera (True lavender), aromatic leaf
Monarda didyma (Beebalm), aromatic leaf
Nepeta mussini (Catmint), aromatic leaf
Paeonia (Peony)

Baroness Schroeder	Kelway's Glorious
Enchanteresse	Mons. Jules Elie
Festiva Maxima	Philippe Rivoire

Phlox (all, whites and pinks best)
Primula vulgaris (English primrose)
Thymus citriodorus (Lemon thyme), aromatic leaf
Valeriana officinalis (Garden heliotrope)
Viola cornuta (Viola or Tufted pansy)
Viola odorata and varieties (Sweet violets)
   odorata Rosina

VI. DROUGHT- AND HEAT-RESISTANT PERENNIALS

Achillea (Yarrow)
Betonica (Betony)
Coreopsis grandiflora (Tickseed)
Dianthus barbatus (Sweet william)
Gaillardia (Blanket flower)
Gypsophila (Babysbreath)
Helianthus (Perennial sunflower)
Heliopsis (False sunflower)
Iris, Bearded
Limonium; Statice (Sea lavender)
Nepeta (Catmint)
Oenothera missouriensis (Evening primrose)
Papaver
   nudicaule (Iceland)
   orientale (Oriental)
Rudbeckia (Coneflower)
Silene maritima (Catchfly)
Yucca filamentosa

VII. SEASHORE HARDIES

High winds, salt spray and sandy soil epitomize the problems
of seashore gardening. Without a tall screen, like a hedge of

beach plum, bay or Japanese honeysuckle and considerable and repeated additions of humus and manure to the soil, few perennials will thrive. When they do, however, they are of unusual size and brilliant color. If in winter lengths of burlap are fastened on uprights to make a temporary screen for well-mulched plants and if other untoward conditions are minimized, many perennials prove extremely tolerant. Patches of binding grass planted beyond the flower bed areas help to prevent shifting of soil.

Althaea rosea (Hollyhock)
Armeria (Thrift)
Aster (Michaelmas daisy)
Campanula (Bellflower)
Centaurea candidissima (Dusty miller)
Chrysanthemum maximum (Shasta daisy)
Coronaria (Rose campion)
Dianthus (Pinks)
Echinops (Globe thistle)
Erigeron (Midsummer daisy or Fleabane)
Eryngium (Sea holly)
Gaillardia (Blanket Flower)
Hemerocallis (Daylily)
Heuchera (Coralbells)
Hibiscus (Mallow)
Iris, Bearded and Siberian
Limonium; Statice (Sea lavender)
Linum (Flax)
Lythrum (Loosestrife)
Monarda (Beebalm)
Phlox subulata (Mountain pink)
Physostegia (False dragonhead)

Rudbeckia (Coneflower)
Sedum spectabile
Silene maritima (Catchfly)
Veronica maritima or *V. longiflora subsessilis* (Speedwell)
Yucca

VIII. CITY DWELLERS

Althaea rosea (Hollyhock)
Alyssum saxatile (Basket-of-gold)
Anchusa myosotidiflora (Forget-me-not anchusa)
Aquilegia (Columbine)
Armeria maritima (Common thrift)
Chrysanthemum
Convallaria majalis (Lily-of-the-valley)
Dianthus barbatus (Sweet william)
Dicentra spectabilis (Bleedingheart)
Dictamnus fraxinella (Gas plant)
Eupatorium coelestinum (Hardy ageratum)
Gaillardia (Blanket flower)
Gypsophila (Babysbreath)
Hemerocallis (Daylily)
Hesperis matronalis (Sweet rocket)
Heuchera (Coralbells)
Hosta (Plantain lily or *Funkia*)
Iberis sempervirens (Hardy candytuft)
Iris, Bearded (if in full sun)
Mertensia (Virginia bluebell)
Monarda (Beebalm or Bergamot)
Phlox subulata (Moss pink)
 divaricata (Wild sweet william)
Platycodon (Chinese balloonflower)
Plumbago larpentae (Leadwort)

Sedum spectabile
Sempervivum tectorum (Hen and chickens)
Tradescantia virginiana (Spider plant)
Viola (Tufted pansy)

IX. GRAY-LEAVED PLANTS FOR BLENDING

Arabis alpina (Rockcress)
Alyssum saxatile (Basket-of-gold)
Artemisia albula Silver King
Bocconia cordata (Plume poppy)
Centaurea candidissima (Dusty miller)
Cerastium tomentosum (Snow-in-summer)
Dianthus allwoodi (Garden pinks)
  plumarius (Grass pink)
Hosta fortunei (Plaintain lily)
  sieboldiana
Stachys lanata (Lamb's ears)
Veronica incana (Woolly speedwell)

X. PALE AND SCENTED, FOR THE MOONLIGHT GARDEN

On pleasant evenings from May to October, a garden planted with pale and scented flowers becomes a sanctuary from both heat and stress. Here in surroundings quiet and remote, the essential dignity of life again asserts itself as our thoughts rise above trivialities and our spirits are fortified by tranquility. Such a garden repays necessarily careful designing and selective planting. Let the background be hemlock, pine and white lilac, the important shade tree an apple or flowering cherry and the perennials such kinds as these.

(Varieties with marked fragrance are starred.*)

For May

Aquilegia chrysantha alba (Columbine—to July)
*Convallaria majalis (Lily-of-the-valley)
Dianthus (White varieties and pale pink)
Hemerocallis flava
Iris
   Snow Flurry
   Helen McGregor
Paeonia
   *Duchesse de Nemours
   *Festiva maxima
*Primula vulgaris (English primrose)

For June

*Astilbe Avalanche, Deutschland
Campanula medium, white (Canterbury bells—into July)
Chrysanthemum maximum Mt. Shasta (Shasta daisy—
   November)
Delphinium (Larkspur—to November)
   chinense album
   Galahad
*Dianthus
   caryophyllus (Carnations—July)
   plumarius (Garden pinks—September)
Dictamnus alba (Gas plant—to July)
Digitalis purpurea alba (Foxglove—into July)
Gypsophila Bristol Fairy (Babysbreath—to October)

Hemerocallis (Daylily)
  Colonel Joe
  Fond Caress
  Judge Orr
Hesperis matronalis (Sweet rocket)
Iris
  Amandine
  Truly Yours
Lupinus polyphyllus alba (Lupine—to August)
Oenothera missouriensis (Evening primrose—August)
Paeonia Kelway's Glorious
  *Baroness Schroeder
  Auten's Pride or Blanche King
Valeriana officinalis (Garden heliotrope)
Yucca filamentosa (Adam's needle)

For July

Althaea rosea, white (Hollyhock—August)
Hemerocallis (Daylily—August)
Iris kaempferi Gold Bound (Japanese iris)
  Golden Moth
  Lark Song
  Vespers
Phlox (to October)
  Mary Louise
  White Admiral
Platycodon grandiflorum album (Balloonflower—October)

For August

Boltonia asteroides, white
Hosta subcordata grandiflora (August lily—September)
Phlox World Peace

For September

Anemone Marie Manchard
Aster Mt. Everest
*Chrysanthemum (pungent)
Liatris White Spire (Gayfeather)

Calendar of Chores

JANUARY

God bless thee
Thy goings out, thy comings in:
Thy home, thy friends, thy kith and kin:
In grief and pain, in joy and cheer;
In all He sends, God bless thy year!

ANONYMOUS

Make a New Year's resolution to plan better and so to work less in your garden. If you attempted too much last year, cut down. Gardens are not meant to be an endurance test but a joy.

Chrysanthemum. On warm unseasonable middays lift the cold frame glass for short periods for ventilation.

Helleborus (Christmas and Lenten rose). Cut generous bouquets from the white, pink and green *H. niger* plants. If you have *H. foetidus*, pick at least one handsome inflorescence.

Convallaria (Lily-of-the-valley). If you have an abundance of these lift a clump or two, pot them, gradually introduce to heat indoors and then to sun. This will result in fragrant flowering in the house.

Make the acquaintance of the perennials this month. Study first a general catalogue like Wayside Gardens' exceptionally well-illustrated one. Then as your interest develops, obtain and read a few special catalogues on peony, iris, chrysanthemum or poppy. Many catalogues are sent free on request. A fee is usually charged for the more richly illustrated ones. If you are an experienced gardener, select a trial few of the newer varieties in your favorite plant group.

Buy or make some wooden seed flats. A good easily handled size is twelve by twelve inches.

FEBRUARY

Tho' stars in skies may disappear,
And angry tempests gather;
The happy hour may soon be near
That brings us pleasant weather.

ROBERT BURNS

Chrysanthemum. Continue to ventilate frame for longer periods as weather permits.

Astilbe, Iberis, Primula, Dicentra (Bleedinghearts). Dig a clump of any of these some pleasant day, pot them and urge them with sunshine, water and warmth to put on an out-of-season show.

Work and rework your garden plans this month. It's a very pleasant fireside occupation.

Get your orders in early to insure prompt delivery of choice material. Remember to include, too, fertilizers, mulching material, stakes, plant ties, tools if you need them, and various oddments. It's so much easier to start equipped than to have to await some necessary item just when you need it most. Order your "sundries" as locally as possible to save delivery costs but buy your plants where the exact variety you want is obtainable. Substitutions are seldom satisfactory to the particular gardener, especially when it's a matter of color.

Don't overlook the season's novelties but don't go all out for them either. The acquaintance of a few each year makes gardening that much more interesting.

Save your wood ashes. Either add them to the compost pit where they will speed humus decomposition or collect them until spring when, scattered on the garden, they will supply potash. To keep their fertilizing value intact when stored separately, place them under cover. You want them "unleached" that is, unweathered.

MARCH

With rushing winds and gloomy skies
The dark and stubborn Winter dies:
Far-off, unseen, Spring faintly cries,
Bidding her earliest child arise:
*   March!*

BAYARD TAYLOR

Chrysanthemum. When you discover green leaves under the mulch in the cold frame, remove the mulch and the cold frame shade. But keep the glass down except during the warm part of the day.

Iris. Examine these and other perennials for signs of heaving. Particularly if your garden has not been mulched, will you need to go over plantings and firm back roots dislodged by frost. If you have had borer trouble, dust with diatomaceous earth this month if new growth is well out of ground.

Late this month poke around a bit and see what goes on under the winter mulch. If green growth appears, loosen mulches to aerate plants. It's not time yet for removal unless the season is unusually advanced.

Buy or build a cold frame.

APRIL

Spring, with that nameless pathos in the air
Which dwells with all things fair,
Spring, with her golden suns and silver rain,
Is with us once again.

HENRY TIMROD

Iris. Clean plantings out by hand as early as possible. Burn old leaves and all debris in which may lie the eggs of the iris borer. Dust with diatomaceous earth a second time.

Dianthus chinensis (Chinese pinks). Thin out plantings made last year.

Peony. If previously buds have blackened, dust or spray with Bordeaux mixture to deter possible botrytis blight. Repeat until buds appear. Set the double tripod supports around the plants before heavy growth makes the task a real chore. Apply a trowelful of wood ashes and one of sheep manure. Triple these amounts for enormous plants.

Chrysanthemum. Lift from the border or cold frame all but the cushion varieties (divide these in alternate years), discard centers and plant fresh single-rooted sections at distances depending on size. "Space plants two-thirds their height apart" is a good old rule. This means twelve to eighteen inches. About the first of the month let the glass or plastic cover over the cold frame plants stay open all day and then at night too, as weather permits. Return separated stock to garden outside as growth develops.

Hardy asters. Lift all plants. Divide most asters each spring. Discard woody centers. Plant three young, well-rooted shoots together to form a new clump. Provide fresh soil with bone meal or select a new site.

Daisies. Divide helenium and shasta the second year into many small sections which will equal the parent in one growing season.

Campanula medium and C. calycantha (Canterbury bell). Transplant to border quarters before buds set.

Delphinium. Fertilize established plants. Transfer youngsters from cold frame to permanent quarters early this month.

Cheiranthus allioni (Siberian wallflower). Transplant to border as soon as bulbs and other early plants are far enough along to permit safe placement among them.

Viola cornuta. Sow this biennial now. It does not care for summer heat.

Remove the greater part of the winter mulch when forsythia blooms. Clean up the remainder or work it into the soil as buds appear on maple trees.

About mid-month apply to all established perennials a balanced commercial plant food in sufficient quantity slightly to obscure the soil. Rake in lightly and water well. (But don't keep so busy with routine that you miss the miracle of spring!)

Set dry twiggy growth cut from pivet or other shrubby material among low-branching perennials like achillea, gaillardia, coreopsis. These will soon hide their excellent supports.

Divide fall-flowering perennials at this time.

Scatter your hoard of wood ashes lightly over the perennial beds in any available amount, particularly on delphinium and pinks.

In the cutting garden allow at least one row there for flowers for the altar. Chrysanthemums 'Avalanche', 'Yellow Avalanche' and 'Betty' would be a lovely white, yellow and pink contribution.

MAY

*Now the bright morning star, day's harbinger
Comes dancing from the East, and leads with her
The flowery May, who from her green lap throws
The yellow cowslip and the pale primrose.*

JOHN MILTON

Iris. Make the acquaintance of Siberians and intermediates. They are worth knowing. If the season is dry, give all iris plantings a thorough soaking to improve flower quality. Cut off any punctured leaves well below noticeable points of attack. Destroy these and any debris around plantings.

Peony. Remove the side buds from each group of three if size rather than quantity is your aim. Otherwise let them all develop. Don't worry over the harmless ants on the buds.

Delphinium. Stake your fast-growing plants before a storm breaks off the lovely spires. They look well with a separate support for each flower stalk.

Phlox. To achieve unusual size, pinch out all but five stems of each mature clump.

Chrysanthemum. When divided single plants have six leaves, pinch out the tops to induce branching. Pinch back branches as each of these develops six leaves.

Late this month or early next, make sowings of spring-flowering perennials for next spring's bloom—arabis, alyssum, columbine, forget-me-not, iberis and primrose.

Around the fifteenth, apply the second dose of balanced plant food to all established perennials.

If you are considering changes which must wait until fall, write yourself a garden note or two and tuck it into the appropriate spot. I use the broad-topped Perfect Labels for this. In September I find such reminders to myself as "Move these hollyhocks to roomier quarters" or "Don't dig here. Remember your mertensia" or "This salmon phlox requests paler companions." It's a useful scheme.

If bleedinghearts are to be divided, mark them now so you can locate them later when they have died down and disappeared.

Keep notes of any color clashes. Later you can improve the situation perhaps by introducing some gray-foliaged plants among the offenders.

JUNE

*To him who in the love of Nature holds
Communion with her visible forms, she speaks
A various language.*

WILLIAM CULLEN BRYANT

Iris. Remove at the ground line all stalks carrying faded flowers. Keep orientals well soaked. Hand-weed clumps as they require. Make a list of any new iris you have seen this year and want next.

Iberis (Hardy candytuft). Prune plants back after flowering to induce thick new growth.

Chrysanthemum. Place around the tall, huskier varieties the tripod supports no longer needed by the peonies. Fertilize lightly the middle of the month. Keep pinching side growth back.

Althaea (Hollyhock). Apply deterrent in Japanese beetle-infested areas. If problem is serious, perhaps it would be better for you to omit hollyhocks for a few years.

Dianthus chinensis (Chinese pinks). Sow these, if you have time, the third week.

Aquilegia (Columbine). Sow seeds every other year. Try Crimson Star or *A. flabellata nana alba* for a change.

Edging plants. Take stem cuttings of rockcress, hardy candytuft, dwarf phlox and pinks when second growth starts. Also, consider, are the edges of your garden fine enough or should they be improved?

Peony. Select new varieties while they are in flower but delay delivery and planting until autumn.

Phlox. Be prompt about snipping off faded flowers. Then you will have a long blooming season and no unwanted seedlings.

Hardy asters. To keep them tractable in the border, pinch out all but three to four shoots in each clump.

Campanula medium and calycantha (Canterbury bells). Sow late this month, preferably in a cold frame.

Digitalis (Foxglove). Sow thinly this month, preferably in a frame.

Dianthus barbatus (Sweet william). Sow this month in an open but protected seed bed or in a frame.

Apply a summer mulch to the border to discourage weeds and conserve moisture. This is especially good for delphinium and anemones.

Fork over the material in your compost pit and soak it with a slow-running hose for a whole day.

Sow now, for early summer bloom next year, seeds of perennial coralbells, lupines, pinks, meadowrue, thermopsis and pyrethrum.

JULY

The Summer looks out from her brazen tower,
Through the flashing bars of July.

FRANCIS THOMPSON

If the weather is very hot, don't read this for a while. Just sit and fan. Remember, gardening is primarily for fun. Doubtless your borders can survive a little neglect at this time.

Iberis (Hardy candytuft). Be alert about spraying this month especially if the weather is hot and dry. You won't see the red spider but a yellowed plant usually means he's been seriously at work on his favorite.

Phlox. Spray for red spider mites and mildew, and give deep soakings if there is little rain.

Linum (Flax). Remove at ground line some of the hardening older shoots which have flowered freely. This will induce new growth.

Althaea (Hollyhock). Watch out for red spider and rust.

Helleborus (Christmast or Lenten rose). A few deep summer soakings are to its liking through dry spells.

Chrysanthemum. Guard against mildew by dusting or spraying, and soak if there is drought. Fertilize mid-month. Stop pinching back early varieties by the fifteenth, later ones by the thirtieth.

Hemerocallis (Daylily) *and Hosta.* Water well in dry weather or bloom may be meager.

Delphinium. If the weather is damp and muggy, be faithful about dusting or spraying to deter mildew and blight. Don't let annuals crowd these plants when they are cut back and small after flowering. Allow a two weeks' rest after flowering, then fertilize.

Biennials. Many of them can be sown late this month or early next. Time this for a cool spell after a rain.

Hardy asters. Stake early, particularly if you are allowing only a few tall shoots for each plant.

Cheiranthus allioni (Siberian wallflower). Sow now.

Violas. Cut back sharply, water deeply and mulch. Maybe they will prove perennial for you.

Fork over the compost pit and soak it well.

If the weather is dry, soak sections of the garden thoroughly and progressively until each section has been moistened six inches deep. Use the overhead sprinkler only occasionally and never at night, to cleanse and refresh plant tops.

This is usually a bad pest and disease month, especially if the weather is muggy. Be watchful and spray to deter rather than to eradicate.

Protect the corners of your garden from careless steps or a dragging hose by short right-angle sections of twelve-inch wire fencing. The hardware man will cut them to your specification. These short bits of fencing also help in the re-education of dogs and children whose short-cut habits need changing.

AUGUST

Every time I go into a garden where the man or woman who owns it has a passionate love of the earth and of growing things, I find I have come home. In whatsoever land or clime or race, in whatsoever language, we speak a common tongue.

MARION CRAN

Iris. If foliage rots at base, lift plants, cut decay from rhizomes; let dry in sun for a day, then coat with diatomaceous earth. If possible, reset in a new location or in fresh soil.

Aconite. Keep well soaked.

Chrysanthemum. Soak deeply if rainfall is slight. This will help check leaf browning. Stake as growth indicates. Three bamboo lengths bound by green raffia will do a neat job.

Phlox. Increase your supply by taking stem cuttings of some favorite varieties. Cut two-thirds back those which have bloomed heavily. They will soon get to work again.

Delphinium. Sow fresh seed (shaken up in packet with clean, sharp sand) some cool day this month. Use a deep flat and keep it in a cool garage or shed.

Lupine. Late this month wake up your resting plants with a good deep watering and a light application of some balanced fertilizer.

Althaea (Hollyhock). Sow now.

Hardy asters. Don't let them suffer drought.

Helleborus (Christmas or Lenten rose). How about making a planting of these this month or next? They will complete your flowering year.

Edging plants. Consider sowing mixed *Dianthus plumarius* for a large supply of fragrant edging plants.

Digitalis (Foxglove). Space six-week-old June-sown plants ten inches apart in row or cold frame. Be careful they do not suffer dryness.

Viola tricolor (Pansy). Sow late this month for a big crop, but they are good biennials to buy.

After a rain, during a relatively cool spell, sow seeds of the summer and fall-flowering perennials—aconite, gaillardia, platycodon, salvia, scabiosa, shasta daisy and stokesia.

Turn over and soak the compost pit once a month.

Take root cuttings this month or next of bleedinghearts, babysbreath, anemone, phlox, sea lavender and oriental poppy.

SEPTEMBER

A spell lies on the Garden. Summer sits
With finger on her lips as if she heard
The steps of Autumn echo on the hill.
A hush lies on the garden. Summer dreams
Of timid crocus thrust through drifting snow.

GERTRUDE HUNTINGTON MCGIFFERT

Iris. Divide and reset crowded clumps. Cut tops halfway back. Plant small divisions of bearded varieties one inch deep and fifteen inches apart. Face rhizomes in the same direction. Set three single pieces of Siberians three inches apart to form one clump. Water regularly if dry weather follows transplanting.

Biennials. Transfer open sowings to rows in a protected reserve bed. Separate cold frame seedlings to stand four to eight inches apart, according to variety.

Primrose. Separate into small but not too tiny divisions or it will disappear.

Anemone. Don't be alarmed if your first-year plants aren't flowering much. They incline to be backward about coming forward until they are well established in your garden.

Phlox. About every third or fourth year divide big clumps into thirds.

Peony. Divide and reset any failing old plants or set out new ones the last two weeks this month. Remember a place in the sun, good drainage and only two inches of soil over the crowns.

Oriental poppy. Set out new plants and divide and reset very thick old ones. You can also take root cuttings now.

Delphinium. Place your new seedlings four inches apart in a cold frame. Use equal thirds leaf mold, top soil and sand.

Aconite. If well-watered plants begin to curl and droop, suspect verticillium wilt. All you can do is discard and burn them. But be sure first that dryness has not produced this sickly appearance.

Chrysanthemum. If you wish to transfer well-budded plants to the border, wait for cloudy weather. Then soak plants the day before and daily for several days after moving. They will bloom on without an indication of resentment. Stake any inclined to be floppy.

Heuchera (Coralbells). Perhaps you can edge a whole bed by dividing several of your large established clumps. Separate by pulling gently apart. Cut from the tap root only sections with some fine roots of their own.

Cheiranthus allioni (Siberian wallflower). Transplant seedlings to a reserve row.

If you haven't one already, prepare a pit in which to start composting autumn leaves. Two by four by three feet will hold a wonderful supply of humus. Over each twelve-inch layer of leaves or other vegetable matter scatter lime or garden fertilizer and a thin layer of soil or sand. Leave a hollow at the top to catch the rain. By spring some of this mixture will be sufficiently decomposed for use. And it is marvelous stuff.

By all means build a cold frame in which to sow seeds early and winter many plants safely.

Any time now you can deal with the spring-flowering perennials which require dividing or transplanting.

If your order of lily bulbs has not come, place stakes among your perennials to indicate proper bulb placement. When some lilies are already present but there are others yet to go in, perhaps next month, mark present locations with wire stakes and future ones with bamboo. Stakes left in place over winter are also a safe guide to early cultivation of perennials, if late hardy plants or bulbs must be worked around.

OCTOBER

Season of mists and mellow fruitfulness!
Close bosom-friend of the maturing sun;
Conspiring with him how to load and bless
With fruit the vines that round the thatch-eaves run ...

JOHN KEATS

Peony. Cut off and burn all foliage. Work in a trowelful of bone meal per plant.

Chrysanthemum. As soon as flowering ceases, cut back tops and lift stock plants of doubtfully hardy varieties. Place these in an open cold frame and water once a week until a hard freeze occurs.

Visit a chrysanthemum nursery or any fair-sized private collection and make your list of varieties for next year. (Forgive me, please, for making so many notes on chrysanthemums. They're my favorite perennials.)

If you plan to mulch the borders with leaves, collect in a corner of the shrubbery border or in baskets all you will need of the type which curl when they fall—oak, birch, beech, hardwood maple, etc. Avoid soggy mulches made by poplar or Norway maple leaves.

Should there be little rainfall this month, as sometimes occurs, soak your perennials finally and deeply about the third week. Plants which have suffered drought incline to winter-kill. Let yours go dormant in good condition.

Early this month is a grand time to redo a badly designed perennial border or one overcrowded by the maturity of its plants. Sometimes I do sections year by year—edging and foreground one autumn, center or rear another. Lift out all plants. Separate those requiring it. Throw away poor varieties or those past their prime. Dig deeply. Work compost and bone meal into the soil. Reset plants. The weather usually favors you and the work is fun. Ensuing satisfaction, tremendous!

NOVEMBER

What is lovely never dies,
But passes into other loveliness,
Star-dust, or sea-foam, flower or winged air.

JOSEPH ADDISON

Iris. After a hard freeze, mulch new plantings lightly the first year. Only in subzero sections continue this practice in subsequent years.

Chrysanthemum. After freezing weather, mulch all plants. After mulching those in the frame, put down the glass and shade it. You may not need to do this until next month.

Helleborus (Christmas or Lenten rose). Examine them early this month. Enough flowers may be open for a first bouquet. Think twice about cutting the evergreen foliage of the variety *niger.* Add bone meal lightly any time now and a thin layer of compost.

Early this month, mulch lightly all young plants just beyond the seedling stage. Do not cover adults until after the first hard freeze.

Plant inconspicuously a few bushes of California privet as a source of neat twiggy supports for coreopsis, gaillardia, veronica, etc.

DECEMBER

Sing we all merrily, Christmas is here,
Day that we love best of days in the year;
Bring forth the holly, the box and the bay
Deck out the cottage for glad Christmas day.

OLD ENGLISH CAROL

Helleborus. Cut these flowers freely for pleasing arrangements with evergreens. When they fade, try a very hot water dip, followed by a cold steeping. This may revive them for your further pleasure.

Iris stylosa. Care for and ventilate this one in the cold frame. And don't be discouraged if flowers do not appear until the second or third year of residence.

After the first hard freeze—not simply a touch of frost—mulch perennials to keep them cold and unstimulated by occasional mid-winter warmth. Pull the mulching material under not over greentopped plants. After the first year, leave uncovered peonies, iris, oriental poppies and delphinium (except in very cold sections). Daylilies never need a cover.

For your garden-mad friends remember that an order for some choice perennial plants is a very fine present.

Merry Christmas and Good Gardening next year!

Sources of Plants

Antique Rose Emporium, Route 5, Box 143, Brenham, TX 77833; catalogue $2.

Kurt Bluemel, 2740 Greene Lane, Baldwin, MD 21013; catalogue $2.

Bluestone Perennials, 7211 Middle Ridge, Madison, OH 44057.

Borboleta Gardens, 15974 Canby Avenue, Route 5, Faribault, MN 55021; catalogue $3. Daylily specialists.

Brand Peony Farm, P.O. Box 842, St. Cloud, MN 56302; catalogue $1.

Breck's, 6523 North Galena Road, Peoria, IL 61601. Hardy bulbs.

Lee Bristol Nursery, RR 1, Box 148, Gaylordsville, CT 06755; catalogue $1. Daylilies.

W. Atlee Burpee Seed Co., 300 Park Avenue, Warminster, PA 18991.

Busse Gardens, 635 East 7 St., Cokato, MN 55321; catalogue $2.

Canyon Creek Nursery, 3527 Dry Creek Road, Oroville, CA 95965; catalogue $1.

Carroll Gardens, Box 310, Westminster, MD 21157; catalogue $2.

Cooley's Gardens, P.O. Box 126, Silverton, OR 97381; catalogue $2. Iris specialist.

The Country Garden, P.O. Box 3539, Oakland, CA 94609-0539; catalogue $2. "The finest flower seeds for garden and cutting."

The Daffodil Mart; Route 3, Box 794, Gloucester, VA 23601; catalogue $1.

Englerth Gardens, 2461 22nd Street, Hopkins, MI 49238. Daylilies, hostas.

Fancy Fronds, 1911 4th Avenue, West Seattle, WA 98119; catalogue $1. Hardy ferns.

Far North Gardens, 16785 Harrison Road, Livonia, MI 48154; catalogue $2.

Foliage Gardens, 2003 128th Avenue, S.E., Bellevue, WA 98005; catalogue $1. Hardy ferns.

Fox Hill Farms, 440 West Michigan Avenue, P.O. Box 7, Parma, MI 49269; catalogue $1. Complete selection of herbs.

The Fragrant Path, Box 328, Fort Calhoun, NE 68023; catalogue $1. Fragrant plants.

Gardens of the Blue Ridge, P.O. Box 10, Pineola, NC 28662; catalogue $2.

D.S. George Nurseries, 2491 Penfield, Fairport, NY 14450. Clematis specialists.

Heritage Rosarium, 211 Haviland Mill Road, Brookville, MD 20833; catalogue $1.

Heritage Rose Gardens, 16831 Mitchell Creek Drive, Fort Bragg, CA 95437; catalogue $1.

High Country Rosarium, 1717 Downing Street, Denver, CO 80218.

Illini Iris, Route 3, Box 5, Monticello, IL 61856; catalogue $1.

Jackson & Perkins Co., Box 1028, Medford, OR 97501. Roses and some perennials.

King's Mums, 20303 East Liberty Road, P.O. Box 368, Clements, CA 95227-0368; catalogue $1. Chrysanthemum specialists.

Klehm Nursery, 197 Penny Road, South Barrington, IL 60010; catalogue $2. Peonies, hardy iris, daylilies.

Lamb Nurseries, East 101 Sharp Avenue, Spokane, WA 99202; catalogue $2. Wide selection of hardy perennials.

The Lehman Gardens, 420 S.W. Tenth Street, Faribault, MN 55021. Specialists in hardy chrysanthemums.

Long's Gardens, 3240 Broadway, Box 19, Boulder, CO 80306. Iris specialists.

Lowe's Own Root Roses, 6 Sheffield Road, Nashua, NH 03062; catalogue $2.

Melrose Gardens, 309 Best Road South, Stockton, CA 95206; catalogue $1. Iris.

Milaeger's Gardens, 4838 Douglas Avenue, Racine, WI 53402; catalogue $1.

Grant Mitsch Novelty Daffodils, P.O. Box 218, Hubbard, OR 97032; catalogue $3.

Geo. W. Park Seed Co., Inc., Cokesbury Road, Greenwood, SC 29647.

Powell's Gardens, Route 3, Box 21, Princeton, NC 27569; catalogue $2.50.

The Primrose Path, R.D. 2, Box 110, Scottdale, PA 15683; catalogue $1.50.

Roses by Fred Edmunds, 6235 S.W. Kahle Road, Wilsonville, OR 97070.

Roses of Yesterday and Today, Brown's Valley Road, Watsonville, CA 95076; catalogue $2.

Schreiner's Gardens, 3625 Quinaby Road, N.E., Salem, OR 97303; catalogue $2. Iris.

Siskiyou Rare Plant Nursery, 2825 Cummings Road, Medford, OR 97501; catalogue $2.

Anthony J. Skittone, 2271 31st Avenue, San Francisco, CA 94116. Rare bulbs.

Spring Hill Nurseries, 6523 North Galena Road, Peoria, IL 61632.

Sunnybrook Farms Homestead, 9448 Mayfield Road, Chesterland, OH 44026; catalogue $1.

Sunnyslope Gardens, 8638 Huntington Drive, San Gabriel, CA 91775. Chrysanthemum specialists.

Thomasville Nurseries, Box 7, Thomasville, GA 31792.

Thon's Garden Mums, 4811 Oak Street, Crystal Lake, IL 60014. Specialists in hardy chrysanthemums.

Andre Viette Farm & Nursery, Route 1, Box 16, Fishersville, VA 22939; catalogue $2.

Wayside Gardens, Hodges, SC 29695; catalogue $1.

We-Du Nurseries, Route 5, Box 724, Marion, NC 28752; catalogue $1.

White Flower Farm, Litchfield, CT 06759; catalogue $5.

Gilbert H. Wild and Son, 1112 Joplin St., Sarcoxie, MO 64862-0338; catalogue $2. Daylilies, iris, peonies.

Some Words to Know

Aeration. This refers to the air content of the soil. One of the reasons for frequent cultivation of a flower bed is to increase the healthful circulation of air in the soil.

Annuals. Their life cycle is completed in one year during which they develop from seed, flower, form seed and die. Some like tobacco and cornflower are said to self-sow, that is, their seed survives the cold and germinates the next year.

Anther. Some flowers like the single peonies reveal prominent little sacs, or anthers, borne on long threads in the center of the blossom. When the cells mature they release golden pollen grains.

Biennials. These come to perfection in the course of two years. The first year the plants develop. The second the flowers appear, and if permitted, the seeds. Then in many cases the plants may as well be discarded.

Cambium. Just beneath the bark of tree or shrub lies a layer of living tissue. This is the cambium. When trees are cut down their probable age can be determined by a count of the annual rings of cambium tissue.

Cold frame. This basically is a box with a bed of soil for the bottom and a sash of glass or plastic for the top. Inserted in the soil in a sunny place it is so set that the front is about ten inches high and the rear twenty. This provides a sloping surface to catch the sunshine.

Corm. This is a short, fleshy, erect, underground stem with scale-like leaves surrounding it. The gladiolus grows from a corm which is often incorrectly called a bulb.

Flat. This is a shallow box in which seeds are sown or seedlings transplanted. The usual size is sixteen by twenty-two and one-half inches with a two- to four-inch depth. Bottom boards are separated one-quarter inch to permit drainage. If makeshift flats of cigar boxes are used, a few half-inch holes are bored in the bottom so that excess water may escape.

Floret. The individual small flowers which make up a thick flower cluster are called florets. They are plainly seen in the make-up of phlox or delphinium.

Germination. When seeds start to grow into little plants, we say germination has taken place.

Head. A dense flower cluster like that of the chrysanthemum is called a head.

Hybrid. An individual resulting from the crossing of two species or of two parents which differ basically in some strongly marked characteristic. Our handsomest delphiniums are the results of such cross-fertilization.

Inflorescence. The arrangement of flowers on a plant, the type of its cluster, is its inflorescence. These may be in heads, racemes, panicles, spikes, etc.

Lath shade. This is a screen to protect soil and plants from direct sunlight. It is frequently made by nailing plaster lath (with alternate open spaces) to a light board frame.

Naturalize. To plant informally in drifts or colonies to simulate nature's own self-sowing is to naturalize.

Organic material. This was once living matter as contrasted with non-living or inorganic matter. Manures, rotted leaves or compost and bone meal are organic fertilizers while commercial fertilizers are largely chemical or inorganic.

Panicle. A loose spire-like flower form such as produced by the astilbe or spirea and phlox is called a panicle.

Perennials. These are root-hardy plants which die down

after frost but green up again each spring and flower seasonally for a period of more than two years.

pH. This is a term describing the sweet-sour condition of the soil the way Fahrenheit readings indicate hot-cold degrees of temperature. Most perennials thrive in a fairly neutral or pH 7 soil with toleration for slight variations either way.

Raceme. A slender elongated flower cluster in which each small flower is borne on a little stalk of its own is a raceme. The bleedingheart and lily-of-the-valley are examples.

Rhizome. An underground stem, usually thicker than the visible stem, with joints from which roots grow is a rhizome. Bearded iris have typical rhizomes.

Species. This is something nature produces. It is a group of plants sharing certain distinctive characteristics which indicate a common parent or genus. In a botanical plant name the first word indicates the genus, the second the species it belongs to, the third the variety as *Phlox paniculata* Miss Lingard.

Specimen plant. A plant grown by itself or prominently placed is often so described.

Spike. A slim elongated flower cluster in which individual flowers grow without stalks and close to the main stalk is a spike. Gayfeather, delphinium and lupine are typical spike flowers.

Stock plant. A plant used to increase one's supply (or saved for this purpose) is called a stock plant. The tender chrysanthemum wintered in the cold frame for propagating in the spring is a stock plant.

Taproot. That long thick root which babysbreath, oriental poppy and lupine develop is a taproot. Plants with this type of root system require extra care in transplanting so as not to injure this main root.

Variety. The slight variations of plants within a species which are noticeable but not important enough to constitute another species are called varieties.

Map labels:

Iberis Purity
Daylily Fond Caress yellow
Phlox World Peace white
Daylily Shooting Star yellow
Aster Plenty
Aster Harrington's Pink
Aster Plenty
Day Autumn

Achillea taggetea yellow
Lily Valencia
Iris Violet Harmony
Lily Regal
L.
Lily Rubrum
L.
Iris Cahokia
Baroness

Veronica holophylla blue
Dictamnus rubra pink
Peony Georgiana Shaylor pink
Aquilegia chrysantha
Phlox Mt. Everest
white
Lily Regal
Aquilegia

Iberis
Tulips Queen of the Bartigons
Shasta Daisy Mt. Shasta
Iris Polar King
Linum perenne
Aster frikarti
Tulips Niphetos yellow
Aster frikarti
Daisy Mt. Shasta
Iris, Pink

Iberis
Iberis
Heuchera pink
Dianthus Her Majesty white
Heuchera pink
Iberis
Heuchera pink
Dian

Legend / plant list:

Aquilegia chrysantha, pale yellow

Asters
frikarti, lavender-blue
Harrington's Pink
Marie Ballard, pale blue
Plenty, lavender

Hemerocallis (Daylilies)
Autumn King, yellow
Cradle Song, creamy-gold
Fond Caress, pale yellow
Lark Song, pale yellow
Shooting Star, creamy-yellow

Heuchera
Rosamundi, pink

Iberis Purity, white

Iris - Intermediates
Paltec, blue
Pink Ruffles, lav. pink
Polar King, white

Iris - Tall
Violet Harmony
Cahokia, palest blue
Great Lakes, light blue
Blue Rhythm, med. blue

L = Larkspur
Giant Imperial
(light blue, lilac, violet)
around Rubrum Lilies

302

Labels within plan:

Aster Marie Ballard · Aster Harringtons Pink · Aster Marie Ballard · Daylily Lark Song yellow · Phlox World Peace · Daylily Cradle Song · Iberis Purity

Iris Great Lakes · Lily Rubrum · Lily Regal · Iris Blue Rhythm · Lily Prosperity · Achillea taggetea

Lily Regal · Phlox Prime Minister · Peony · Aquilegia · Peony Walter Faxon rose-pink · Dictamnus alba · Veronica blue

Aquilegia · Aster frikarti · white · Aster frikarti · Shasta Daisy Mt.Shasta · Iris Paltec · Linum perenne · Tulips Insurpassable lavender · Iberis

Linum perenne · Tulips Niphetos yellow · Neuchera pink · Dianthus Ner Majesty · Neuchera pink · Iberis · Iberis

Neuchera pink · Iberis · Neuchera pink

Lilies

    Lilium regale, white
    Prosperity, lemon-yellow
    Lilium speciosum rubrum, rose
    Valencia, orange-gold

Peonies

    Georgiana Shaylor, pink
    Baroness Schroeder, white
    Walter Faxon, rose=pink

Phlox

Mt.Everest, white, rose eye
    World Peace, white
    Prime Minister, white, red eye

Tulips

    Insurpassable-
        lavender, followed by
        white petunia, Paleface
    Niphetos-yellow, followed
        by petunia, Yellow Gleam
    Queen of the Bartigons, peach-pink,
        followed by petunia, Pink Beauty

Veronica holophylla, blue

DRAWING BY KATHLEEN BOURKE

0   1   2.   4   6   8 feet

303

Index

(See also Lists for Ready Reference, 251 ff.)